Robert Pickering Ashe

Chronicles of Uganda

Robert Pickering Ashe
Chronicles of Uganda
ISBN/EAN: 9783743384361
Manufactured in Europe, USA, Canada, Australia, Japa
Cover: Foto ©ninafisch / pixelio.de

Manufactured and distributed by brebook publishing software (www.brebook.com)

Robert Pickering Ashe

Chronicles of Uganda

BY THE REV.

R. P. ASHE, M.A., F.R.G.S.
Author of " Two Kings of Uganda"

WITH PORTRAIT AND TWENTY-SIX ILLUSTRATIONS

NEW YORK
A. D. F. RANDOLPH & CO.
182 FIFTH AVENUE
1895

To

THE VEN. ARCHDEACON WALKER.

My Dear Friend—

I venture to dedicate this book to you and your fellow-workers before I can receive your reply to my request for permission to do so.

Since you have not even seen the book you are in no sense sponsors for it. I can therefore only hope that when it reaches you it may meet with your approval; for, armed with that, I shall have little fear of other critics less qualified than yourselves to pronounce upon my work.

Believe me,
Yours affectionately,
ROBERT P. ASHE.

PORTISHEAD,
SOMERSET,
November 1894.

To
ROBERT HENRY WALKER
AND
HIS FELLOW-MISSIONARIES
I DEDICATE
THESE CHRONICLES,
AS A TOKEN OF MY SYMPATHY
WITH THEM IN THEIR WORK
UGANDA.

PREFACE

WHEN writing these Chronicles of Uganda I was well aware that there were already in existence a good many books dealing with Uganda, and that a considerable literature has gathered about the region of Africa wherein Uganda lies; yet I felt that there was still a distinct need for some book which should represent, as a continuous story, the chief events which led up to Uganda's becoming an English Protectorate; and this need I have endeavoured to supply in the following pages.

In some measure, at least, I have tried to write from the standpoint of the native actors in the scenes which I describe.

In reading of the early days of Mwanga's rule, the tragic horror of that period will only be appreciated by those who will go back in imagination to that time when the Uganda king was an impersonation of relentless cruelty and absolute power. His very silliness and weakness at that period lent a further feature of horror to the situation of those who had the misfortune to find themselves in his clutches.

I have necessarily been obliged to mention the names of a number of persons whose views I could not always endorse, and whose policy I could not in every point approve. I trust that I have, however, avoided attributing to them any unworthy motives, and I venture to hope I have been able to show that a good deal of what hasty partizanship or sheer misunderstanding may have put in a sinister light, is capable of a more charitable, and, at the same time, a more natural interpretation.

I should like to remind my readers that, unless one is prepared to exercise a good deal of self-restraint in perusing a story of this kind, there is always a tendency to forget that we are in possession of facts and data which were necessarily absent from the minds of those whose actions we are considering, and from our standpoint of complete knowledge we are apt to form harsh judgments upon those, who, if they erred at all, may have done so largely owing to ignorance.

Moreover, I think I have been able to show that the Uganda troubles of 1892-3 were due in some measure to the uncertainty entertained in Uganda as to the ultimate action of England with regard to withdrawal.

Preface ix

Though I have not considered it within the scope of the work to chronicle only the events connected with the Church Missionary Society's Mission, yet this Mission, with its wonderful story of the triumphs of the Gospel, necessarily finds a prominent place.

And here let me say that although Christendom—divided on so many other questions—has almost universally sanctioned a resort on the part of Christians to the extremest violence provided that it be perpetrated from conscientious motives, yet after reading such a record as this of Uganda, one is driven to exclaim " The pity of it ! " that even the very remotest result of the coming of the heralds of " The Prince of Peace " should have been such shedding of blood by Christians as I have described.

I must acknowledge my indebtedness to the pages of the *Church Missionary Society's Intelligencer*, especially for the period when I was not myself in the country. I cannot help hoping that the vast mass of deeply interesting and valuable material relating to Uganda contained in this periodical may some day be collected and published by the Society.

I must also acknowledge the value, as an independent contemporary record of events during 1891-3, of the second volume of Captain Lugard's book, "The Rise of our East African Empire." (Messrs. Blackwood & Sons.)

I have availed myself of this interesting work in writing of the period which it covers, though not always taking the same point of view. I have also availed myself of a small book of the greatest interest, being a work in the language of Uganda, called "The Wars of the Ba-ganda" (people of Uganda), written by the present Prime Minister, Kagwa Apolo, who was a prominent figure in the wars of which he tells the story.

For the majority of the illustrations I am indebted to the kindness of my friends, Mr. J. P. Nickisson, Church Missionary Society of Nassa, and Mr. R. H. Leakey, of Uganda, to whose skill in photography I owe the pictures, excepting that of the Lions, which was not taken with a camera.

For the representations of Uganda implements, utensils, etc., and the descriptions, I am indebted to Dr. Basil Woodd Walker, and his brother, Dr. Cyril H. Walker, who arranged and photographed the collection.

Nor must I omit to mention the help of another old friend, Mr. J. Spencer Hill, in furthering my undertaking.

ROBERT P. ASHE.

PORTISHEAD,
    SOMERSET,
        November, 1894.

CONTENTS

BOOK I

INCIDENTS OF TRAVEL

I. FROM LONDON TO MAMBOYA   3
II. MAMBOYA TO USAMBIRO   21
III. USAMBIRO TO UGANDA   39

BOOK II

A RETROSPECT

I. KINGS MUTESA AND MWANGA   55
II. REVOLUTION AND EXPULSION OF MWANGA   85
III. THREE KINGS   111
IV. SCRAMBLING FOR UGANDA   131
V. A NEST OF HORNETS   149
VI. BRINGING OF THE SUDANESE   171
VII. UGANDA POLITICS   193
VIII. THE BATTLE OF MENGO   215
IX. THE TRAGEDY OF BULINGUGE   237

BOOK III

UGANDA REVISITED

I.	THE FLIGHT FROM BUDU	. 261
II.	ENGLISH INTERESTS AND GERMAN OFFICIALS	. 283
III.	THE KING'S RETURN	299
IV.	THE MUHAMMEDAN QUESTION	. 317
V.	THE RAILWAY SURVEY	. 331
VI.	A JOURNEY TO KAVIRONDO	. 343
VII.	QUESTION OF UNYORO AND UVUMA	. 373
VIII.	THE MUHAMMEDAN REVOLT	. 393

BOOK IV

FROM UGANDA TO ZANZIBAR

I.	PERILS OF WATERS	. 415
II.	PERILS IN THE WILDERNESS	. 437

APPENDICES

A.	INSTRUCTIONS TO THE LATE SIR GERALD PORTAL	. 455
B.	LETTER OF THE LATE SIR GERALD PORTAL ON MISSION EXTENSION	. 457
C.	THE WAR AGAINST UNYORO	. 459
D.	CORRESPONDENCE RELATING TO TORO AND UVUMA	. 460

LIST OF ILLUSTRATIONS

	PAGE
THE MISSION BUILDINGS AT NASSA, ON SPEKE GULF .	40
REV. E. H. HUBBARD AT NASSA.	42
NOVEL COMPANIONS .	45
UGANDA WEAPONS, IMPLEMENTS, MUSICAL INSTRUMENTS, UTENSILS, ETC.	58
THE ISLAND OF UKEREWE .	61
KING LUKONGE OF UKEREWE AND HIS WIFE	64
KING MUTESA'S GREAT BURIAL HOUSE, NABULAGULA	65
MWANGA, KING OF UGANDA, 1893	91
AN UGANDA MARKET .	113
BUYING AND SELLING.	115
MATAYO THE MUJASI, REV. H. W. D. KITAKULE, WASWA THE MUKWENDA, KAGWA THE KATIKIRO WITH HIS WIFE AND SISTER .	137
NIKODEMO POKINO, AFTERWARDS SEKIBOBO .	201
KING MWANGA'S FLIGHT .	253
UGANDA IMPLEMENTS, UTENSILS, ETC.	264
REED WALL BEHIND "EDGAR" SHOWS THE UGANDA METHOD OF BUILDING .	333
HE LEFT WITH ME TIMOTEO	337
THE GREAT CHURCH OF ST. PAUL, ON NAMIREMBE HILL, UGANDA .	345
INTERIOR OF ST. PAUL'S CHURCH, SHOWING THE COMMUNION TABLE AND RAILS .	349

List of Illustrations

	PAGE
CHURCH FURNITURE, ST. PAUL'S, UGANDA.	351
MR. WILSON OF THE IMPERIAL BRITISH EAST AFRICA COMPANY, AND F. C. SMITH OF CHURCH MISSIONARY SOCIETY	359
SOME OF MY HOUSEHOLD	367
NASSA MISSION BOYS, ENKOKO, HALF MUHUMA, MUBASSA, HALF MUHUMA, HENRY MUKASSA, UGANDA TEACHER	417
KAPONGO THE CHIEF OF NASSA	421
"EDGAR," SHOWING ALSO UGANDA ENTRANCE AND DOOR BEHIND	425
REV. J. C. PRICE'S MISSION CHILDREN. THE GIRL HOLDING THE BOOK IS DAUGHTER OF THE UGOGO CHIEF OF MPWAPWA	443
TIMOTEO, MUDEMBUGA, R. P. ASHE, BADUBAZE, KAGWA, KANGIRI JIMMY, ALBERT NAMENYEKA, A CHIEF	447

BOOK I

INCIDENTS OF TRAVEL

CHAPTER I

FROM LONDON TO MAMBOYA

Last News of Mackay—Our Party—A silent City—Port Said—Fiasco of Railway Point—The Trowser Question—Zanzibar—In the Hands of Carriers—Serious News—Return of Greaves—The Iron Donkey—Deserted Villages—Avoiding a Mother-in-Law—Vicarious Medicine—Thieving Porters—Arrive at Mamboya.

CHAPTER I

FROM LONDON TO MAMBOYA

IN the year 1890 the sorrowful news reached me of the death of Mackay, my friend and former companion in many troubles, the great pioneer missionary of the Nyanza. The last news received of him had been most hopeful. Stanley and Stairs had left him the preceding September full of life and energy, doing his work of teaching and translating in the evenings, and busy by day erecting storehouses, boat building, forging bolts, and riveting the boiler for the steamer which he desired to put upon the Lake. And now to hear that he is gone, stricken down by fever from the Usambiro swamps. The news had been received by telegram. A little later, and there came a letter in the well-known hand—that kindly hand which would never more hold a pen or wield a hammer. It was the letter of a valiant worker, which, while it told of bitter disappointment, yet breathed a steadfast purpose and an undying hope.

As I read Mackay's last letter the longing rose up within me to go back to the Nyanza—to see his grave, to clasp once more the hands of old and tried and faithful friends, to see once more their kindly dark faces, to hear once more their strange tongue becoming almost unfamiliar to me from want of use. Accordingly a month or two later I notified to the Committee of the Church Missionary Society my intention of returning to Africa, and my willingness, should they invite me to do so, to return to Uganda as their agent. The result was that the Committee cordially invited me to work for the Society, and to go with a reinforcement of missionaries, which they were about to send out in the following May (1891) to the Victoria Lake.

Our party of five was made up as follows: Dr. Gaskoin Wright, who had relinquished a lucrative practice to become a medical missionary; the Rev. G. Greaves, a young Cambridge man, who had held an important curacy in Birmingham; Mr. (now the Rev.) E. H. Hubbard, a student of the Church Missionary College; and Mr. Walter Collins, who had formerly been a local preacher of the Wesleyan body.

There is always more than the ordinary sadness of farewell in embarking for the shores of Africa. And we experienced a sense of relief when the last words were spoken, and the sorrowful good-byes uttered, and we had at length bidden England a final farewell. Wright, Hubbard, and myself, in order to gain a few extra days, had arranged to join our steamer at Naples. Our journey thither presented a strong contrast to the African wastes and wildernesses which we were shortly to traverse on our way to the Victoria Nyanza.

We left London on May 17th, 1891, and travelled

night and day to Rome, where we could only spend a few hours—enough, however, to visit the Colosseum, the awe of whose stupendous ruin seems to oppress one's mind with a sense of the vanity of man's most solid handiwork; to enter St. Peter's, and to stand for a few minutes beneath its glorious dome; then a hurried visit to the Vatican Gallery, to have rather a dream of its wonders than to realise what they really are. From Rome we went to Naples, where we spent two days, taking the opportunity of visiting Pompeii, where in imagination one can re-people with busy life those deserted streets and grass-grown temples, and empty, dismantled palaces. In the magnificent museum of Naples, and at Pompeii itself an unmistakable hint of what the moral tone of that ancient city was is conveyed by some of the pictures portrayed upon its walls, and by the objects of art recovered from its houses, so that one can understand the meaning of that desolate and silent city over which Vesuvius hangs in the glorious clear air, with its faint white cloud of smoke floating upon the summit; the ruined city and the mountain from which poured the molten lava that destroyed it, both enduring witnesses to the wrath of God against the unrighteousness of men.

Bidding farewell to Naples, we went on board the steamship *Madura* as second-class passengers. We did not complain so much of the dirt and bad food on this ship as of the horrible foulness of the air of the place in which we were condemned to be while the hatches were battened down during rough weather. Our fellow-sufferers were a number of sergeants, private soldiers, and servants connected with the various expeditions which were to leave Zanzibar at about the same time as ourselves. In spite, however, of the many discomforts, they and we had a pleasant time together.

The late Captain Stairs of the Katanga expedition was also on this steamer, and I had the pleasure of making his acquaintance. Though he appeared to be naturally quiet and reserved, yet when he spoke of Africa and the Africans his whole manner would change, and his face light up with eager interest, as he compared notes with other travellers, or told of what he had experienced during his eventful journey with Stanley. His early death, which took place not long afterwards, means the loss of a true-hearted friend to the cause of Africa.

On the fifth day out from Naples we reached Port Said, now an important place, owing to its position at the entrance to the Suez Canal; but an evil city, and the common sewer through which east and west seem to pour their vileness and their filth. Gaming hells, dancing saloons, drinking bars flaunt on every side, while young boys accost the stranger, inviting him to these haunts of vice, or endeavour to sell him obscene pictures. Since I first passed through the Canal in the year 1882 Port Said has more than trebled in size, and contains now, I believe, a population of 36,000 souls. There are, I understand, twenty-five Romish priests at work here, while Protestant Christianity is represented by only one person, an agent of the British and Foreign Bible Society.

Leaving Port Said in the evening, we passed through

the Canal with the aid of the electric light, and reached Suez the following day. Six days through the Red Sea brought us to Aden, and in eight days more we reached Mombasa, the headquarters of the British Imperial East Africa Company. I had left England full of enthusiasm for this Company. The fact that such men as Sir Fowell Buxton and the late Sir William Mackinnon were prominent directors of the undertaking was an ample guarantee that, as far as they were personally concerned, the Company was primarily, if not a philanthropic undertaking, at any rate one which chiefly sought the development and civilisation of the countries to be administered, and not one to attract hungry investors desiring dividends.

On closer acquaintance with this corporation, however, I came to the conclusion that there were other interests than those of philanthropy represented, interests which, though perhaps legitimate in themselves, could not but be out of harmony with a benevolent undertaking. I must confess after what I had read of the cutting of the first sod of the railway, and of the grand doings on that occasion, and of the intention on the part of the Company to hasten on the work, I was shocked, on visiting " Railway Point," to find the railway what might not unjustly be termed a sorry *fiasco*. The work accomplished was of the puniest and most paltry description, and even what there was appeared to have been abandoned.

At Freretown, near Mombasa, we were kindly entertained by our fellow-missionaries. I learned here, to my surprise, that the "trowser question"* was a somewhat burning topic. Some of the missionaries considered it within their province to dictate to those to whom they preached the gospel what kind of clothing their converts might or might not wear. A small matter, but very significant for a student of modern missions. The converts were up in arms against this senseless piece of arrogant tyranny. I do not know how the controversy ended, or whether the trowsers or the missionaries were victorious. Considered æsthetically, one might hope that the missionaries gained the day ; but considered morally, one wishes that the converts were able to vindicate their liberty.

Another day in the steamer brought us to the town of Zanzibar, beautiful with its dazzling white buildings set in the deep green of the luxuriant tropical vegetation which surrounds them on all sides. The little island of Zanzibar, or Unguja as the natives call it (from which place the start for Uganda was to be made), is so well known that there is little need to describe it here in detail. Gathered into the town is a very large population, consisting of Arabs, Indians, and Negroes, with a few European traders and the members of the Consular staff of every nation which has representatives in the island. The Negro portion of the population, which is the largest, lives chiefly in thatched huts on the outskirts of the Arab town.

Zanzibar, now a free port, has vastly improved in late years, owing to the efforts of various British

* Native converts at Freretown were forbidden by the missionaries to wear trowsers !

Consuls and the energy of the Sultan's European advisers, of whom at present the chief is General Sir Lloyd Mathews.

The present Sultan, with whom I had the honour of an interview on my return from Uganda, was placed upon the throne by the English. He seems a man of considerable refinement and enlightenment, and is, I believe, something of a scholar. But his position is really an anomaly, and there are many reasons which would make the abolition of the Sultanate and the annexation of the island desirable.

To the disgrace of England, who has always posed as the liberator of the slave, slavery is actually recognised in the law courts of Zanzibar, which is a British protectorate, though in India legalised slavery has been abolished as repugnant to humanity. In 1873 the import of slaves to Zanzibar was absolutely forbidden by a decree of the Sultan, which, however, has been more or less of a dead letter. And now the Arab and Swahili slave-owner is upheld in the Consular Courts in his position of slave-holder on the ground that he is a protected person, while the slave, also a protected person, is denied his rights in the law courts.*

---

* A writer in *Blackwood* for June 1894 has put this matter very clearly. He says :—
" The large community of British Indians resident in East Africa are not subjects but 'protected persons' (from Cutch). They are not, and never were, allowed to fly the British flag on their vessels. They were almost entirely Muhammedans, and under the law of the Sheria. And their case was exactly identical with the present status of the protected Arabs and Swahilis. Yet in spite of the fact that the British Indians were domiciled in a foreign

We had not been in Zanzibar very long before we were all in the hands of the doctor. Our indisposition was no doubt induced by the extreme discomforts of the voyage which we had made in the *Madura*.

Thinking the mainland would prove healthier to my companions than Zanzibar, I suggested that three of the party should cross to Sadaani, and make their way to the rising ground on which the village of Endumi is built. Endumi is the first stage of the journey to the interior, and is situated some five miles from the sea. In the meanwhile I remained with Collins at Zanzibar to look after the caravan.

I found a system in vogue, for which the Imperial East Africa Company were largely responsible, of paying the caravan porters three months' wages (in our case all they would receive) in advance, by which means the unhappy traveller finds himself entirely in the hands of his carriers, who, to do them justice, use their power with remarkable moderation ; yet, taken at its best, the system, as may well be imagined, is most unsatisfactory. I strongly objected to taking the men on such terms, with the result that they all simply

country (Zanzibar), in which we had then no jurisdiction, we arbitrarily compelled them to release their slaves without compensation, not merely refusing to recognise their rights of ownership at law, but enforcing total emancipation, and making it criminal for an Indian to hold a slave. Why, then, do we hesitate to apply the same ruling to the Arabs, now that by our proclamation of a protectorate over Zanzibar their status has become identical with that of the British Indians ?"

It is to be hoped that such a state of things may soon be put a stop to, and some serious effort made in the interior for the suppression of the slave trade.

walked off, and I was obliged to give way and eat humble pie, and request them to come back again on their own terms. This a few of them deigned to do. The rest had joined some of the other caravans, and the work of supplying their places proved a further cause of delay. A whole book might be written upon the difficulties, delays, annoyances, and miseries of organising an expedition such as ours. We had the serious disadvantage, moreover, of a mixed caravan, one half of our porters being Zanzibaris, while the other half were Wasukuma natives from Nassa on the Nyanza. The result of this blending of nationalities was that the two parties disagreed so badly together as sometimes even to come to blows. We were always obliged to have two camps—one for each division.

Our missionary companions had not been gone more than a few days, when a letter came from Hubbard containing the serious news that Greaves and Wright were down with severe dysentery, and that he himself was far from well. I was myself in the hands of the doctor, and Collins also was indisposed, so that things looked not a little depressing. However, Collins and I made all haste to embark in an Arab dhow, and cross to the mainland, which we reached the following day, and landed at Sadaani at about 11 P.M. Here we succeeded in borrowing a lantern from an Indian merchant, who was acting as our agent, and by the light of the lantern we walked the five miles to Endumi, where our sick friends were encamped.

To our deep sorrow, we found that Greaves was in a very dangerous condition, but Wright was slightly better. Next day there was no improvement in Greaves, and we all felt that the only hope for his life lay in taking him back to Zanzibar, where he would have the advantage of careful nursing and attention. We therefore placed him in a hammock, and carried him to Sadaani. The German officers stationed there showed us every kindness, and lent us the Government dhow to convey our sick friend across to Zanzibar, whither Hubbard accompanied him. Greaves was received and tenderly nursed by the Sisters of the Universities' Mission, but in spite of every attention which kindness could suggest a week later he passed peacefully away.

Hubbard, as soon as he had placed his sick companion in the care of these true and generous friends, rejoined us at Endumi. We had arranged that Greaves, if well enough, should follow us with Roscoe, another missionary who was to leave England for Uganda a month later.

There was nothing now to prevent our making a start, and we finally began the long march into the interior July 9th, 1891. The impossibility of procuring carriers had made it necessary for us to leave many of our loads behind, and, to add to our difficulties, Dr. Wright and Collins were too ill to walk, and had to be carried.

During my former journeys I had sometimes thought that a bicycle might be utilised upon much of the beaten caravan tracks, which connect village with village and tribe with tribe, and on which the traveller might cross the whole continent; oftentimes, moreover, one finds long reaches of level road worn perfectly smooth by the feet of passers-by. But what in earlier days had been simply an interesting theory was made not only possible, but highly practicable, by the invention of the safety bicycle ; and so on this occasion a good new safety bicycle, with cushion tyres, formed a very important part of my equipment.

It was with a certain degree of trepidation I unpacked the machine at Sadaani, and took it from the great wooden case in which it had been conveyed thither. There were some thousands of Wanyamwezi carriers belonging to Stokes encamped near the town, who viewed with unfeigned astonishment this, to them, marvellous contrivance, which they soon named the " enzobe ya chuma "—iron donkey. I mounted, and, to my great satisfaction, found that it went well on the narrow footway leading out of Sadaani to Endumi, where our tents were pitched. Knowing, however, that I should come to many places where it would be impossible to ride the machine, I hired a porter to follow me, and to hold himself in readiness to carry the bicycle over any rough places, rivers, ravines, or rocky hills which we should meet with on our way. The carrier selected very soon found that he had made a good bargain, since for the greater part of the distance his office proved a lucrative sinecure.

The route we followed lay entirely through German territory, the road passing near the important station of Mpwapwa, two hundred miles, and Unyanyembe, five hundred miles from the coast.

For the first few days we passed through low-lying,

rich, open, park-like land, well watered with small rivers, and gradually rising until the magnificent scenery of Mamboya and Mpwapwa is reached, from which point the country sweeps up to the great plateau of Ugogo and Unyamwezi, and on to the waters of the mighty Lakes.

As our small party advanced we found that every village we came to was deserted, for the people had not yet recovered from the effects of the war waged by the Arabs against the Germans in the year 1888. Moreover, they knew too well the thieving proclivities of the caravan porters whom European travellers are obliged to employ. To my great disappointment, I found the village of a native chief called Mazengo, where I had spent ten days some three years before, almost entirely deserted, and that the kindly folks with whom I had been on the most friendly terms had all disappeared. On the morning of our arrival at this place I had a deplorable accident with the bicycle. A root, hidden by the grass, caught in the front wheel, causing it to be twisted into all shapes, also bending the fork in a frightful manner. As I viewed what appeared, at first sight, an almost total wreck, I despaired of being able to repair the damage. However, I succeeded during the day in bending the twisted parts sufficiently back to make the machine once more capable of being ridden. In the evening I went alone to a village at some distance, which had not been abandoned, and asked the inhabitants about some of my old friends at Mazengo's, especially mentioning by name a little boy called Kilimo.

Next morning I heard voices outside my tent, and on making my exit I found Kilimo himself and some of the villagers. This led to friendly relations with the chief, who was eventually prevailed upon to return with the other villagers.

While in this district we had a curious illustration of a widely prevalent African custom. In one of the villages inhabited by some members of the Wakamba tribe Dr. Wright was making good use of his medical skill in treating some cases of ophthalmia. While he was busy with a woman I saw a young man standing at a distance, who had evidently come for treatment, but who hesitated to approach. Supposing he was afraid of the white doctor I called to him to come near. The bystanders now explained that it was not the doctor but the patient whom the young man feared. She was his mother-in-law. The villagers were quite pleased with me for appreciating their feelings on the subject, which I did, not from my own personal experience, but from knowing that the curious custom of holding it improper in the highest degree to approach or even look at a mother-in-law prevails among many tribes, the people of Uganda among the rest. The Bahuma and Basoga* are notable exceptions.

Dr. Wright's method of treatment was rather more successful than a case I had dealt with in this neighbourhood some years before. A man had come begging me for *dawa*, medicine; but as he did not

* The prefix Ba or Wa means people. Wa-Swahili means Swahili people. Ba-ganda, people of Uganda.

appear to be seriously unwell, I thought I would give him some "Eno's Fruit Salt," which if it did him no good would probably not do him any harm. I therefore prepared a cup of the mixture, but seeing him hesitate about swallowing it, I had, with some asperity, to insist upon his doing so while it effervesced. When he had drained the cup I told my interpreter the patient might now, if he desired, give his symptoms more in detail, which he proceeded to do, explaining, however, that the medicine was needed for his wife, and not for himself at all! I have little doubt he was quite satisfied that this was the white man's usual method; and if the poor woman eventually recovered, the *dawa* of the white doctor, swallowed by the husband, was most likely credited with the cure.

On July 28th we reached the Kifwi Pass, leading through the mountains into Mamboya, where we fell in with Captain Stairs' caravan, which had started from Bagamoyo, a town on the coast considerably to the south of Sadaani, our own point of departure.

Our respective camps were pitched about half a mile apart. In the afternoon my companions and I took a walk on the surrounding hills, and to our surprise we saw the people flying in the greatest terror. We succeeded in enticing one elderly man to approach us, when he told us—the Swahili language being our medium of communication—that the caravan porters were raiding the whole country-side. On returning to our camp we saw two of the Zanzibar carriers come in leading four goats. The men admitted they were stolen, but pleaded in extenuation that Stairs' men had made the raid, and they had merely joined them. On searching our camp we found it was full of the little household utensils of the poor people of the neighbourhood, and that our friend's story in the afternoon was perfectly true.

I went at once to Captain Stairs and told him what our people had done. He replied that he was well aware of it, and that he had already flogged some of his men for the thefts; but he added that the natives themselves were to blame for the losses, since they had no reason to fly, thus leaving their little villages to be looted. I told him, however, how frequently they suffered from the depredation of passing caravans, and we both agreed to pay compensation, which we were enabled to do through our Church Missionary Society's missionary, Mr. Wood, who lived at Mamboya.

Before starting next morning we collected all the household goods we could find in the camp into a great heap, and I waited behind until both caravans were well on their way to Mamboya, to see that the rightful owners recovered the lost property, and not some of the Wanyamwezi tribe, who had a village in the neighbourhood.

I was rewarded after a while by seeing the natives (Wamegi) coming down the hills, and appearing like rabbits from their burrows. I sat quite motionless at a little distance with the bicycle. Soon the old women were busy identifying the various articles and in a very short space of time there was nothing left. I then mounted the bicycle and rode away.

What the natives thought of me and the "iron donkey" I do not know, but I was soon out of their ken, and a little later I reached the beautiful district of Mamboya, where the caravan was by this time encamped.

CHAPTER II

MAMBOYO TO USAMBIRO

Death of Greaves—Muganda Makali——A Rescue Party—Booty recaptured—The Iron Donkey again—Robbed by Highwaymen—A widespread Plague—Parting Company—Attacked by the Tetze—The Lord of Flies—A narrow Escape—" It is not a Man "—Repairing the Bicycle—Mackay's Grave—Men who knew how to die.

CHAPTER II

MAMBOYA TO USAMBIRO

A PLEASANT surprise awaited me at Mamboya for an hour or two after our arrival in walked the Rev. E. C. Gordon, an old companion in travel, and, like myself, one of the members of the party of missionaries who accompanied the late Bishop Hannington on his first journey to the Nyanza. Gordon was now on his way home from Uganda, which he had left some two months previously.

We were obliged to remain at Mamboya for eleven days, waiting for Mr. Roscoe and the loads which he was bringing on, and which we had been forced to leave behind us. While here we received the mournful intelligence of the death of Greaves at Zanzibar.

Mamboya is about one hundred and sixty miles from the coast; the scenery surrounding it is truly magnificent. The Church Missionary Society's station is high on the hills looking down on rich and fertile valleys, while glorious mountains tower far above the misson. Here a pointed peak of naked rock rises from its bed of living green, there a great dome, wreathed with snow-white clouds, looms through the misty morning air.

One chiefest charm of Mamboya is the grand view of the illimitable expanse of the vast Masai plain rolling away northward to the far horizon.

Leaving Mamboya, we made our way through mountain passes to Mpwapwa, a distance of fifty or sixty miles. During this part of the journey I found the bicycle of little use.

Mpwapwa, the point at which many of the great caravan routes to the interior converge, is an important place, and is a station of the German Government. On leaving Mpwapwa our way led through a waterless wilderness, the Muganda Makali (bitter water), so called from the strong saline springs at each end of it.

The day before we entered this wilderness, which leads to Ugogo, we had our first adventure connected with African highwaymen, or Ruga ruga. About midday a number of Wanyamwezi travellers came into our camp looking extremely excited, and told us a sad tale of murder and robbery. They said that shortly before they reached our camp they had been attacked by a number of predatory Wahehe (an important tribe in this region), who had killed their leader, and carried off two tusks of ivory and between thirty and forty goats which they had been taking to the coast. I thought, if we lost no time, it might be possible to overtake the thieves, who probably could not have got away very far with their booty. The poor fellows were delighted when they saw we were willing to assist them, and soon a band of volunteers was ready to start. Wright, Hubbard, Collins, and myself, with a band of porters, formed the rescue party, while Roscoe stayed behind to take care of the camp. We started at a rapid pace, but I had not run more than a few yards when my mind misgave me as to the scene of the murder being quite so close at hand as our Wanyamwezi friends had represented it to be. At any rate, I thought it would be worth while attempting to use the bicycle, so I turned back for the machine, and soon overtook my companions. Our guides followed a perfectly smooth path for nearly six miles, keeping up a good round pace. Lest I appear a monster of selfishness, I must mention that none of my companions knew how to ride a bicycle, so I had always a clear conscience when I saw them panting along, as at present, or wearily trudging forward on the daily march, while I went easily on wheels.

All at once our guides stopped, and led us off the beaten track into the bush. The bicycle bearer was now called into requisition, and we followed our guides out into the plain. We saw nothing, however, and could not distinguish any track of the goats, but still our guides held on. Suddenly we heard what seemed the bleat of a kid, but to our disappointment a curious bird rose up whose singular cry had deceived us. By this time we were approaching a scrubby bit of ground, and began to fear we had come on a wild-goose chase, when my boy, Songoro, suddenly shouted "Look there!" and soon we were racing at full speed across the plain, and in a few moments plunged into the thicket, where we suddenly came on all the goats in a small clearing. On one side lay the two ivories, while close at hand was a large calabash of fresh water, which the robbers had left in their hurried flight. The sight of an armed band of Europeans had terrified them, and they fled, leaving their ill-gotten booty behind them. They were, probably, as I have said, a small band of the great Wahehe tribe, which later proved so hostile to the Germans, almost totally annihilating a large military expedition of the latter. Had there been, however, any large muster of the tribe in our vicinity, we should almost certainly have heard of it, so that our little relief expedition was not attended with much risk.

Next day we crossed the long wilderness of Malenga Mkali, some thirty miles in extent, and entered Ugogo. Ugogo is a thirsty land, a land of sweeping winds and driving dust, an inhospitable land of poverty. And yet it has a kind of indescribable charm about it— the spell so subtle and yet so strong which every part of Africa, each in its own way, and after its own manner, seems to weave about the traveller's imagination, making him desire to return to it as the moth returns to the flame that destroys it.

Ugogo is a country consisting of forests and vast plains, enclosed by mountain ranges. These plains are dotted here and there with small " tembeys," or villages. These are long, low, narrow, mud-roofed buildings constructed of interlaced wattles, plastered roughly with clay, which form a square, into which the cattle are driven at night. Cultivation is carried on, and the people are also keepers of cattle and goats. The huge Baobab trees which dot the great level plains are a striking feature of Ugogo. These trees are of vast growth, the wood soft and useless, though the bark is largely used for making trunks or bandboxes.

The women of this country are modestly clothed with skins; young girls wear a small apron of bead-work or cotton cloth. The boys* and men are naked, though they sometimes have a leather bib in front covering their chests, or a piece of leather hanging behind to sit upon. They pierce their ears, and gradually distend the lobe, so that the men can wear large wooden discs, about half an inch thick, and about three or four inches in circumference, and the women a smaller kind, often beautifully ornamented.

As I was passing through one of the forests with the bicycle I met a party of natives in the path. On seeing me they exhibited the wildest terror, flung down their calabashes of water and flour and other articles, and fled right and left among the trees. I stopped immediately, and called to one elderly warrior not to be afraid. He came near with much caution. When he saw that I laughed, and when I had explained that the bicycle was only an "iron donkey" (endogoi ya kyuma), he was greatly reassured. The people had heard the report of the Germans' machine guns, and I suspect thought the bicycle was something of the same sort. I was dreadfully sorry for the fright I had

* The boys are circumcised at about eleven or twelve years of age, and some corresponding rite is performed on the girls at the same period.

unwittingly given, and for the broken calabashes, but the caravan was far behind, and I had nothing with me to give the poor frightened creatures to make good their loss. I think they were very glad, however, to have passed me without having been butchered, or, at least, bewitched.

A few marches further on we had a more unpleasant experience of highway robbers than our little rescue expedition had proved.

A number of these gentry suddenly rushed out upon the caravan from the thicket, on both sides of the path, uttering shrill war cries, and brandishing their spears in the faces of the frightened porters, some of whom were women. The boxes and bales went down like a peal of thunder, dropped in sudden panic by the terrified porters, who scattered right and left. The robbers whipped up four loads before any of the white men could arrive upon the scene, and vanished with them into the thicket as quickly as they had come.

The wily carriers improved the occasion by reproaching me for not having served out gunpowder to them, asserting that had I done so they would have valiantly defended the loads. Gunpowder and gun-caps mean a handy little bit of ready money in East Africa. I was informed that the method robbers employ is for one of their number to secrete himself in the branches of a tree near the path, and if he sees a weak place in the caravan which the band intends to rob, or a wide interval between the porters, as often happens during a long march, when many become tired out and lag behind, he gives a whistle like the call of a bird, and his concealed companions then rush out. On this occasion one of the men behaved with great coolness, and saved his load. He sat on the box he had been carrying, and when a warrior came to despoil him he raised his empty gun. Once or twice the robbers made at him, but each time his threatening gesture and firmness made them sheer off.

All along the line of march, but in Ugogo especially, we came on hundreds of dead cattle. The plague had swept the whole country from Uganda to the east coast, but strange to say, passing over the Sesse Islands in the Nyanza, as if the water were in some way a barrier to the infection. Buffalo, giraffe, and other big game had also suffered severely from the disease.

It took fifteen days to pass through Ugogo counting Sundays and other resting days. We emerged from this country by climbing the mountain wall which leads to the still higher plateau of Unyamwezi, between which region and Ugogo lies the Muganda Makali, the "Terrible Garden," a long wilderness which occupies six days to pass through. On each side of this wilderness are settlements of the Watuturu tribe—a very good-looking people, who have long silky hair, and the better types of them have handsome, regular features, like the royal Wahuma tribe, whom they resemble in being cattle-keepers.*

We reached the far side of the Muganda Makali in safety, and entered Unyamwezi, the country of the great carrying tribe of East Africa. Here we found our

* The Watuturu, like the Wagogo, Wakamba, and Masai, practise the rite of circumcision, but not the Wahuma.

supply of the calico cloth used for buying food so short, that it became necessary to purchase a fresh stock.

We had reached a point not more than a week's journey from Unyanyembe, the important Arab trading centre now in the hands of the German Government. We therefore decided that the caravan should move on, while I should strike in a more westerly direction towards Unyanyembe, taking with me a few men to carry the small bales of cloth, which I should be able to obtain from the Arab merchants. I was to rejoin the others at the large district of Usongo, where an old friend, the ivory trader Stokes, had his headquarters.

My way lay through the forest desert, where years before a midnight lion adventure had befallen us on my first journey to the Nyanza with Hannington, so humorously described by the Bishop in his Journal.* But though I neither saw nor heard lions I was the victim of the attack of creatures not so large as lions, but much more ferocious. I mean the tetze fly—fatal to domestic cattle, and most hostile to men. The first day of my journey to Unyanyembe I did not leave camp until late, but the following morning I started before sunrise, and, mounting the bicycle, was soon far ahead of my little party, whom I intended to wait for under some wayside tree. I soon learned, by experience, that when there is a company of people the flies distribute their favours; but if there is only one solitary wretch by himself he may expect something extremely

* "James Hannington," p. 227.

unpleasant.* Bloodthirstiness is a mild term to express the frightful craving for blood which characterises these pests—flies only a little larger than the common house-fly, but somewhat longer and of a light grey colour. They have a long, hollow, needle-like proboscis in a kind of sheath, which opens to display the weapon with which they stab, and through which they suck the blood of their victim. The sensation they cause is at first like the faintest prick of a very fine needle. The tetze, however, has a great advantage over the mosquito, in that its prick leaves no irritation.

The flies came about me in dozens, and I was streaming with blood in several places. I killed them in scores, but it was a continual battle; they grew fiercer as the sun became hotter, till at length what at first had seemed merely an intolerable nuisance began to assume an aspect which was absolutely horrible. What if I should become faint, and unable to continue the battle with them. They might drain a man as dry as a red herring. I had been told a fearful tale of a traveller in Iceland who, with his horse, had been actually eaten alive by flies, the flies finishing both man and horse in one day. What if these tigerish pests should actually make an end of me! Between nine and ten o'clock I had accomplished about twenty miles, and so I determined to dismount,

* I believe it not unlikely that large heads of domestic cattle, or numbers of horses together, might be brought in safety through a fly district, where one or two would suffer so much as to lead to their death. It is remarkable that big game, which is always found in herds, does not suffer from the fly fatally.

since I found that guiding the bicycle and keeping in the narrow path prevented my dealing in a satisfactory manner with my persistent enemies. In getting down, however, my hat fell off, and in an instant my head, which was closely cropped, was covered with the enemy. I recovered my hat, wheeled the bicycle with one hand, which was being bitten all the time, while I battled with the other till I reached a tree.* Here, freed from the bicycle, I renewed the engagement with vigour, and, to my great joy, after I had killed a few dozen of the flies, they seemed to become more shy. I now lighted a great fire with a box of matches which I always carried in my pocket. The wind blew the hot flames near me; and though the sun beat down from above, I preferred the heat to the enraged foe. Under these conditions I battled with the enemy for something like three mortal hours. As the tetze grew less persistent in their attacks their place was taken by the small common house-fly, and for the first time in my life I was quite pleased to see them. Presently a new winged foe came up in the shape of a minute bee-like fly, which makes straight for the eyes, no doubt attracted by the moisture. The late Bishop Hannington once remarked that he never understood, until he came to Africa, the meaning of " Beelzebub, lord of flies." And on this occasion Beelzebub certainly attacked me with as much vigour as ever

* One of those gigantic spurges which are common in this region. In some districts the natives dread to sit under them, saying it is unlucky, and the milky sap is said to be used as poison. None of my followers, however, seemed to have any superstition about this tree.

the devil did Luther. While I was enduring this waking nightmare of flies my men came up. By this time it was two o'clock in the afternoon. I had begun to fear I had come too far, and passed the water and camping-place by mistake, but the men said it was not so. I was able to give them some water which I carried in two tins, which I had slung to the bicycle ; and so, after the men had rested for a while, we resumed our journey, but did not reach our camp till evening ; and even then we could not obtain enough water to cook our food, but had to go some three or four miles to find the precious liquid.

The following day I narrowly escaped a disagreeable accident. While taking our mid-day rest the men set fire to the grass and scrub, and as the flame went rolling away into the forest, in its course it burned away the trunk of a half-rotten tree near the path, so that it was exactly timed to come crashing down as I passed by on the bicycle. I saw too late as I came up to it that the tree was in the act of falling; but I could not stop myself. It was a moment like a nightmare, but I kept on, and the falling giant just missed me, though I could feel the wind of it as it crashed down behind.

But I was not destined to reach Unyanyembe without accident, for the very next day, while tightening one of the bearings of the front wheel of the bicycle, the end of the fork, which had been slightly cracked, broke completely off, and the machine became perfectly useless. I had, therefore, to come down to tramping.

The disabled bicycle was now carried by the porters whom I had taken to convey the cloth I hoped to buy from the Arabs. I had great hopes of finding a Zanzibar blacksmith at Unyanyembe or Taborah, as the Arab settlement is called, who would be able to repair the damage.

While still some distance off I fell in with Mr. Deekes, one of our missionaries on his way home from Nassa. He had been with Mackay during his last illness, the melancholy details of which he related to me. Deekes himself had suffered much from this deadly Usambiro fever, and was on his way home for a much-needed change. As he required a few necessaries for his coastward march he came with me to Taborah, where, on arrival, we were courteously received by the German Governor, Mr. Siegel, as well as by the Arab merchant from whom our purchases were to be made.

Mr. Siegel and I had some conversation upon African character in general, and the Wanyamwezi people in particular. His verdict was frightfully against the Africans. Of the Wanyamwezi, he said, " It is not a man; it has not the feelings of a human being." I thought he spoke rather more strongly than he felt. Presently he produced the picture of a fair European lady and a young black girl by her side. The lady was his wife. The picture was all on my side, so I knew that Mr. Siegel agreed with me more than he allowed. I was gratified to hear, that after visiting Europe, on his return to Taborah his wife accompanied him; and from what I saw myself, and heard from others, I should say he was one of the most successful Governors of the Imperial German East African staff.

At Taborah I was fortunate in finding a blacksmith, and he and I, between us, were successful in repairing the broken bicycle. Meanwhile, the bargain for the required calico was satisfactorily concluded with the Arabs, and we bid farewell to Taborah. Deekes and I parted here—he for his long tramp to the coast, and I to join my companions at Usongo, which I reached, with the help of the bicycle, a few days later, September 19th.

Usongo is the chief town in a very populous district —a district which, when I passed through it last, had suffered from a hostile raid, and instead of smiling cornfields and pleasant villages was a howling wilderness, dotted here and there with blackened ruins. But now, once more the villages were rebuilt, and the land cultivated. The king's village was enclosed by low, solid, mud-roofed, " wattle-and-daub " houses, forming a large square within which was a second stockade, enclosing several of the conical-roofed, circular houses, built with a wide verandah all round. These houses have a rough attempt at comfort. Some of them are very clean, and are furnished with bedsteads covered with skins, and with low wooden stools. Hospitality is a characteristic of these people. It is the custom of the Unyamwezi, when they make war, on preparing for hostilities to put patches of white clay upon their faces. The curious body dance is common among the women, who contort and twist themselves in a rhythmic dance to the incessant sound of two drums beaten by women. The girls gradually work themselves up into a kind of ecstatic state, gradually approaching the male bystanders, until one of the dancers touches the person whom she selects, who is then expected to give her some small present.*

Leaving Usongo, we followed Speke's old route for ten days through Nindo and Salawe, and on October 1st, 1891, reached Usambiro, the now abandoned Church Missionary Society's station, and the scene of Mackay's latest labours. How desolate and deserted the place seemed. No echo of clanging anvil and clinking hammer broke the stillness, no sound of busy life and pleasant work, for the chief workman was gone; no kindly smile of welcome as there had been when Walker† and I had arrived at Usambiro in 1887. I had passed on ahead of the caravan with the bicycle, and on reaching the station my first act was to go to the little burial ground, now containing three new graves. Mackay's last resting place was marked by a rude wooden cross surmounting the heap of stones which covered the grave. I knew that he whose body had been laid here had been misrepresented, unappreciated, misunderstood—not indeed by Christian England, which broadly looked upon his noble life, and which rightly estimated him as worthy to be reckoned with such names as Carey, Livingstone, Moffat, and Selwyn, but by those whose privilege it might have been to

* This practice among the people nearer the Nyanza has, I have been given to understand, an improper significance.
† Archdeacon Walker, missionary in Uganda.

help him, sympathise with him, and generously support him. How little his committee really understood him may appear in the fact, as he had often told me himself, that four separate times they endeavoured, on more or less frivolous charges, to remove him from his work by recalling him home.*

I turned sadly from these graves—two of them of men whom I did not know,† and of whom the world knew nothing, and the Church only that they, as well as Mackay, Bishop Parker, and Blackburn, knew how to die.

* Mr. Eugene Stock was always on Mackay's side, and strongly opposed his recall.
† Mr. H. J. Hunt, who died November 14th, 1890, and the Rev. J. W. Dunn, who died November 21st, 1890.

CHAPTER III

USAMBIRO TO UGANDA

Two Problems—Removing Stores to Nassa—The Overland Route—Methods of Travel—Lions as travelling Companions—Wild Animals which I saw—The Bicycle in Request—Sunrise on Kiyanja—Arrival at Bukoba—King Mutatembwa—A curious Superstition—On Uganda Ground once more.

CHAPTER III

USAMBIRO TO UGANDA

FOR the next few days we were busy paying off our caravan, and providing the carriers with calico for food money to take them back again to Zanzibar. Their agreement with us was now concluded. Very few of them had abused the somewhat harsh terms they had exacted from us by running away; they were all anxious to return to their beloved Unguja (Zanzibar); and at any rate, we could not afford to keep more than one or two of them to help in organising the expedition from Usambiro to Uganda.

We now found ourselves face to face with two somewhat difficult problems—the first, how to reach Uganda; and the second, how to carry out the decision of the Church Missionary Society to abandon the Usambiro station, the buildings of which, indeed, were all tumbling into ruin, and how, and to what place, to remove all the valuable property stored in the rickety mission buildings.

The first question of how we should reach Uganda was partly met by out having secured the use of a boat belonging to Mr. Stokes, the trader, the old mission boat having become a total wreck, and the new vessel, the *James Hannington*, had not yet been placed on the Lake. Hence, we had only boat accommodation for two Europeans; and so it was decided that Wright and Collins should go in the boat as soon as possible, and that Roscoe and I should remain

THE MISSION BUILDINGS AT NASSA, ON SPEKE GULF.

behind, pack up and send the heavy iron goods to Nassa, on Speke Gulf, the station to which Mr. Hubbard, already mentioned, had been appointed.

When the work of removing the Church Missionary Society stores up to Nassa was finished, Roscoe and I hoped to accomplish the journey by land to Uganda, going by the western shore of the Lake, and carrying with us the less bulky and most valuable property, containing, among other valuable articles, some scientific instruments and several cases of drugs. This costly journey was necessary, since it was almost impossible to obtain canoes. The Roman Catholic faction in Uganda had, somehow or other, succeeded in getting hold of nearly all the boats on the Lake, and hence it was with the greatest difficulty that our missionaries could get any canoes at all. So much was this the case, that many of the English missionaries in Uganda had been waiting eighteen months for their necessary stores, which were lying at Usambiro. A fortnight after our arrival, Dr. Wright and Collins started for Uganda, leaving Roscoe and me alone to our work of packing up the goods and organising the caravan, Hubbard having already left for Nassa.

Our preparations for the journey to Uganda were nearly completed, when, on November 6th, twelve canoes, which had been sent by our missionary friends at Mengo, arrived to take us across the Lake. The canoes, however, were very small, and not capable of containing one-tenth of our loads, so that we decided that Roscoe should avail himself of the water transit, while I should take the caravan round the western shore of the Lake, as already arranged. So I bid Roscoe farewell, and started on a journey which was destined to have a somewhat disastrous conclusion.

I had with me two Zanzibari headmen—Mnubi, who had acted in this capacity on the march to the Nyanza, and Hamesi, a tailor. I had also a young Wanyamwezi headman, with fifteen porters, who had agreed to accompany me to Uganda, while as guide I obtained the services of the headman of a small village close to the mission station at Usambiro, whom I had known years before. It will thus be seen that I had only fifteen regular carriers for the two hundred loads which I had to convey to Uganda. My plan was to move

REV. E. H. HUBBARD AT NASSA.

from district to district, hiring fresh porters at every place I came to. This was an undertaking of much difficulty, and yet, owing in great measure, I think, to the fear which the natives entertained for the Germans, who had lately occupied this region—a fear which all Europeans, more or less, shared with them. The chiefs on the road treated me with the greatest respect, and in return for the presents I gave them provided porters to carry my loads. These porters I paid with calico, at so much per head. I think the possession of the bicycle proved a strong point in my favour, for the people suspected it to be a machine gun—and, at any rate, were quite certain that it was a piece of the white man's magic. But to whatever I owed it I happily succeeded in accomplishing the journey to within a few days of the German station of Bukoba, near the frontier of Uganda. As soon as the German officers heard of my approach they sent to my assistance, and for several marches transported the whole caravan free of cost.

The route I followed was for some distance that by which Stanley had reached Usambiro on his latest journey. I was still able to use the bicycle, though, as I neared Uganda, the hills and swampy valleys made that method of locomotion more and more difficult.

While journeying between Usambiro proper and a place called Bumbeke I had a novel, and I think I may call it an unique experience. One morning, at about ten o'clock, I was far ahead of the porters, and was moving along upon the bicycle over a fairly good path, when my attention was suddenly attracted by hearing some large animals galloping by my side. I was marking my path carefully at the time, but on looking to my right hand, where the animals were, I discovered that the creatures which were accompanying me were three magnificent lions. Though I had heard the roar of lions close at hand in the darkness,

I had never before actually seen one face to face. My novel companions kept up with me, going parallel with me for about a hundred yards. They were distant some twenty or thirty yards. Presently they stood still, looked at me for a moment, and then slowly bounded off at a right angle, from time to time stopping and looking back, till they finally disappeared in the long grass, while I held on my way. My men, when they came up, discovered, not far from the path, the partially devoured carcase of a zebra, which the lions had pulled down. My silent and sudden appearance had disturbed them at their feast, and, I doubt not, the extraordinary vision of the bicycle had given them fright. I did not feel any alarm myself, for such creatures, however dangerous they may be if on the defensive, seldom attack human beings unless they can come up to them silently, and spring unseen from behind. There is a great deal of game in the region round the Lake. The wild animals which I saw in this district included zebra, giraffe, rhinoceros, ostrich, and various kinds of antelope.

On November 18th, after a week's journey in a westward direction, I came once more to the Nyanza. Formerly it was not known that the Lake came down to this point, Ukome, until Stanley's latest discovery. The country was very beautiful. I spent ten days here with a little chief called Roga while waiting for my scattered caravan to come up. The boy chief was intensely interested in the bicycle, and was continually bringing me some one to race with. He would come, saying, " See, I have brought you a man ;

"MY NOVEL COMPANIONS KEPT UP WITH ME, GOING PARALLEL WITH ME FOR ABOUT A HUNDRED YARDS."

STAN·BERKELEY

he is a very good runner ; try if you can beat him." There was a good piece of pathway close at hand, and whether it was the speed of the bicycle, or the modesty of my competitors, it always happened that they were the first to give up.

My friend the little chief willingly supplied me with carriers, and, leaving his village, we passed on, still in view of the Lake, to a beautiful place called Nyamirembe, opposite an island called Bugando. The bicycle was still in request, and most useful. The people in this district are not of a very high type, but the chiefs seem more or less of the Wahuma race. The men and young girls do not wear clothing. Still continuing by the Lake, I came to a country called Kimwanyi, of which an old chief named Kazuma was king. I had sent messengers on ahead to him to ask for porters, which, to my great surprise and delight, he sent, and more than a hundred men returned with my messengers. I spent some days with Kazuma, and then made my way into the magnificent country of Ihangero, called by the people of Uganda, Jangero, and ruled by a Wahuma king, Nyalubamba. He certainly was one of the most dignified men I have seen—handsome, tall, and proud, yet courteous and polite. He was highly pleased with my performance on the bicycle. The king in these countries sits in front of his chiefs, and not as in Uganda, where the chiefs sit facing the king, or else in rows on both sides. Many travellers have spoken of the glory of African sunsets, but at Nyalubamba's I saw a sunrise more gorgeous than any I can remember.

Some distant hills, called Kiyanja, were illumined with a splendour so strange and beautiful, that one might dream that it shone from that " City which has the Glory of God, whose light is like a stone most precious as it were a jasper stone clear as crystal."

From Kazuma's I had sent to Bukoba, to tell the German officer, Captain Langheld, of my approach. He at once sent his second in command, Sergeant-Major Kühne, to meet me. This gentleman showed me the very greatest kindness, and at once relieved me of all further care and anxiety as to the caravan. Mr. Kühne and I had our Christmas dinner here. Our medium of communication was Swahili. He told me of one or two hairbreadth escapes when attacking African stockades ; and how on one occasion, when he felt his small following must be overpowered, he took out his notebook to scrawl a hurried line of farewell to his mother. But on that occasion he escaped, and lived to reach the Fatherland, where he only stayed, however, a few months, and returned once more to Africa, to fall at last fighting before a stockaded village.

Christmas Day was brightened by the arrival from Uganda of a young sub-chief, with some dozen followers, who had been sent all this distance to meet me, and to welcome me. Letters came also from my friend Walker, now living at Masaka, the capital of Budu, and the seat of the important chief Pokino Sebwato (Nikodemo), the foremost man among the Protestants of Uganda, and practically their leader.

On passing out of Ihangero we reached the country

of a chief named Kahigi or Kaizi—healthy highlands overlooking the Lake, while westward was a fine view of a hilly plateau, which terminated in a sudden declivity. We could see in the distance a sparkling stream pour its waters over the rocks, a sheer fall of between one and two hundred feet.

At the end of December we reached Bukoba, where I was kindly welcomed by Captain Langheld, who gave me hospitality for nine days. From here I sent letters to Walker to tell him of my arrival at Bukoba, and then prepared to wait patiently for the Uganda canoes or the carriers, whom I hoped he would be able to send for the loads which I had with me. The German fort was built in the territory of the Baziba, a large nation bordering on Uganda, but, unlike Uganda, under a number of independent kings, or Bakama, as they are called. Mukotanyi was the name of the king near whose chief village the German fort had been built. It commanded a view of the Nyanza looking east, while far west were the hills of Karagwe.

My time at Bukoba passed pleasantly. I succeeded in teaching both my kindly entertainers to ride on the bicycle, while I was able to contribute to their amusement in the evenings by producing a musical box which I had with me, and which played a large number of tunes. Our conversation naturally turned on Uganda, and my German hosts were not very sparing of their criticisms of the action of the English Company's officers; and it certainly did appear very strange to me, knowing as I did the strong and loyal following they had in the country, that they should hold the

4

weak position which my hosts implied that they occupied. I had not been very long in Uganda itself when I discovered the reason for such an unsatisfactory condition of affairs; but enough of this for the present.

In the month of January I left Bukoba, accompanied by Captain Langheld, who intended to pay a visit to a frontier chief, named Mutatembwa, whose territory lay on the south bank of the Kagera River, which is the geographical boundary dividing the English and German spheres in this region. The second day from Bukoba brought us to Mutatembwa's capital. The Germans had previously had a fight with the people of this chief, but their arms of precision, and the fact of Mutatembawa's political isolation, soon brought the fighting to an end, and the chief was glad to come to terms with the white strangers, by paying five hundred head of cattle and a considerable amount of ivory. Captain Langheld's visit on the present occasion was of a friendly and a complimentary character. The chief collected something like two thousand of his warriors in honour of his guest, and came himself from his village to pay a visit of state. He wore upon his head a tall beaded crown, which seemed to have a continual tendency to fall off. Two warriors, one at each side of him, held a long shield so as to protect his person. He seemed very suspicious, uneasy, and nervous, but he could not restrain his admiration and surprise on seeing a donkey we had brought with us; but his astonishment knew no bounds when the bicycle was produced, and I mounted and showed him how it was used. I also showed him the musical box, which so impressed him that he sent to borrow it, and offered, if I would sell it, to give me a tusk of ivory (worth about £25). A few more days, and I had lost the musical box, with most of my other property, including the bicycle !

That night the king's great drums were beaten without intermission, and a watch kept, since the people entertained no little fear and suspicion of their European visitors.

All this country, from Ihangero to the Kagera River, is generally called Kiziba. The people wear a kind of long fringe round the waist and shoulders made of the fibre of the wild palm, and speak a language very similar to that of the Baganda. They have a curious superstition regarding snakes, and pay them a kind of worship, allowing them free access to houses, never killing them unless the snake should bite one of the inmates of the house, in which case only it appears lawful to kill the unpleasant though sacred inmate.

Next day we reached a place called Bugombe, where I bade farewell to Captain Langheld, and went on to a point on the Lake where I hoped to obtain canoes to take me from the mouth of the Kagera to Bali, the landing place nearest to the Pokino's capital of Masaka, where my friend Walker had established himself. On my way to the place of embarkation, the chief on the Kiziba side of the Kagera sent to say he would like to see me—he called himself the Kokino —so I turned aside and went down to his village.

He was quite a young fellow, son of Mutatembwa, and expressed himself as anxious to learn the white man's wisdom and religion. The Baganda had frequently visited him—in fact, all this country on the south of the Kagera had formerly been a regular raiding ground for these people.

The next evening, January 13th, I pitched my camp at a place called Bwendi, in Budu, on the Uganda side of the Kagera, so that after an absence of nearly five years I stood on Uganda ground once more. And here for a time I must pause to say something of the story of Uganda, and to take a retrospective view of the strange vicissitudes through which the country had passed since its first discovery in the year 1862 by Captain Speke, the famous explorer.

BOOK II

A RETROSPECT

CHAPTER I

KINGS MUTSEA AND MWANGA

*H. M. Stanley's Letter—Description of Uganda Weapons, etc.—
First Missionaries reach Nyanza—Christ or Mukasa—" La ill
aha ill 'Allah"—A rash Speech—King Mutesa's Death—Status
of Princes—Mwanga as King—Stormy Outlook—Printing
Press at Work—The Masai Route—Unsuspected Dangers—
Capture of Bishop Hannington—Expecting instant Death—
Ominous Precautions—Messengers from Mwanga—Murder of
Bishop Hannington—We are doomed to Death—Redeeming
our Lives—Christianity asserts its Power—Persecution—The
Crowning Deed of Blood.*

CHAPTER I

KINGS MUTESA AND MWANGA

MUTESA has been described by so many writers, from Speke downwards, myself * among the number, that I need do no more than give a short outline of his relations with his European visitors.

In 1862 Uganda was entered by Speke, whose journal of the discovery of the source of the Nile contains a vivid picture of the country in its pristine state. It was visited thirteen years later by Stanley in his memorable journey described in his book "Through the Dark Continent."

These travellers found that Uganda presented a striking contrast to the surrounding tribes; and though a land where the direst cruelty and most callous indifference to human life or human suffering prevailed, yet not wanting in a certain kind of civilisation of its own. Here was a people whose rulers exacted the most scrupulous modesty on pain even of death. Both men and women were clothed in the beautiful red

* "Two Kings of Uganda." (Sampson Low & Co., 1879.)

embugu, or bark-cloth, for the manufacture of which Uganda has always been famous—the men wearing it as a graceful robe knotted over the right shoulder, the women wrapping it round them under both arms, and securing it by a cincture of the same material fastened round the waist. People of the upper class wore shoes made in the country, while the reed-built and thatched houses displayed the greatest neatness and skill in their construction.

In consequence of a letter from Stanley the Uganda Mission was undertaken by the Church Missionary Society, under the enthusiastic direction of the late Rev. Henry Wright, Mr. (now the Rev.) Edward Hutchinson, Mr. Eugene Stock, and others, who in simple faith determined to embark upon an enterprise the importance of which only true wisdom could have realised, and the difficulty of which only true faith could have dared to face.

In response to their appeal for missionaries, Shergold Smith, a retired naval lieutenant, Alexander Mackay, Dr. Smith, Rev. C. T. Wilson, Mr. O'Neill, and others volunteered for the work. Of this party only four, in the first instance, succeeded in reaching the Lake—the two Smiths, Wilson, and O'Neill. Of the rest some died, others were invalided home, while Mackay had been carried back to the coast from Ugogo by the doctor's orders—a piece of discipline in which his dauntless and eager spirit found it difficult to acquiesce.

The others reached the Nyanza in 1877 after very great trials and sufferings. Lieutenant Smith, the

UGANDA WEAPONS, IMPLEMENTS, MUSICAL INSTRUMENTS, UTENSILS, ETC.
(*For description, see note, p.* 59.)

leader, wrote, "It seemed to me that all Satan's force was allied against us. The men deserted by fifties. Lies, thefts, false reports—all were used to delay us ;

DESCRIPTION OF ARTICLES ON PREVIOUS PAGE.

1. Neck ornament, red and white beads.
2. Uganda knife with black wooden handle.
3. Usukuma harp with figure ornament, made of one piece of wood. The strings are one continuous piece of twisted gut.
4. Lubare spear, entirely of iron, one of many which are used standing in rows before the tomb of a deceased king of Uganda.
5. Magic horn used by the medicine man. To it are attached charms of all sorts.
6. Uganda spear as used by a chief. The central ridge and the edges only are polished.
7. An Uganda chief's staff (upside down) of white wood.
8. A Lubare shield from Busoga. This is made of one bit of wood, cut to shape, and covered *entirely*, excepting on the two prominences, with fine wickerwork. Very long black and white goat's hair is sewn round the edges.
9. Uganda harp, covered with fine leather, which supports the eight strings, and is laced with ornamented gut to the leather at the back. The rings near the pegs are made of lizard skin.
10. Spear used in Uganda by the Wahuma, or cattle-herding tribe—much lighter than the ordinary Uganda spear.
11. The right shoe, or sandal, of an Uganda chief, made of ornamented buffalo hide, the thongs being of otter fur.
12. A polished black clay bottle from Uganda, used for strong drink by the highest chiefs only. This is made by hand without the use of a potter's wheel.
13. A large basket made of grass, one of a pair as used for containing cooked food.
14. A large war drum, made of one piece of wood, hollowed out, and covered on top and bottom with raw cow hide, with the hair on outside. This is thonged together by strips of twisted raw hide, which also has the hair remaining. The strap of ornamented leather is for carrying round the shoulders. The cushion of sheep's skin to the left is for use when the drum is balanced on the head during a journey. Each of these war drums was, as it were, consecrated by the cutting of a man's throat over the wooden part before the cover was fastened on. These drums are of various sizes.
15. A wooden board used in a well-known game (Mweso), which is played with beads or counters.
16. A solid wooden stool made of one piece without joints, from Kavirondo. This supports an Uganda adze. The handle is of wood, the heavy blade of iron, so arranged that it can be used crossways or lengthways as required.
17. An Uganda hand drum—a hollowed piece of wood, covered with goat's skin.
18. A small stool cut from a single piece of wood from Unyamwezi.
19. Uganda adze. For description, see No. 16.
20. The ordinary Uganda spade or hoe as used by the women. The blade is wrought iron, hammered out on a flat stone. It is tied to the handle, which is a natural angle in the growth of the wood, selected specially.
21. Vessel for milk or cider, from Kavirondo.
22. A white rope of plaited (square) "bow-string hemp," used formerly by the king's executioners.

B. WOODD WALKER.

and it took us six weeks to accomplish that which can easily be done in sixteen days (*i.e.*, the journey from Taborah to Kagei at the south of the Nyanza). Trouble seemed to follow trouble as wave follows wave in a stormy sea. First Dr. Smith, a young and devoted Scotchman, succumbed to dysentery, and his sorrowing companions laid him to rest by the waters of the sunlit Lake. Shortly afterwards followed the massacre of Lieutenant Smith and O'Neill on the island of Ukerewe by its chief Lukonge. The missionaries had become involved in a quarrel between a half-caste Arab trader Sungura and the chief. The Arab, finding himself attacked by Lukonge's warriors, took refuge with the two missionaries, who chivalrously afforded him protection, and, as a consequence, lost their lives in what I fear was the Arab's unjust quarrel.

Later came Mackay, and at great personal risk visited Lukonge, who expressed his sincere regret at what had happened, saying he never meant his white friends to be harmed.

After this Mackay crossed the Lake, and reached Uganda, that country where his great work was accomplished.

Mutesa received him kindly, and soon learnt to respect the single-hearted missionary, and, like Herod with John, Mutesa heard Mackay gladly, and did many things; but he would not do the one thing needful— yield himself to be the servant of Him who sits above kings. Mackay, in his letters home, has powerfully described what may be regarded as the great crisis in Mutesa's life. The matter arose regarding the visit of

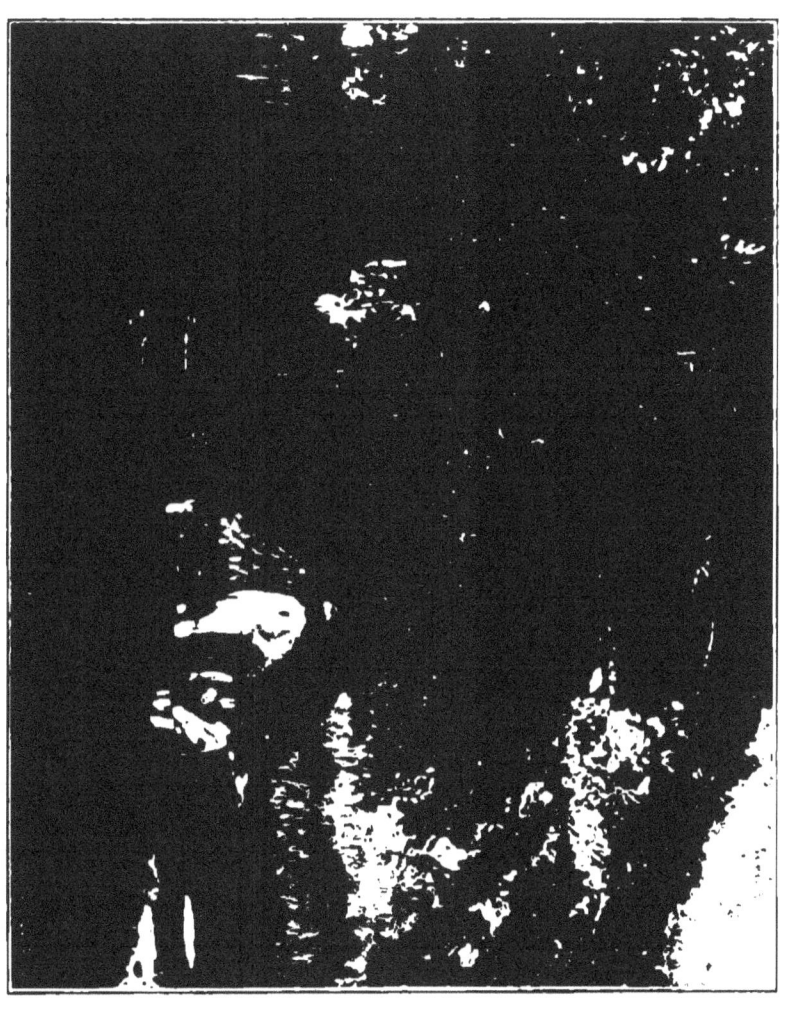

ON THE ISLAND OF UKEREWE.

the priests of Mukasa, the tutelary divinity of the Nyanza, in solemn pomp to the king's capital on Nabulagula Hill. In conversation Mutesa admitted to Mackay that he knew the heathen deities were false, and that the priests deceived the people, and for a time strenuously opposed their approach to his enclosure; but the influence of his queen-mother, the " Namasole," and of the chiefs prevailed, and the king gave way to the storm which his opposition to the religion of the country had raised, and from that time Mutesa left the ranks of earnest inquirers after truth, to become an amused and cynical listener to religious discussions and arguments in which he appeared to find much entertainment.

King Mutesa, or Mukābya, as he was commonly called, was an object of the deepest reverence, and even superstitious dread, to his people. Before the coming of white men to his country he had practised the horrid rites of the Kiwendo, when thousands of victims were ruthlessly slaughtered in the performance of the sanguinary religious rites of Uganda. It was said that when Mutesa rebuilt his father Suna's tomb, the throats of two thousand unhappy human victims were cut at the dead king's grave.

Mutesa had also inaugurated the system of religious persecution against the Muhammedans, which his son and successor Mwanga put in operation against the Christian Church.

Arab traders had come to Uganda in Suna's time, and, later, had been eagerly welcomed by Mutesa, who even learned to read the Koran. The young pages, sons of the chiefs who were in attendance on the Emperor or Kabaka, seeing that their royal master looked favourably on the new teaching, took every opportunity of learning all that they were able from the stranger Arabs, and soon Mutesa's lubiri (enclosure) echoed with the confession of the Mussulman faith—

KING LUKONGE OF UKEREWE AND HIS WIFE.

"La ill āha ill 'Allah Muhammed rasul Allah" ("God is God, and Muhammed is His prophet"). But the young pages went further than the king, and eagerly accepted the initiatory rite of Islam.

Then they refused beef from the king's table, saying beef from a bullock not slain by a true Muhammedan is food only fit for dogs. This rash speech was duly reported to the royal tyrant. His large eyes flashed, while a grim smile played on his lips. "Is my beef only fit for dogs?" asked Mutesa. And forthwith he summoned Mukajangwa, the head executioner, who, with his myrmidons with cords round their heads, and strings hanging over their faces to give them a terrible

KING MUTESA'S GREAT BURIAL HOUSE, NABULAGULA.

appearance, awaited the king's behests. "Go," said the king, "and seize every uncircumcised man or boy in the country, that we may slay them." The order was promptly obeyed, and that same night two hundred unhappy youths were burned to death.

I had reached Uganda early in 1883, and the following year Mutesa died. The burial of Mutesa may be taken as one instance of how old customs were breaking down. Mutesa was the first king placed in a coffin, and interred in a grave.*

On the death of Mutesa one of his younger sons, named Mwanga, was chosen to succeed him. This lad had often visited the two missions, though his father, I believe, had forbidden him to do so. Most of his elder brothers were kept under the strictest guard, being immured in a large enclosure under the charge of a chief called Kasuju. These princes had their own gardens and estates in the country, the fruits of which were duly brought to them by their slaves and dependents. This system had only been introduced by

* On the accession of a king in former times the custom used to be for a long fuse to be ignited by a man named *Senkole*. The fuse was wound round a post, and each day *Senkole* added more to the length of the fuse. When the king happened to die it became the part of *Senkole* to extinguish the fuse, and to whisper mysteriously to the *Katikiro* (prime minister), "The fire is out," the formula by which in Uganda the death of the king is expressed. At first the king's death is kept secret, but soon the terrible fact becomes known, whereupon the death-wail goes up from the multitude of women in the king's vast enclosure. No one who has ever heard it can forget the sound of that great cry, as it suddenly breaks forth upon the midnight stillness, now rising to a shriek of anguish, anon sinking to a wail of plaintive despair.

The corpse of the deceased king in former times was taken to a place called Merera, the *butaka*, or possession of an old landed proprietor called *Sebandeke*, and some eight hours' march west of Mengo. Here the lower jaw was cut off and placed in an ant-heap (kinyomo), that the ants might eat it perfectly clean. The body, despoiled of its lower jaw, was not interred, but carried to the house of a peasant on the estate, and laid there; the house was immediately broken down, so that the heavy thatch and *débris* might completely cover the dead king's corpse; strong

Mutesa ; for in former times the sons of the kings had held high chieftainships throughout the country; but, on the death of the reigning ruler, this had resulted in so much anarchy and fighting, that the plan of immuring the princes was adopted by Mutesa to prevent any trouble as to the succession. Mwanga, who was strikingly like his father, had been allowed by the king to be at liberty, as also the eldest son Kiwewa, who by the immemorial custom of Uganda might not sit upon the throne.

The missionaries, both English and French, were pleased when they heard that Mwanga had been elected to the kingship. We had dreaded lest his

stakes were driven in side by side all round the house to keep off wild animals; and then the king's chief butler or brewer (*Seruti*), his chief baker or cook (*Kauta*), the chief of the Bahuma herdsmen (*Sebalija*), and his second in command (*Sensalira*), were put to death there. The third ruler of the Bahuma, however, was left alive; but *Mulamba*, the king's doormaker, was killed; also his lady cook and his lady brewer.

To return now to the jaw, which is called *lwanga*. It was carefully removed from the ant-heap, and presented before the new king; after which it was handed to *Manoga*, the king's tailor, who covered it with beads worked in patterns. Then on a site chosen in Busiro, the government of Mugema, in which the capital is always built, a *kigya*, or sacred temple, used to be erected, surrounded with a fence of reeds, wattled or woven, not laced, side by side, as in an ordinary enclosure. This enclosure was capable of containing some three hundred houses, which were inhabited by the dead king's widows, and was guarded outside by old men. The jaw, *lwanga*, was kept by the head widow, who had been formerly the head wife, or *Kadu Lubare*, of the dead king; and the late queen sister, the *Lubuga*, became the head of the old establishment, but lived in a separate enclosure of her own outside.

elder brother Kalema might have been chosen—that same Kalema who afterwards became Sultan of the Muhammedans when Kiwewa, who took the kingdom when Mwanga was expelled, had in his turn been driven out. Kalema's ruthless and savage cruelties help one to understand how in comparison Mwanga was called Mutefu ("The Mild").

Thus, then, the clever though unstable lad Mwanga found himself suddenly raised from what was little more than the position of a well-to-do peasant to the autocratic power of an African emperor. How he filled his great position the following pages will show.

It very soon became evident that the young king had allowed himself to fall completely under the influence of Arab traders and the old heathen chiefs. The latter hated equally all foreigners and their ways, while the Arabs detested the missionaries, who, besides being unbelievers in Islam, were of that same race whose people at the coast showed such bitter hostility to the slave trade, from which the Arab almost entirely derives his living. English cruisers at Zanzibar seized and confiscated the slaves which the Arabs had taken such great expense, pains, and trouble, either to buy, as in Uganda, or to raid, as in the Nyassa and other districts. To this hostile Arab influence in the councils of Mwanga may be traced nearly all the disasters which gathered round the work of Christian missions during the early part of his reign.

The first two years of Mwanga's rule were marked by three distinct outbreaks of persecution, aimed either at the missionaries or the converts whom they taught.

The first took place early in the year 1885, when the outlook on all sides was stormy and uncertain.

Vague rumours of an advancing tide of European aggression filled the hearts of king and chiefs alike with uneasiness and dread. In the north the great white Egyptian pasha (Gordon), towards the latter part of Mutesa's reign, had shown signs of a desire to seize Uganda; and one of his officers in 1875, M. Linant de Bellefonds, had actually entered the country with a few hundred soldiers, and flaunted the Egyptian flag in Mutesa's capital. The Germans had already begun operations on the east coast, and tidings of their high-handed doings had reached Uganda, while undefined rumours came from the west of white men advancing by the Congo, while both the English and French had various mission stations in the Unyamwezi country, to the south of the Nyanza; hence from all quarters of the compass white men seemed to be converging on Uganda.

The Arab slave-traders were not slow to take advantage of any news they received of what they represented as European aggression, and were able so cleverly to work on the king and his chiefs, that their fears and suspicions were at last thoroughly aroused, which led them to treat us with marked hostility—a hostility which at last culminated in a personal outrage upon Mackay and myself, and the burning to death on January 31st of three of our young converts, whose only crime was that they had been taught by us, and were our friends.*

* A full account of these martyrdoms is given in my "Two Kings of Uganda." See p. 145. (Sampson Low & Co.)

This cruel outrage seemed for a time to satisfy the anger of the chiefs. It had not been resented. There was no way in which it could be resented. But all of them heard how deeply it had affected us; not indeed in the way they had imagined, for it had stirred us to sorrow rather than to anger. We were an insoluble mystery to these rulers. So they let us alone, contenting themselves by forbidding any of their people, upon pain of death, to come about our place. But this order was very soon disregarded, and, like Nicodemus, first one came at night to sympathise with us in our trouble, and to listen to our teaching, then another; then one or two would steal in quietly in the daytime. Mackay and I wrought hard meanwhile at the printing press during this lull in our work of teaching, so that as opportunity offered we might have some printed matter to put into the hands of the people. When a month or two had passed the storm seemed to have blown over, and we were once more surrounded by crowds of eager learners and listeners; and the three of us * had our hands full from morning till night with our work of preaching and teaching.

But as the year drew to a close the dark clouds a second time gathered about us, and soon we were to suffer the loss of the brave Bishop Hannington, which meant in my case the loss of a warm personal friend. We had reached the Nyanza together in 1882, but continued fever had obliged him to return to England

* The Rev. P. O. Flaherty was the third English missionary in Uganda.

for a time to recruit. He soon, however, came back to East Africa as bishop, and took up his residence at Freretown, where rumours reached him of the troubles which I have mentioned.

Hannington had suffered much on the journey up to the Lake from what he supposed was the unhealthiness of the Unyamwezi route, though the probabilities are that more suffering was caused by want of experience and insufficient supplies than from any particular unhealthiness of the German Protectorate. He therefore determined to try the more direct route to the Nyanza which had been traversed by Mr. Joseph Thompson. He was anxious to lose no time in reaching Uganda ; for though we had been unable to send any letters for something like six months after the sad martyrdom of our young converts, yet uncertain tidings of the trouble had reached the bishop, and the chivalrous desire to share our dangers, and to give us his sympathy and help, made him hurry on his preparations for his journey to Uganda. The sad story is soon told. He passed triumphantly through the dreaded Masai, the tribe which had been considered the great bar to this route, only to fall at last in Busoga, a victim to the fears and terrors of Mwanga and his chiefs. As soon as we could find opportunity we wrote to Hannington, warning him against the danger of either entering Uganda, or sending any more missionaries until the suspicions of the people were more allayed. We also explained to him the political complications in the country, which made the very greatest caution absolutely necessary. Our letters, though they reached the coast only a fortnight after the bishop left on his last journey, were not forwarded to him. The British Consul-General at that time had also been fully informed by us of the danger, and yet no messengers were sent after Bishop Hannington to warn him of the terrible peril into which he was running; and so he came on in ignorance of the causes disturbing Uganda, which made his coming at this time doubly dangerous, but his coming by the most jealously guarded frontier of the Nile actually fatal.

But though we had been unable to communicate with Hannington, he had written to tell us of his intention of coming to Lower Kavirondo, and asking us to send the boat to meet him. On Mackay's informing Mwanga that the bishop hoped to come and pay him a visit, and had asked that the mission boat should be sent to meet him, Mwanga asked, suspiciously, to what point he would come, "He will come to Kavirondo," was the reply. No one knew where Kavirondo was. (The Baganda call Kavirondo Bukede.) "Would he come to Busoga?" The answer was in the negative, and so very reluctantly the king sent two of his men with the boat—these were Mika Sematimba and Matayo (now Mujasi)—with orders to seek for the stranger white-man, and when they found him to convey him, not direct to Uganda, but to Msalala—the English mission station at the south of the Nyanza—after doing which, they were to come back and report upon Hannington. The king further said, that if the report of the messengers were favourable, he would then send for the bishop to come to Uganda. The French missionaries, on being questioned, gave it as their opinion that it would not be advisable for the English bishop to enter Uganda. In the meanwhile, Hannington had made his way to the Nile, which was guarded at the point he reached by the chief Luba, who had orders from Uganda, on pain of death, to permit no one to pass. The sad story is but too well known how Luba obeyed his orders to the letter, and seized Hannington by force and imprisoned him. As soon as the capture was accomplished, he sent post-haste to inform Mwanga of what he had done, and to ask for instructions. The news of Hannington's arrest was followed by the holding of a hasty council of the Uganda chiefs, with the result, that men were sent with orders to kill the bishop and all his following (between forty and fifty men *) ; and this deed of blood was carried out on October 29th, 1885, just nine months after the first martyrdoms.

The bishop's diary was subsequently recovered in which he had written a graphic account of his capture and sufferings in prison. I give a few brief extracts.

On October 21st Hannington had reached Luba's villages, where he pitched his camp ; and in the afternoon he and his man Ibrahim had climbed a neighbouring hill. He writes : " To my joy I saw a splendid view of the Nile only about half-an-hour's distance, country being beautiful . . . when suddenly, about twenty ruffians set upon us. They violently

* The main body of porters, some one hundred and fifty, had been left at Mumia's, under the Rev. W. H. Jones.

threw me to the ground.... Twice I nearly broke away from them, and then grew faint with struggling, and was dragged by the legs over the ground. I said, 'Lord, I put myself in Thy hands, I look to Thee alone.' Then another struggle, and I got to my feet, and was thus dashed along.... The exertion and struggling strained me in the most violent manner. In spite of all, and feeling that I was being dragged away to be murdered at a distance, I yet sang 'Safe in the arms of Jesus,' and 'My God, I am Thine,' and then laughed at the very agony of my situation, my clothes torn to pieces, wet through, strained in every limb, and for a whole hour expecting instant death; hurried along, dragged, pushed, until we came to a hut, into the courtyard of which I was forced. Now I thought, 'I am to be murdered.' As they released one hand I drew my finger across my throat, and understood them to say decidedly, 'No.' We then made out that I had been seized by order of the Sultan."

"*October 22nd, Thursday.*—I found myself last night on my bed in a fair-sized hut, but with no ventilation, floor covered with rotting banana peel and leaves and lice, in a feverish district, fearfully shaken, scarce power to hold up a small Bible. Shall I live through it? 'My God, I am Thine.'"

"*October 23rd, Friday.*—I woke full of pain and weak, yet they guard every move as if I were a giant. I don't see how I can stand all this, yet I don't want to give in; but it almost seems as if Uganda itself was going to be forbidden ground. Though I am far in the dominion, I have yet only looked upon the country itself. The Lord only knows."

"*October 24th, Saturday.*—Thank God for a pleasant night. The day passed very quietly. I amused myself with Bible and diary."

"*October 25th.*—Still a great deal of pain in my limbs. When I was beginning to think of my time in prison as getting short, the chief has sent men to redouble the fence around me. What does it mean ? Has a messenger arrived from Mwanga? The look of this has cast me down again. My guards and I are great friends, almost affectionate, and one speaks of me as ' my white man.' My men are kept in close confinement, except two, who come daily backwards and forwards to bring my food. This they take in turns, and implore, so I hear, for the job."

"*October 26th, Monday.*—I am heavy and sleepy. If I mistake not, signs of fever creep over me. To-day I am very broken down in health and spirits."

"*October 27th, Tuesday.* (Sixth day as a prisoner.) I am very low in spirits, it looks so dark. I have been told that the first messengers [to Mwanga] would return at the latest to-day. I don't know what to think, and would say from the heart, 'Let the Lord do what seemeth Him good.' I am very low, and cry to God for release."

"*October 28th, Wednesday.*—A terrible night ; first, with noisy, drunken guard, and secondly, with vermin which have found out my tent, and swarm. I don't think I got one sound hour's sleep, and woke with fever fast developing. O Lord, do have mercy upon me, and release me. I am quite broken down and brought low. Comforted by reading Psalm xxvii. ('The Lord is my light and my salvation, whom shall I fear?' etc.

"Evening ; fever passed away. News come that Mwanga has sent three soldiers, but what news they bring they will not yet let me know. [It was the news of his intended murder.] Much comforted by Psalm xxviii. : ' Unto Thee, O Lord, will I call. . . . The Lord is my strength and my shield, my heart hath trusted in Him, and I am helped.' "

" *October* 29*th, Thursday.*—I can hear no news, but was held up Psalm xxx., which came with great power."

The above is the last day's entry. He will write no more sorrowful words. His life's lessons are over. The contradictions of men must seem small now, for a great power possesses him. In faith he has uttered the words, " O Lord, my God, I cried unto Thee, and Thou hast healed me." Renewed, he can call for praises to Him whose anger is but for a moment, in whose favour is life. God has taken him now into His keeping, has loosed his sackcloth, and girded him with gladness, and the glorious song dies away in a pæan of praise. " O Lord God, I will give thanks unto Thee for ever."

He is led forth to die—a weary road amid hostile faces, a babel of strange voices sounding in his ears. He is weak and weary, and worn with fever. On through the bright banana groves his captors lead him until they reach an open space; here they halt. A signal is given ; it is the firing of a gun. Another moment, and Bishop Hannington has fallen pierced by the spears of that race to which he had devoted his life.

But we must leave the painful incidents of this journal, and the absorbing interest which centres round the brave hero who thus had given his life for the good cause, to return to his fellow-missionaries in Uganda. We had heard with horror the cruel intention of Mwanga, and had sought in vain to intercede for the Bishop's life. When the sad tidings of Hannington's death reached us, Mackay wrote : " The worst seems over ; our dear brother is happy ; we remain in the midst of death. Lord, Thy will be done."

The reader will clearly see how serious our position had become. Hannington, by a change of plan, had made his way to the Nile instead of adhering to his original intention of waiting for the boat at Kavirondo ; while Mackay's assuring Mwanga that the bishop would not come to Busoga being followed so soon by his arrival there, made us appear to the suspicious chiefs in the light of persons who were engaged in a deliberate plot to seize the country from the Nile. Further, I think there can be little doubt that Luba greatly exaggerated to Mwanga the resistance made by Hannington, in order to excuse his own rough treatment of the bishop, while the caravan of some one hundred and fifty men, which the bishop left behind him at Mumias, in upper Kavirondo, was probably magnified into an army of invasion.

For many days we waited in suspense for some definite news as to what had really occurred ; at last we could not doubt the fact of the murder from the circumstantial accounts which had reached us.

The question was discussed in the King's Council of what should be done to us, since, it appeared, we were in the plot to seize Uganda. Had we not told lies about the bishop's coming ? It was therefore decided that we should be killed. One of Mwanga's sisters, named Nalumansi, however, who was learning to read, hearing of this plan, sent down a significant message to us saying : "You had better make friends with the king, and redeem yourselves." This, in Mackay's view, meant we had better send Mwanga a present. O'Flaherty urged that it would be useless, since when we were dead the king could take all that we had. But Mackay remembered an instance in Mutesa's days which made him think otherwise. A small sub-chief for some offence or other had been condemned to death. The executioners had even seized him, and were dragging him off to kill him, but Mackay heard the prisoner say as he was dragged past the king : " Nkuwade ente ana " (" I will give you forty cows "). " Set him free," said the king, and he was immediately released, and came back to say, " Neanze, neanze ge " (" I thank, I thank you "), then quietly returned to his seat among the courtiers.

We therefore sent nearly all that we possessed to the king and the two principal chiefs, who we knew were principally concerned in the murder of the bishop. These were the Katikiro Mukasa, and Kyambalango, the Pokino. We were immediately summoned to the king's presence, and plied with questions as to who had told us they intended to kill us. What the present was for? Who had told us about a white man in Busoga? Then they threatened us, the king saying he would put us in the stocks, and he challenged England and all Europe to rescue us! Had Lukongo not killed our brothers? Had Mirambo (an important Unyamwezi chief) not also killed white men? What harm had befallen them? For more than two hours the interview was protracted. At last the king ordered us to receive a couple of cows, which meant that we were acquitted.*

After this, things soon began to settle down again. Mr. O'Flaherty was allowed to leave just before Christmas; and the departure of even one of us was looked upon with satisfaction by our Arab enemies, who, now that Mwanga had committed himself by killing a European, seemed to gain more influence over him than ever.

But though there were a few months of comparative quiet, and a new year had begun brightly, there were indications that the suspicions, which had never slumbered, were once more assuming an acute phase. The Mumbeja, or princess, who had saved our lives by her timely warning, now flung away her Mayembe, sacred horns and charms. This example was followed by others; but in June of 1886 a circumstance took

* Formerly it was the custom that when the king killed a man his nearest relatives or friends must at once send the king a considerable present, to redeem or purge themselves, and to show that their hearts were white, and that they were not harbouring evil thoughts of malice and revenge. Their failing to do so was an offence visited with death. Hence the importance of the timely warning to us to send the king a gift to " redeem ourselves."

place which suddenly brought the Christians and Muhammedans into violent contact.

The Christians were accused of becoming insolent and disobedient. The fact was, they had begun to set themselves against the evil practices of Mwanga's shameful court.*

The matter soon came to a climax. Mujasi, who was chief of the king's bodyguards, and who had been the murderer of the first young martyrs, urged on Mwanga that he was not king in his own country if his slaves even dared to refuse the king's orders. Further, it was said that both we and the French priest were gradually filling the country with our teaching, and making the people our disciples by hundreds, that we called them our children, and that unless some strong measures were taken the whole country would soon be in the hands of the foreign white teachers. The boy Matia was threatened with instant death, but eventually escaped with a beating. But the King had received a rebuke, and the Muhammedans had been put to shame, so at their instance Mwanga gave the order that all the Christians in Uganda should be seized and put to death. The king set the evil example by attacking one of his Christian attendants with a spear. The poor lad was dragged out, and immediately despatched by the executioners; next Mwanga turned

* One of the pages, a lad named Matia, had the courage to refuse to participate in some of those evil doings, which were practised as a matter of course by the professors of Muhammedanism. Matia's refusal was made to a Muhammedan chief, named Kauta, who was acting with the permission of the king, whose page Matia was.

upon Kagwa Apolo (the present Katikiro, or Prime Minister), and struck him with the spear, and gashed him on the head with it. But probably the king's passion had spent itself upon his first victim, and Apolo's life was spared.

Others were clubbed to death and speared, and many were seized and put in the stocks; many were mutilated in a manner which in some cases proved fatal.

At this time of trouble a Russian traveller, Dr. Junker, who had come down from Wadelai, and who brought news of Emin Pasha and the doings in Equatoria, entered Uganda from Unyoro. He told us how he had seen strewing the roads many mutilated corpses of murdered Christians, or rather perhaps of men suspected of being readers.

Most of the Christians, as soon as the outbreak of persecution became known, went into hiding; one or two, however, determined to stand their ground, and to allow themselves to be taken before the king to plead their cause. There were three especially whose names deserve to be remembered—Kidza Musaali, Munyaga Byenju, and Walukaga. The first was a sub-chief under Mujasi. Now this man Mujasi, though he hated Christianity, had yet a kindly feeling for his dependent Kidza, who was a faithful officer, and even warned him to fly, but Kidza refused; he was therefore taken, and, at the King's order, clubbed to death. Munyaga was also taken, tried, and condemned; he was first of all dismembered, and then burnt. But the climax of the persecution was reached when Walukaga and some thirty other Christians were brought forth to die. A vast heap of firewood and inflammable reeds was piled about them as they lay bound hand and foot, and heavily laden with the Kaligo, a long forked branch, which secured their necks. The executioners brought flaming brands, and simultaneously at several points ignited the vast bonfire.

This was the crowning deed of blood in the persecution, which seemed in this last act to have spent its force; for from that day it quickly subsided. In that awful hour Christianity had proved its might, and from that hour it steadily grew and spread.

Mwanga had tried conclusions with the new teaching, but had failed to stamp it out. The Namasole, his queen-mother, absolutely refused to give her attendants up to be massacred by her son's insolent executioners, so that persecuted in one quarter, the Christians were protected in another, and openly continued their teaching. Mwanga had effected nothing; but he had indeed proved his own weakness—a weakness which, coupled with his cruelty and growing tyranny, at last led to his own overthrow.

CHAPTER II

REVOLUTION AND EXPULSION OF MWANGA

Mackay's Departure and Gordon's Arrival—On the Way to the Court—Walker's Reception—The King of Uganda—A Course of Oppression—Enormous Fines—A Prescient Priest—Opposing Forces—The King's Jealousy—An Ancient Religion—A diabolical Plot—Observing the Omens—Mujasi's Excuse—Another Day's Respite—The Death Drum—Mwanga threatens—Open Rebellion—The King baffled—Decision to dethrone Mwanga—A King wanted—Making a King by Force—Cross and Crescent unite—Mwanga deposed—A Modern Ulysses.

CHAPTER II

REVOLUTION AND EXPULSION OF MWANGA

THE persecution of 1886 finally decided the momentous question as to the impossibility of stamping out the Christian faith in Uganda. Mwanga had steadily obeyed the behests of the Arabs, though listening at times to the French priests. He had followed the advice of the priests that it was inexpedient to allow Bishop Hannington to enter Uganda, then the advice of his old heathen chiefs in murdering him, and lastly, he had followed the advice of the Arabs and heathens in murdering and burning the Christians, both Protestant and Roman Catholic. The state of mind of this unhappy ruler was almost frantic. He could trust no one, while he feared all parties in his kingdom. The murder of Hannington haunted him, not with remorse at the deed, but with craven fears of the consequences. At this time the Arabs were in Uganda in force, and the letters written from the Consulate in Zanzibar, and sent through the Arabs, demanding freedom to come and go for British subjects, were falsified by them into a summons for Mackay, who was alone in Uganda at that time, to return to Zanzibar to answer for crimes which it was alleged he had committed on the road up country. The Arabs were no doubt skilfully interweaving, with their lying interpretation of the letters, some old matters in which the Consul-General at Zanzibar years before had acted in a most extraordinarily injudicious manner, with reference to a difficulty Mackay had experienced with some mutinous Zanzibari carriers.

The most interesting narrative of this trying time is fully given in Mackay's journals.* Suffice it to say, that he felt it wiser, owing to the suspicions entertained against him, to withdraw from Uganda for awhile; but he succeeded in obtaining permission from the king to send back as his substitute from the south of the Lake the Rev. Cyril Gordon, who had remained in that district since his arrival with Hannington nearly six years before. Gordon, with the devotion that has always characterised him, immediately started for Uganda, which he reached on August 18th of the same year (1887), and was politely received by the king, and warmly by the converts. He then bore remarkable testimony to the spirituality of the Christians whom he found in Uganda, and who had escaped the massacres inflicted the previous year upon the infant Church. "All who have visited me," he wrote, "seem to be truly taught of the Spirit."

The Rev. R. H. Walker joined Gordon in Uganda in April. He had been sent for by the king, who had heard of his arrival at Usambiro. The king was

* *Church Missionary Intelligencer and Record*, January 1888, p. 18, *et seq.*

afraid of Mackay and me, who were both at the south of the Lake. He knew that we had suffered much at his hands, and dreaded that we might bring some "ill-luck" upon him, and hence his request for the new Englishman.

The king had heard with dismay that another bishop (Parker) had succeeded Hannington, and received a letter from Hannington's successor with every expression of hostility. He now formed the plot of killing both Gordon and Walker, if the latter should be the bearer of any further communication from Bishop Parker. Walker, however, brought the tidings of the bishop's death, which, strange to say, proved the salvation of the two missionaries in Uganda, as well as of their numerous converts. The king, as soon as he heard of Parker's death, and that there were no more letters from him, relinquished his sanguinary scheme of vengeance, and for a time left the missionaries to work in peace.

Walker, in his letters home, gave a vivid description of his first interview with King Mwanga. He and Gordon were summoned one morning almost as soon as it was light, and at half-past seven they set off for the court. Crowds of people passed them hurrying to the same place. The road for some three hundred yards to the great entrance gates of Mengo was lined with armed warriors, holding spears and shields, and many of them with faces coloured red. As the missionaries passed the drums beat, and all of the warriors shouted and kept up a tremulous cry, quivering their spears as they held them above their heads. On

entering the first gate they found the courtyard inside
full of soldiers (some three or four hundred), dressed in
white and armed with guns; many of them carried red
and white flags. At a given word the soldiers marched
quickly past the strangers on both sides, and returned
behind the first rows, thus making their numbers
seem very great. After passing through several doors
in the high reed fences they came to the king's straw-
built reception house. This house was a circular
building, the roof coming down to the ground; but
being some twenty or thirty feet high, the walls inside
had only a slight curve. The roof was supported on
trees for pillars, and the walls consisted of fine
white reeds tied side by side, making a smooth clear
surface. The floor was covered with clean fine
scented grass, carefully dried, and neatly laid down.
The throne was of white wood, in imitation of a
European chair, on which was spread the royal leopard
skin. At the feet of the king was a polished elephant's
tusk.*

The bodyguard was drawn up in front of the reception house. As they entered, stepping over the raised
doorstep, all in the court rose to their feet, the Arabs,
the chiefs, and the king himself. The band now
struck up. It consisted of a big drum, two kettle

* This tusk is called "kasanga." Each king has his own
kasanga, as a mark of his honour. Under the great gateway,
called "wankaki," leading into the royal enclosure, there is also
a tusk of ivory forming a kind of doorstep; hence the saying,
"Tainza kubuka kasanga" ("He can't leap the kasanga"),
implies that the person spoken of is merely an unsophisticated
country cousin.

drums, a bugle, and several horns and trumpets formed of the long-necked gourds of the country. Walker advanced up the centre aisle towards the king, who placed his hand on his breast, and bowed towards his two white visitors, who acknowledged his salute in the same manner. The king and chiefs then sat down, while Gordon and Walker were ushered to their seats (camp stools) some ten feet from the king's right hand. The court was crowded. All along the walls soldiers were ranged with guns pointed towards the door. The king spoke kindly to Walker, and criticised his personal appearance. He asked him if he came in the place of the bishop. Gordon, who acted as interpreter, assured the king that Walker had come in no sense as the bishop's representative. Mwanga then asked if Walker were a smith or a carpenter, and on being told he was simply a teacher he seemed quite satisfied. And when Walker's presents were produced, a large carpet and a chair (a chairman's chair, high-backed, stuffed, and covered with crimson leather), he looked pleased. The court lasted some three-quarters of an hour, and then the king rose, and as the band played left the court-house.

Walker's description of the king in many respects might serve for his picture now: "A man with a weak-looking mouth, and rather a silly sort of laugh and smile; he raises his eyebrows very high, and twitches them in surprise, or in giving assent to a statement. He looks a young, frivolous sort of man, very weak, and easily led; passionate, and, if provoked, petulant. He looked as if he would be easily frightened, and possessed of very little courage or self-control." *

A guard of honour conducted the two missionaries part of their way home, and thus ended a momentous crisis in their lives, and in the history of the mission.

This same year, 1888, saw the formation of the Imperial British East Africa Company, afterwards destined to play so important a part in the history of Uganda.

The king now embarked upon a course of oppression, cruelty, and tyranny, which made his rule intolerable, and eventually led to revolution, which cost him his throne.

He made a royal progress through his dominions, which proved nearly as disastrous to his unhappy subjects as a foreign invasion, since he ruthlessly robbed and raided his own people. In the province of Chagwe he raided hundreds of cattle, and numberless women and children. Then he marched through Singo, carrying terror and dismay wherever he went, seizing women, children, and cattle, in vast numbers. He finished the raid in Budu, the most southerly portion of his kingdom.

On his return to Mengo he distributed the spoil amongst his worthless favourites; but his action had made him hated through the length and breadth of the land.

His next move was to summon all his chiefs to the task of enormously extending an artificial pond which

* The above account of Mr. Walker's reception is taken almost verbatim from his letter in *Church Missionary Society's Intelligencer*, November 1888, p. 700, *et seq.*

MWANGA, KING OF UGANDA, 1893.

he had made, and in which years before I had been called upon to exhibit what skill I possessed in swimming, an almost unknown accomplishment in Uganda. The chiefs came with extreme reluctance, many of them smarting from the loss of their wives and other valuable property extorted from them during the king's progress. The tyrant now initiated a system of petty annoyances, frequently rising at dawn, and hurrying down to the pond, when, if he found the chiefs had not arrived, he inflicted enormous fines upon them, demanding something like one thousand women in all, besides valuable coloured cloths and guns. By giving these to his dissolute personal following he succeeded in surrounding himself with a mercenary band of reprobates, whose numbers, for a time, prevented any organised resistance to his tyrannical proceedings.

Ever since he had murdered Bishop Hannington Mwanga dreaded that the English would seize Uganda, as the Germans had seized part of the coast; nor had Gordon's position been made much easier by the presence of the prescient Père Lourdel, who informed the king and chiefs that they had nothing to fear from the English, at any rate, for some five years!

Early in 1888, the king began to show hostility to the Arabs, as well as to Gordon, whose people were imprisoned and beaten. The old Katikiro, however, promised redress.

At this time, there were many forces in the deadliest opposition to the English mission, any one of which was strong enough to have caused its overthrow, and even the murder, of the solitary Englishmen who maintained it; yet these opposing forces preserved a kind of equilibrium maintained by the mutual jealousy of those who represented the strongest elements in the country. The chiefs were chafing under the tyranny of the king, while the king began to suspect the Arabs of plotting to seize the country, and hence the precarious safety which Gordon and Walker enjoyed.

The king had treated Bishop Parker's letter (see p. 81) as a challenge, and ashes were placed upon it as a sign that Mwanga accepted the arbitrament of war, and defied the English to invade his country. At the same time, he maintained that it was the people of Usoga, and not his own people, who had murdered Hannington. A vivid picture of this troublous period is given in Gordon's letters.*

Things were in this condition when the irritation and the anger which Mwanga's evil rule had aroused in the minds of his people suddenly burst forth into open rebellion.

Several Christians were holding important chieftainships. Isaya Kijambo was the Gahunga, Albert Kibega the Mutusa,† Kagwa Apolo (the present Prime Minister) was Omwanika, and Nyonyi Entono the Musalo-salo. These chiefs also denounced the abominations which the king was in the habit of practising. Moreover, the king saw with chagrin and jealousy the handsome houses and

---

* *Church Missionary Society's Intelligencer*, September 1888, p. 587.

† Gahunga, chief of Sesse; Omwanika, storekeeper; Musalo-salo, engineer; Mutusa, an office named after the late king.

neat fences which these young men built for themselves. It had been usual in early days, as now in Usoga, for the chiefs to keep their places in a wretched condition, so as not to seem to wish to compete in magnificence with the royal surroundings. As regards the Arabs, and those whom they had gathered round them, Mwanga was quite quick enough to see that they were a very real danger to his power. The Arabs had overthrown many native rulers, and the young Muhammedans were now growing insolent and again refusing to eat the king's meat ; but Mwanga dared not deal with them as his father had done. The Muhammedan readers, though up to the present they had escaped massacre at the hands of Mwanga, were nevertheless in disgrace, and were furious at the work* forced upon them by an uncircumcised heathen, as well as at the exactions to which they were obliged to submit. They made no objection to the king's levying fines upon, or murdering his Christian subjects, but they resented most bitterly that they themselves should be the victims of his extortion and tyranny.

Thus while both Christians and Muhammedans were coming more and more into opposition to Mwanga, some of the shrewder of the old heathen party saw in this an opportunity of endeavouring to prevail on the king to exterminate all who professed the new religions, and thus to rehabilitate the heathen system of Lubareism, the national religion of the country, which of late years had wofully declined.

* The cause of the final expulsion of the Muhammedans from Uganda was their refusal to perform legitimate work for the king.

This religion was an ancient and awful superstition, richly endowed, and made doubly terrible by the holocausts of human victims frequently sacrificed to carry out its fearful rites.*

The heathen party had in truth a very powerful system behind them, and they hoped, by securing the co-operation of the king, to effect their purpose of banishing the new customs in favour of the old.

The person more deeply versed in the heathen system of Uganda than any of the other chiefs was Ntanda, now Nicodemo, who had also learned much of Muhammedanism. Strange to say, at the present time he is baptised and a professing Christian.

* The worship paid to demigods is curiously exemplified in the case of two who may be mentioned—namely, Budo and Kibuka. All that is mortal of these ancient heroes is still extant in the form of two carefully preserved mummies.

Budo is the corpse of a gigantic man wrapped in bark-cloth, all except the head, which is bare. He has long hair, and his eyes are closed, and he is in a sitting posture. He is kept behind the curtains of the temple where he resides, guarded by a virgin honoured as his wife, and whose sacred person no one dare approach. The frightful dread of the vengeance of the god is a perfect safeguard to the chastity of the priestess—a proof of the fallacy of the statement sometimes put forward, that Africans had no idea of female chastity till the modern and late introduction of Christian morals among them. The mummy Budo sits on a bed draped with bark-cloths, and on certain days drums called " kikase " are beaten, when he is brought from behind the curtains to hold a reception in his temple, at which the neighbouring chiefs and important people attend. They kneel before him extending the palms of their hands, and crying out, "Asinze" ("He is great"), speaking of him in the third person ; whereas, to a living king, they say " Osinze" (" You are great").

Kibuka, like the other mummy Budo, is the corpse of a very

He and Kyambalango, the Pokino (ruler of Budu who also could read both the Koran and the New Testament), together with a man named Tebukuza, gained the ear of the king, and persuaded him that neither he nor his kingdom would ever flourish as long as the new religions were tolerated in the country.

The result was, that Mwanga and these men hatched between them a diabolical plot, which had for its object the annihilation of all the readers in Uganda, both Christians and Muhammedans. The old prime minister, Mukasa, would have nothing to say to the scheme, affirming that "the readers" were too numerous to be destroyed.

The conspirators now summoned the Mandwa, or priests of Lubare, who duly proceeded to slaughter

tall man wrapped in bark-cloth, but he is in a lying posture, with his face covered. His guardian virgin wife is called Nagalamede, and his receptions are held as described above in the case of Budu. Kibuka, the story goes, was a mighty warrior of old times, who lost his life fighting for the king in Ganda. (Ganda is the name the country was first known by.) Kibuka killed multitudes of the people of Unyoro with his arrows, but subsequently married a woman of that nation, who, pitying the plight of her people, betrayed the mystery of her warrior-husband, and warned them in the next engagement to aim their arrows at a black cloud, which they would see hanging over the battlefield, and that then they would kill Kibuka. In the next battle they did as she had directed them, and the corpse of Kibuka rolled before them, having fallen from the cloud, and Kibuka *living* ceased to trouble them; though from that day to the present his shade has inspired them with so much dread of vengeance, that no man of Unyoro will pass Embale, where Kibuka's temple stands; and when the reigning king wishes to send either wives or slaves to Kibuka's priest, care is taken that no Unyoro person shall be among them.

cattle, and take the omens regarding the success of the plot. If the blood of the slaughtered animal flows out in several divergent streams the omen is good ; but if it pours out in one full stream it is bad. This is called Kulagula (to foretell). For several days the omens were observed with the most satisfactory results, and the Mandwa declared that the issue of the plot would be satisfactory ; and in this they were right, though the satisfaction was to be enjoyed by those whom they desired to put to death. The plot was as follows: Mwanga was to give out that he had determined to destroy the worship of Lubare in the country, and that he intended to begin by stripping the Mandwa of all their wealth, and that his first step would be a raid on the Island of Bugala, which belonged to the priests, and on which was much cattle. He was then to summon all the fighting men in the country who had guns, and who were all either Christians or Muhammedan readers. The old heathen warriors still clung to their ancient weapons, spear and shield. The assembled readers were then, on some pretext or another, to be landed on another bare and desert island, and there left to perish miserably. The canoes were to be withdrawn, and the waters of the Lake watched, to prevent any canoe reaching the hapless victims of this outrageous scheme of vengeance. Like everything that Mwanga planned or did, this plot partially leaked out, and the intended victims learnt enough to arouse their worst suspicions.

The king now ordered the Gabunga, who had charge of the canoes, to collect all the boats in Sesse, while he ordered Mujasi, a cruel and fanatical Muhammedan who commanded his bodyguard, to march the soldiers to the point of embarkation on the Lake. Mujasi sent back to say he was dreadfully ill, and his eyes were so much affected that he could not see, while another Muhammedan chief plastered some of the rotten fruit of the banana on his leg, which he exhibited to the king's messenger as a frightful ulcer, affirming the while that he was quite unable to walk. Musalosalo and Omwanika, the two principal Christian chiefs, also received orders to march to the Lake with the Christians. Omwanika, or Kagwa Apolo, was the leader of the Bazungu or English readers, while Musalo-salo, or Nyonyi Entono, was chief of the Bafransa or French readers.

The Christians slept that night at Kitebe, halfway to the Nyanza. Mukasa, the old Prime Minister, sent to tell Nyonyi Entono not to embark in the canoes, for that the king intended to murder all who did so.

Next day they reached Entebe (Fort Alice), the point from which the king meant to start, and where all the canoes had been collected. The king now arrived on the scene. But at this point a difficulty arose, for Lukoto, the Chief Judge of the Prime Minister and a great devotee of Lubare, informed Mwanga that the Mayembe (sacred horns) were not in spirits. These awful symbols of the faith had shown some mysterious sign that something unpleasing to Lubare was taking place.

And so it was, for this happened to be the sacred day of Bwerende, the monthly Sabbath of the Baganda, which is fixed by the appearance of the new moon, and on which no cultivation is done nor work undertaken. The king, though chafing at the delay, was nevertheless obliged to acquiesce in this objection of his accomplices, who were fervent votaries of Lubare. He therefore agreed to put off the departure of the canoes till the morrow. Thus the host of condemned readers obtained another day's respite.

That night, at Mwanga's orders, Mutamanyang' amba Kisiga, the chief executioner, beat the peculiar and terror-striking tattoo on the drum, which told the horrified hearers that the Bamboa (executioners) were abroad to secure victims for a kiwendo—the vast human sacrifice paid by Uganda kings to the horrible god Lubare.

Before the awful death drum rolled out its dismal warning the people had said, " Surely the king cannot mean to make the attempt to murder all the vast host of readers in the land " ; but the weird and dreadful notes of the drum dispelled any doubt as to the king's intention, and soon a fearful and anxious crowd gathered round Nyonyi Entono and Kagwa Apolo, and another chief Lubanga, who was a Muhammedan. There was a hurried debate, which resulted in the determination of one and all to resist the king by force.

Nyonyi Entono was accordingly despatched to Mwanga, to remind him that it was contrary to Uganda custom for the king to visit Lubare's island without due religious rites, and that if he went accompanied only by his younger chiefs, and evil were to befall him at the hand of Lubare, that then the whole country would seize them and their families and burn them with fire, and further to implore the king not to risk himself in such a dangerous visit.

Nyonyi Entono accordingly went to the king, who seemed impressed by what he said, and changed his mind, and declared that he himself would not go to the island, so he sent Kisiga, the executioner, to tell Nyonyi Entono that as soon as the drums beat he was to embark the whole body of Christians in the canoes, and that any one found loitering in the camp should at once be put to death.

Before dawn broke the drums rolled out the signal to embark. A few of the people repaired to the canoes, but far the greater number remained sullenly in the camp.

Nyonyi Entono had slept within the king's temporary fence, and as he waited, Lutaya, Mwanga's Muhammedan favourite, came out and said : " Follow the king ; he has gone to the boats." Nyonyi Entono took no notice of Lutaya's words, knowing that Mwanga was still inside, but remained where he was, together with all the king's pages and his own followers. On this the king came out of the royal hut, and made his way to the Lake. It was now daylight, and the king saw that only a few of the more timid had entered the canoes ; by far the greater number, disregarding his orders, were standing on the beach. Thereupon the king entered his own noble canoe (named *Waswa*), followed by Nyonyi Entono, who came unarmed, whispering to his personal attendants not to accompany him. *Waswa* was now paddled out a little distance into the Lake, none of the other canoes following. The king turned, and ordered Kagwa Apolo to enter another canoe. This he slowly did, whispering to his followers the same order as Nyonyi Entono had given, that they should not embark with him. The king then commanded one of the smaller chiefs to get into a third boat, but he stoutly replied, " I will not." Next the king ordered the Muhammedan Lubanga, already referred to, to enter the canoe—he replied that he must first go for his gun, and turning his back walked into the long grass to await what should befall. Sekyeru, another Muhammedan, was appealed to, and he flatly refused, saying, " I will not embark." Nyonyi Entono now addressed the king, saying, " All Buganda refuses to take you to Sesse. There is no old chief here, and we are not able to take you."*

At this the king, with a gesture of anger, snatched a gun from the bottom of the canoe. Whereupon Lubanga and Sekyeru cried out, " Let us kill him." Kagwa Apolo, however, restrained them, saying, " No, let us not do so without sufficient reason. If he kills any of us then we will kill him ; but if we kill him now all nations will be against us, saying, ' They have slain their lord.' "

The king, now seeing how matters stood, though he did not hear the talk about killing him, called to the Mumyuka † of Musalosalo, saying, " I see the canoes

---

* The great god Mukasa is lord of Sesse, and will kill any person intruding on his dominions. He calls the King of Uganda his slave, and the king, when he sends to perform religious rites, must do so through the chiefs, Sabaganzi and Gabunga.

† Mumyuka, the second in command in every chieftainship, is called the Mumyuka.

here are not enough to hold us all. Do you take the people back to Mengo, while I return by water to Munyonyo." Munyonyo is the landing-place about eight miles from Mengo Entebe (Fort Alice), where the mutiny took place, being more than twenty miles from the capital. As soon as Mwanga came back he sent post haste to tell the old Katikiro that the whole country was in rebellion. The answer he received was that the plan to kill the readers had been against his, the Katikiro's, judgment and advice. When old Mukasa's messenger had delivered the message the king was silent. Meanwhile the Muhammedan readers sent messengers to the old Prime Minister, and to Nyonyi Entono and Kagwa, the two leaders representing the French and English readers, saying, "We had better depose Mwanga, since he is certain to renew his attempt upon our lives." And to this the Katikiro agreed, and it was accordingly determined to place another king on the throne. Then came the question of who should be chosen as Mwanga's successor, and they decided upon Mwanga's brother Kalema, a man who, it appears, was more or less favourably inclined towards the Arabs and the Muhammedan faction, and who afterwards played so important a part in the politics of Uganda.

Two messengers were accordingly despatched to fetch Kalema from the enclosure where the royal princes were guarded by Kasuju, the keeper of the king's children.

The messengers were afraid, however, that their tidings might not be well received by Kasuju, and that they might lose their lives. So they returned, saying it was impossible to reach Kalema, and that it would be better for a strong armed party to go and take him out of his prison palace by force.

On hearing this, Nyonyi Entono suggested that it might be better to secure the king's eldest brother, Kiwewa, who lived in an open enclosure, and whose person was sacred, although it was the immemorial custom of Uganda that the eldest son might never succeed to the throne. Nyonyi Entono argued that as the Christians and Muhammedans were people of "*dini*" (religion), and had turned their backs on heathen customs, they need not regard this old superstition. In this he was supported by a Muhammedan chief named Katabalwa. The others agreed to the suggestion, and forthwith a man named Buga Ekwagala, with three others, were sent to fetch Kiwewa, that he might be proclaimed king. On arrival they found him in his house; but on communicating their message he flatly refused to accompany them, saying that the thing was impossible. But his visitors would take no denial, and actually forced him out of his house, and led him towards Rubaga Hill, doubtless impressing on him as they went the ease with which he might step into Mwanga's great position. The rebels now secured the royal drum, Mujaguzu,* on which they beat the royal tattoo in honour of the new king. Mwanga, to his dismay, heard the king's drum booming out on

* This drum was kept in a house on the top of a hill, from which could be seen the first appearing of the new moon. As soon as the new moon appeared Mujaguzu was accustomed to be beaten, that all men might understand that the day of Bwerende, the Uganda Sabbath, had come round.

Rubaga Hill, opposite his own enclosure, and the site of the French Mission.

Mwanga now issued from Mengo, and hurried down towards the king's pond, which lay in the hollow between the Hill of Mengo and the loftier eminence of Rubaga. He was followed by a number of the conspirators, among whom were Kyambalango (the Pokino), Lukoto, Entanda, and Wakibi, the Munawa ; and a number of his insolent young pages clad in white. His sister Nasiwa * also accompanied him.

Mwanga asked Nasiwa had they not better take refuge at the French Mission on Rubaga with Mapera,†

* Nasiwa, the eldest princess and nominal wife of Mukasa, the Divinity of the Nyanza. Every Mumbeja (princess) is supposed to be a vestal virgin and nominal wife of a Divinity, but unlike the truly virgin keepers of Budo and Kibuka (p. 96), their virginity is only nominal, since the Bambeja (princesses) used to be notorious for their amours, and for the utter licentiousness which characterised them. In Mutesa's days Princess Nakamanya was wife of god Kibuka, Princess Nasolo of god Wanga, Princess Kagere of Lwanga, Princess Nakati of Budo. In the olden time, when Kibuka was killed, god Mukasa had asked the reigning king for his daughter, and the king gave him his daughter, Nasolo (the name which the eldest of the princesses is always called, as Kiwewa is that of the eldest of the princes). Nasolo, like Kiwewa, has the royal title of Kabaka, and is over all the princesses, who are not kept in durance like their brothers. The god Mukasa, as a return for this princess, sent to the king the famous warrior Kibuka, whose legend I have given on p. 97. Thus Princess Nasolo is wife of god Mukasa, Princess Nabweteme is wife of god Nende, Princess Nabaroga is wife of the Lubare of Musongole, etc., etc.

† Mapera, name of the French missionaries, but also word for Guavas. " What is your name ?" the people had asked the first French missionary. He had replied, "Call us ' Mes pères.' " The natives immediately called him by the nearest word which they knew of a similar sound, which was Mapera (Guavas.)

Nasiwa replied, "By no means, since it is his children who are fighting with you. He will seize you, and give you up to them." Mwanga then returned to his Lubiri or enclosure. He came out and stood by the great entrance gate—the Wankaki—with about a hundred of his boys, who were armed, many of them, with breech-loading rifles, and a few with Winchester repeating rifles.

The Prime Minister's enclosure is on the lower slope of Mengo, to the left-hand side as you approach the king's gateway. Mwanga sent some of his boys to implore old Mukasa to come to his aid, but the Prime Minister sent a polite message back that he would fight for the king where he was, and hold the lower slope of Mengo. Meanwhile two columns advanced with the beating of innumerable drums and wild shouts of triumph upon Mwanga and his little following of boy pages—one column being the Christian readers under Nyonyi Entono, and Kagwa, the other, the Muhammedan readers under Mujasi who was destined in a few more days to meet a bloody death from the very man he was now leading in triumph to the capital. Thus the Cross and the Crescent closed in on heathenism. As represented by Mwanga and his boys, it made its last stand in Uganda.

No sooner had the two columns advanced up Mengo than old Mukasa's contingent, so far from showing fight, went over *en masse* to Kiwewa without firing a shot, and Mwanga saw that he was betrayed. For a few more minutes the king and his white-robed boys

CHAPTER III
THREE KINGS

New Chiefs—Retirement of the old Katikiro—A royal Privilege—The new King—Muhammedan Influence—An Arab Plot—A treacherous Coup—Missions sacked and looted—Shipwrecked on the Nyanza—Plot and Counterplot—Mujasi's Elation—Mujasi killed by the King—Kiwewa deposed—Misunderstandings among Christians—Mwanga invited to return—Stokes aids Mwanga—King Kalema despatches an Army—Defeat of Christians—The Irony of God's Answer.

CHAPTER III

THREE KINGS

THE revolution which set King Kiwewa upon the throne had been effected without any serious fighting, and the frightful tyranny of Mwanga's rule passed away like an evil dream. Kiwewa "ate Buganda"* in August, and immediately set about officially appointing the chiefs who the successful Christian and

---

* "Eating Buganda"—*i.e.*, becoming its Chief or Kabaka. Another form of it, "Alide eng oma" (" He has eaten the drum "). Some of the ceremonies of eating the drum, or becoming king, are of interest. Since the days of a former King Mulonda, his chair, or stool, called Namulonda, is always brought to the capital for the new king to be seated in. It is kept at other times in the province of Singo, at the village of Mugulu, and is in the hands of the clan whose *totem* is the buffalo (embogo). The people in charge of the chair (entebe) are called Ba-tebe or chairmen. But before the enthronement, as soon as the candidate for the throne has been declared successor to the deceased king by duly placing a square of bark-cloth, called Kabugo, on the dead king's body, he hastens off at full speed to a village called Budo—where I suppose the demi-god mentioned on p. 96 resides. Here there is an anthill; and whichever of the prince candidates succeeds in first climbing this and standing thereon is looked upon as king. Near this anthill is a house called Bu-ganda, where the successful candidate spends two days. During this period a monster python is procured, and the king is handed a

Muhammedan factions had arranged should be given the principal offices in the kingdom.

Nyoni-entono became Katikiro or Prime Minister. His Christian name was Honorat. He was a Roman Catholic and a confessor, having suffered cruelly during the persecution. His was a fine character, and his death, which took place a little later on, was a heavy loss to the cause of Christianity in Uganda. Kagwa Apolo, the present Katikiro, or Prime Minister, was made Mukwenda, Chief of Singo. Mujasi, the Sabadu, of Stanley,† who had been the first originator of the massacres and murders of the Christians, was a furious and fanatical Muhammedan. He was subject at times to wild fits of passion, when he would lose all self-control, and scream himself hoarse with rage. Such was the person who was selected to be Kangao, or Chief of

royal spear of brass, which he sharpens on the python's living body, the people holding it securely the while. The serpent is then set free. The queen sister, the Lubuga or Nalinya, is then brought, and a piece of cane-like fibre, used for making baskets, and called luyulu, is presented to her with a lukato, a kind of skewer or bodkin used in piercing the holes through which to pass the fibre which binds the basket. These are the implements and materials for a woman's work of basket-making. She is also given a knife called najolo, unlike the ordinary Uganda knife, which resembles an English chisel or bradawl in the manner it is fixed into its handle; but najolo is made like a spear, for the wooden handle fits into the iron socket as in an English spade.

Najolo and the lukato and fibre are then presented to Nalinya with the words, "Go and bind a basket, that you may dish up in it your husband's food." Nalinya is called the new king's wife until the women belonging to his predecessor have been allotted to him. None of those who have borne children are among this number.

† "Through the Dark Continent."

Bulemezi.* Bugala, another Muhammedan, became Kimbugwe, or Keeper of the King's enclosure. This post

AN UGANDA MARKET.

was the second chieftainship in the kingdom. The old

* Kangao of Bulemezi. Kangao is Chief of Bulemezi, the northern province of Uganda, which was formerly an independent kingdom. Hence Kangao is permitted to retain the Mujaguzu (royal drum), and may beat a kingly tattoo in his own province.

Katikiro, Mukasa, retired to Mutesa's tomb at Nabulagala, the place where Mutesa's old chiefs were wont to retreat when they were succeeded by his successor's appointments. Kyambalango, the old Pokino, and copartner with Mwanga in his diabolical plot, took flight, and his place was looted.

At this time the English Mission was represented by Messrs. Gordon and Walker, while Monseigneur Lavinhac, Pères Sourdel and Denoit, and a lay brother occupied the French Mission on Rubaga. As soon as the murderer and tyrant Mwanga had disappeared numbers of persecuted Christians came out of their hiding-places.

Many flocked to the king to seek employment about his person, trade revived, and the markets were crowded with buyers and sellers, while the Missions were thronged with busy learners and eager inquirers.

Writing of this short but happy period, Gordon described the Ba-ganda as coming about the station like swarms of bees.

The new king held a grand Baraza (Durbar), and summoned the European missionaries and Arab traders to attend. The Europeans were given the precedence. Kiwewa was most prodigal in his promises. To the Arabs he would give freedom for their trade, and would open the road to Unyoro. Their religion might be taught, and he would build them a mosque. The Europeans should have full liberty to teach and to preach without let or hindrance. The people should no longer suffer from tyranny such as that just broken ; and the new monarch graciously ordered that his executioners should be armed with sticks, and not with those deadly pliable cords with which their victims were bound before being put to death. And many offences formerly considered capital were now to be visited with a milder punishment.

BUYING AND SELLING.

But King Kiwewa fell more and more under Muhammedan influence. There were numbers of Arab traders in the country, who naturally threw all their influence into the scale against the Christian chiefs, and eagerly fomented the feeling of jealousy with which the Muhammedan faction saw these Christians occupying so many of the important positions in the country. The Arabs also were much vexed at the appointment of Nyonyi Entono as Katikiro in the place of the deposed Mukasa, for the Katikiro had great interest in the ivory trade of the country, and they were bitterly aggrieved that this important post had not fallen to one of their own co-religionists. There is little doubt that these Arabs, from the first, had planned to seize Uganda for themselves; indeed, without their aid the native Uganda Muhammedans could never have formed the strong faction in the kingdom which their party was soon to become.

The Arabs very soon succeeded in forming a plot to overthrow the Christian chiefs, and sought for a fitting opportunity to put it into execution. They first of all cleverly worked upon the fears of the king, persuading him that the Christians meant to depose him, and put in his place one of his sisters, who was a Christian; "for," said they, "is not the chief nation of Europe governed by a woman, Queen Victoria? and therefore the Christians in Uganda are seeking to establish the same custom here." As the Muhammedans had been chiefly concerned in placing Kiwewa in power, he doubtless felt more or less bound to listen to their counsels, and to wink at the treacherous plot which they had hatched against the Christians. Accordingly in October of this year the Muhammedans in open baraza accused Nyonyi Entono, the Katikiro, of being concerned in a plot to depose Kiwewa. He vehemently denied it, and left the Baraza in great indignation, and repaired to his own enclosure. Certain negotiations stood their ground as the long wave of rebels surged onward towards them in a deep line. As customary in Uganda warfare, each side reserved its fire until within a few yards of one another, then, with a sudden volley, the rifles blazed out, and one of Mwanga's faithful boys fell dead beside him pierced with a bullet. This was enough for the king, who turned and fled, followed by his wives and a multitude of pages. The former, with the exception of four, he sent back again, and, followed by some two hundred of the boys, he hurried to Munyonyo on the Lake, and embarked his followers in several canoes. But as he paddled out into the lake, first one of the canoes dropped behind and forsook him, and then another, until he was left alone with the occupants of the canoe which he had entered himself. The victorious insurgents had allowed no pursuit, which accounts for Mwanga's having reached the Lake in safety. The Baganda have a superstitious horror of killing a king, and this no doubt contributed to Mwanga's escape.

The voyage of this modern Ulysses was not without adventure. Neither he nor his companions knew the Lake; but they were fortunate in capturing a native of the Sesse Islands, who was familiar with the route to the south of the Nyanza, and who acted as their steersman. Twice south of Kagera River the little party had to fight for their lives, for more than once they were attacked by armed bands of the Baziba; but these soon sheered off when they found that this canoe was filled with people all of whom had breech-loading rifles, which they freely used. At last the exiled king reached Magu, on Speke Gulf, where he took refuge for a time with some Arab traders. He could hardly have selected a more dangerous place. But we must leave him for the present to follow the fortunes of Kiwewa, the new king.

were then entered upon, and messengers were coming and going between the Katikiro's enclosure and the lubiri (king's courtyard). An important Muhammedan chief was actually within the Katikiro's fence as a hostage. He had been sent in this capacity to carry assurance that no treachery was intended, and some of the Christian chiefs, not suspecting evil, trusted themselves within the lubiri. A murderous volley was suddenly opened upon them, and one or two of them fell, and the rest fled. Directly the shots were fired outside the Muhammedan hostage was instantly shot dead, and Nyonyi Entono came out with his following, only to meet a thoroughly well-organised attack. The Arabs were there, and personally took part in the encounter. The Christians had been taken unawares, and after making a short, but ineffectual, stand, they retreated; and their two leaders, Nyonyi Entono, the Katikiro, and Kagwa Apolo, the Mukwenda, led the more earnest converts in good order out of the country. Their number was not great, and King Entare (lion) of Nkore or Busagara, gave them an asylum at a place called Kabula.

The Muhammedan power was now completely in the ascendant, and a re-distribution of chieftainships took place. A new Katikiro was appointed, while Mujasi, the Kangao, became Mukwenda.*

But with the new order of things it fared ill with the European missionaries, who were immediately arrested, brought up to the Katikiro's enclosure, and

* Mukwenda, chief of Singo, a large province north-west of Uganda, bordering on Unyoro.

immured in a filthy prison, where they were kept for a whole week. The two missions were meanwhile sacked and looted, and on the eighth day the missionaries were brought down to the Lake, and put on board the English mission boat, the *Eleanor*, or *Mirembe*. Walker was even stripped of his outer clothing. The French priests were allowed to take on board some cowrie shells with which to buy food, and then the little party sadly bade farewell to the land of so many sorrows and triumphs of the Gospel.

But though they had escaped as by a miracle from the hands of their enemies, a sudden disaster befell them from a totally unexpected quarter. The boat was stove in by a hippopotamus, and capsized. They were near an island, and most of the party were able to make the shore. The French priests, however, had a number of children with them, and five of these little ones found a watery grave in the Nyanza.

The boat was recovered, and towed to land with the help of some native canoes, and Walker, though without proper tools, succeeded in repairing her in a manner anything but to his own satisfaction, yet sufficiently to make her float again.

The little band then renewed their doubly dangerous journey, and by the good hand of God upon them, after a voyage of seventeen days, succeeded in reaching the south end of the Nyanza, and put in at Bukumbi, the French mission station. Next day Walker and Gordon went on to Usambiro, where they were kindly welcomed by Mackay.

Having thus got rid of their Christian rivals, the

Plot and Counter-Plot

Muhammedans now determined that the whole of Uganda should profess Islam ; and in order to accomplish this resolve, they realised that it was necessary to begin by converting the king. The Katikiro (Muguluma), and Mujasi the Mukwenda, with others, accordingly waited upon the king, and broached their ideas to him. Kiwewa now saw that he was in the hands of fanatics of the worst type, and began bitterly to regret that he had suffered these Muhammedan bigots to drive from the kingdom his Christian chiefs, who, at any rate, had not proposed baptism to him, as the Muhammedans were urging upon him the initiatory rite of their religion.

Kiwewa declared point blank that he would never consent to the rite, and that he would rather be deposed, as Mwanga had been, than agree to its imposition, and the baffled chiefs left him to consult as to what was best to be done. They then formed the extraordinary project of seizing the king, and imposing the rite by force,* and twelve of their number were appointed to carry out the undertaking, of whom Bugala and Mujasi were the principal men. But, like so many Uganda plots, this scheme leaked out, and Kiwewa got wind of it, and sent to say he had reconsidered his determination, and was prepared to become an out-and-out Mussulman, and appointed a day when he would undergo the initiatory rite at the

* This imposition of the rite of circumcision by force made the Muhammedans hated and execrated by the heathen peasantry, and accounted largely for the numbers that flocked to the exiled Christian chiefs.

hands of those whose religion he was about to profess. It is stated that the unhappy king had made an abortive endeavour to poison some of his fanatical chiefs.

Nine days had now passed since the treacherous attack upon the Christians, and the day had come when Kiwewa would finally witness his belief in Islam.

Mujasi, though anxious, was yet elated. He had thus far been a sharp sword in the Prophet's cause, and had prospered. He could look back upon a long series of what he considered triumphs of the faith, which were due almost entirely to him. To him had belonged the honour of having shed the first Christian blood in Uganda, though it were but the blood of children. His voice had counselled Hannington's death. It was at his instance the frightful massacres of Christians in 1886 were carried out. It was his hand that had helped to expel Mwanga when he had turned against the followers of the prophet, and now, the final triumph of Islam was about to be assured in Uganda by the present king's submission to that rite which Mujasi had been the foremost in forcing him to accept.

Mujasi and his assistants accordingly presented themselves at Kiwewa's enclosure, and were admitted with their following, and the outer gates were closed. The king had, meanwhile, made his own preparations, and behind the bark-cloth hangings in the house of reception had placed a large number of his executioners ready with their cords, waiting to spring out and seize the chiefs when the time was come.

The haughty Muhammedans entered, and the King politely received them. "Mutuse banange" ("You have come, my friends"), he said. Then something of this sort occurred. Suddenly rising, he turned to Mujasi, and said, "So you have eaten Buganda, and you will make the Kabaka your slave?" Mujasi and the Katikiro were instantly pinioned from behind, and Kiwewa killed the former with his own hand. There was wild confusion. The Katikiro's boy, who was sitting in the doorway, fired a gun at the king. On this the gates were burst open, and the Muhammedans and Arabs who were waiting outside rushed in. Kiwewa ran from his enclosure and fled to his father's tomb, accompanied by a number of the old heathen chiefs.

But neither Mukasa nor the guardians of the grave would give him any countenance or afford him any help. They even showed him violence, and five of his people were killed. He then fled to a place called Kyebango, accompanied by the chiefs still faithful to him; and there he spent the night.

The Muhammedans meanwhile brought Kiwewa's younger brother, Kalema, who, to gain the kingdom, willingly embraced Islam. He was a very different man from Mwanga, and as brave as Mwanga was cowardly. Next day he sent to attack Kiwewa, whose chiefs advised him to give battle. Kiwewa was, however, quickly routed, and some twenty of his followers were killed. He himself was made prisoner, and brought back to the capital, where he was put into the stocks and strongly guarded.

The Christian chiefs, Nyonyi Entono and Kagwa, had gone to Enkore or Busagara to the country of the Muhuma, King Entare (lion). Entare was a great friend of one of the chief men among the Christians, Sebwato Nikodemo, who had formerly been sent by the old Katikiro to sell ivory at Enkore. Nikodemo conducted his fugitive fellow-Christians to Entare, who hospitably received them owing to his former friendship with Nikodemo.

But Entare would not welcome a daily growing host of fugitives unless they could make it worth his while to do so: his guests, therefore, set to work bridging swamps, and making raids on Uganda as well as on the neighbouring Banyarwanda, who were themselves great cattle raisers, and also cattle raiders. News now reached the exiled Christian colony that Mwanga had fled from the Arabs and taken refuge with Mackay, and was learning the Protestant religion, while at the same time one of the Roman Catholics told his companions the English disciples were about to attack them.

A hasty council was thereupon held by the French converts as to whether it would not be better to forestal the expected attack by immediately falling on the Protestants. Word soon reached these last of the discussion, and they went in hot haste to ask what it meant, indignantly denying that they had any hostile intent. The difficulty was for the time smoothed over, more especially as it turned out that Mwanga was not with Mackay, but with the French priests at Bukumbi, to which place he had gone having made his escape from the Arabs at Magu.

The Christians were now growing so numerous that it was debated among them whether it might not be feasible to return to Uganda and overthrow the Muhammedan power.

Kalema was hateful to the Bakopi, or common people, who fled in daily increasing numbers to join the Christian fugitives, among whom dissension was growing rife, while famine seemed to stare them in the face. It was suggested that they should invite Mwanga to return, since with him as their head they would soon have a very large following throughout the country. They therefore sent messengers to ask the advice of both the English and French missionaries, who were at the south of the Lake, as to the best means of carrying out this project. Some of the exiles had a plan for making an expedition to Uganda in order to seize another of Mutesa's sons, all of whom, with the exception of Mwanga, were now in Kalema's hands. The more prudent, however, prevailed upon them to wait the return of the messengers sent to invite Mwanga's return. Some of the Protestants were doubtful about having anything to say to Mwanga, and seem to have written in this strain to Mackay and Gordon ; but it is quite evident that a formal invitation was sent from the whole body to Mwanga to come back.

These envoys to the missionaries started early in March, and made their way to Bukoba, which had not as yet been occupied by the Germans, but belonged to King Mukotanyi, who supplied them with canoes. In these they made their way to the French mission at Bukumbi, and presented the invitation to Mwanga to return. Stokes, the ivory trader and quondam missionary, had just brought up to the Nyanza a boat in sections, and put her together. He visited Ukumbi, and was implored by Mwanga to give him a passage in his boat to Uganda. Mwanga promised a heavy reward in ivory if Stokes would help him in this way, and also supply him with ammunition and guns. Stokes accepted the offer, and, with the help of the French priests, an expedition was organised and armed, having for its object the restoration of Mwanga. The deputation, or rather the Protestant portion of it, went on from Bukumbi up the creek to Usambiro, accompanied by two of Mwanga's lads, to ask Mackay to lend him the mission boat, the *Eleanor*, to take with him on his expedition. The members of the deputation somewhat guardedly asked for advice. Mackay and Gordon's advice was that their converts should on no account have anything to do with restoring Mwanga. Mackay sent to Mwanga, advising him to stay where he was, and wrote to Monseigneur Livinhac, telling him that the English missionaries would have nothing to do with Mwanga's scheme. To this letter Monseigneur Livinhac replied as follows:—

"BUKUMBI, SOUTH OF VICTORIA NYANZA,
"NOTRE DAME DE KAMOGA,
"*April* 30*th*, 1889.

"MY DEAR FRIEND,—

"I thank you for your news, and for telling me frankly what you think concerning Buganda.

"I had already told Mwanga and his people that their project is a dangerous one. All replied that they knew the danger, but that would not hinder them; that they did not mean to raise 'rebellion,' nor a war for religion, but only an 'expedition' in order to expel a usurper and the foreign invaders (Arabs), and to restore the rightful king, as also to allow to return to their own country those who had been unjustly driven away, and who were suffering from hunger in exile.

"I do not know if they will be able to land in their country, and to join their brethren. Perhaps in a few days we shall see them come back as they went.

"I do not know what your converts will do, but one of them, 'very influential,' has written to us, begging us to allow Mwanga to go, if he is with us, as he is the heir of Mtesa, and if he promises 'liberty.'

(*Signed*) "LEON LIVINHAC."

Gordon had also written strongly to Stokes, urging him to refrain from taking Mwanga in his boat, or otherwise aiding him to regain his throne. But the expedition had started before Gordon's letter arrived at its destination.

Meanwhile news had reached Kalema that messengers had gone to invite Mwanga to return, and that Mukotanyi had provided them with canoes. Kalema immediately despatched an army to attack Mukotanyi, who, as soon as he heard of the advance of the invading force, sent off post-haste to implore the aid of the Christian party, since, he urged, it was to benefit them he had incurred the hostility of Kalema.

The Christians, therefore, on hearing of the intended

invasion of Mukotanyi's country, marched into Budu, and intercepted the Muhammedan army under Wamala the Mukwenda before it could reach Bukoba, and inflicted upon it a severe defeat. Wamala returned in disgrace, and Kalema then sent his Katikiro with a still larger force to oppose the victorious Christians, who were advancing in two divisions on the capital. The Muhammedans awaited the approaching host in the plantations, and a fierce encounter ensued. One division of the Christians was victorious, and eight of the Muhammedan leaders fell ; but the other division met with disaster, and the young Roman Catholic Katikiro, Nyonyi Entono, was killed, with many others, the Christians losing some two or three hundred killed. This battle was fought at a place called Mayuki.

The Christians now retreated, followed by their victorious adversaries, who pursued them until they had driven them over the frontier.

Tired out and dispirited they returned to Kabula, to hear that Mwanga had actually arrived, and was even now at Dumu on the coast of Budu. This was early in May.

There can be little doubt that Kalema kept his spies in the Christian camp, for news seems to have reached him of the scheme to carry off one of the remaining princes ; so to make this impossible, he immediately put the unhappy Kiwewa to death, and secured every prince (Mulangira) and princess (Mumbeja), remembering the plan formerly suggested, that the Christians might even seize a princess, and make her queen. And these unfortunate people their ruthless brother burned to death. This shocking atrocity was hardly perpetrated when he heard of Mwanga's arrival with a large following at his gates, a piece of news which may well seem to carry with it the irony of God's answer to that fearful crime.

CHAPTER IV

SCRAMBLING FOR UGANDA

A Reverse for Mwanga—" They that take the Sword shall perish with the Sword"—A dignified Death—A brilliant Feat—Zakaria appeals to Stanley—An Act of Christian Virtue!—Battle of Nasenyi—Battle of Kitebi—Battle of Kinakulia—Imperial British East Africa Company—Dr. Carl Peters—Preparations for fighting—A solemn Compact--Death of Mackay—Victory of Bulwanyi—Arrival of Dr. Peters—Arrival of Jackson and Gedge—Failure of Imperial British East Africa Company's Treaty—The First Christian Church—Palm Trees lift up their slender Stems.

CHAPTER IV

SCRAMBLING FOR UGANDA

THE messengers who had been sent to ask Mackay's advice returned with the king, and brought the letters which Mackay and Gordon had written to the Protestant party, strongly urging them to have nothing to do with the scheme of replacing Mwanga.* But already the matter had been settled for them by the Muhammedan attack upon their ally Mukotanyi. They therefore decided to go to Mwanga's assistance, though with extreme vexation that they appeared to be rejecting the advice of Mackay.

Meanwhile Kalema collected another army which he

* Mackay, in writing home about the advice he and Gordon had given, observes: "Should the scheme succeed, I fear greatly that Mwanga, once in power, will wreak a terrible revenge on the Christians, who were the chief agents in driving him from Bugunda, and especially on the Protestants for declining to help to restore him. Here, too, we shall not be safe from Mwanga's malice, which will not be less when he has Romanists as his chief advisers. Even Père Lourdel is reported to have already given out that when Mwanga is restored, we need never expect to be allowed to set foot again in Buganda, seeing that we refused to aid in accomplishing his restoration.

sent to attack Mwanga. The Sesse Islanders had all declared for Mwanga, and as they were the sailors of Uganda, this gave the Christian faction the command of the Nyanza. Mwanga and his following, now swollen to many thousands, advanced inland from Dumu to Badja, some twenty miles from the Lake. They had between one and two thousand guns, and a large following of spearmen, but they had not recovered from their last defeat, and their lack of enthusiasm for their anything but valiant king no doubt contributed to the unhappy result of the first encounter; for they were badly beaten. The Muhammedan Baganda were led by Arabs, whose courage, as well as the possession of breech-loading rifles, no doubt contributed to the victory which they obtained. I do not think there was much loss of life in this encounter. Mwanga's chief leader, Muemba, was killed, whereupon his followers immediately fled, not so much, I imagine, from craven fear, as that probably they thought the white man Stokes and their king ought to have led them in person, and not have watched the course of events from a safe distance. Fighting, however, was not in Stokes' contract, and Mwanga had no stomach for the risk it entailed. When the day was lost, Mwanga fled back to Stokes' boat with some two hundred of his people. The people embarked in canoes, while he himself travelled in the boat, and made his way to the Sesse Islands, where he was enthusiastically received by the islanders, and where for a time he made his camp. The main body of Christians retreated once more to Kabula, to await further developments.

There was one remarkable feature in this strife, exemplifying our Lord's words, " They that take the sword shall perish with the sword," since, one way or another, nearly all those great chiefs who had been persecutors had met their deaths. Mujasi, who, as we have seen, had treacherously killed the Christians, had himself been treacherously killed by Kiwewa, while Kiwewa, who had countenanced the murder of the men who were hostile to the Muhammedans, met his own death at the hands of his Muhammedan brother Kalema. Kyambalango, the old Kimbugwe, who had counselled the murder of Bishop Hannington, and had been involved with Mwanga in the plot to slay the Christians, was subsequently wounded in one of the battles against them. He fled, and was pursued by a number of heathen spearmen, and burnt to death by them in a hut in which he had taken refuge. There remained only the old Katikiro, who had refused help to Kiwewa when he fled to Mutesa's tomb, and who, through all the troubles, had succeeded in keeping on the winning side. This man had penetration enough to see that the Arabs would not be able to hold their own against the Europeans; nor is it unlikely that rumours had reached Uganda that white men were on the march to Usoga. This must have been the Imperial British East Africa Company's expedition under Mr. Jackson. The old Katikiro seems, therefore, to have made some kind of overtures to Mwanga. At any rate, Kalema, suspecting his loyalty, sent men to murder him. When the messengers came he behaved with much dignity, and met his death with the greatest courage. He saw that his murder was intended, and made no resistance. He was shot, and his body cast into one of the houses, which was then set on fire, so that all that was mortal of him thus perished in the flames. This man was one of the most remarkable Africans I have ever met. He possessed an astonishing insight into character. He was as courteous and polite as an Arab. Emin Pasha called him the one gentleman in Uganda. When not carried away by the cruel passion of revenge he could take a statesmanlike view of affairs. I have a vivid recollection of his proud and handsome face, which yet was so difficult to read.

But underlying all his suavity and politeness there was a determined and bitter hatred for foreigners; and whether it was consummate acting or genuine feeling, he displayed a touching fidelity to the memory of his old master, King Mutesa. Though he could read a Gospel, and knew something of the Koran, he died as he had lived—an adherent of the old Uganda religion.

Meanwhile Mwanga proceeded with his fleet of canoes along the coast of Uganda, pillaging and burning, and made his way round Entebe Point—now Fort Alice—and up Murchison Bay to the famous islet of Bulinguge, where he formed his camp. Stokes left him at the end of June; but before doing so wrote on behalf of Mwanga to the Imperial British East Africa Company, explaining the position of affairs, and begging for assistance. These letters, which were dated June 7th, lay for some time in Kavirondo, and Mr. Jackson did not receive them till November 7th, when he arrived at the east side of the Nyanza in that month.

Mwanga's people meanwhile had several successful skirmishes with the Muhammedans, and succeeded in the brilliant feat of destroying an Arab dhow which was carrying arms and ammunition to Kalema. On board this vessel was an Arab named Halfan, who was made prisoner, and who was ransomed only on his friends depositing with Mwanga five hundred pounds of gunpowder, seventy muzzle-loading guns, and nine bales of calico. This ammunition subsequently came from the Arabs at Magu, on the south of the Nyanza, who despatched it by Stokes' boat.

Mwanga now sent two important deputations to the French and English missionaries at the south of the Lake, inviting them to come back and give Christian instruction to his followers. I give his letter to Mackay :—

"BULINGUGE, *June 25th*, 1889.

" *To* MR. MACKAY,

" I send very many compliments to you and to Mr. Gordon.

" After compliments, I, Mwanga, beg of you to help me. Do not remember bygone matters. We are now in a miserable plight, but if you, my fathers, are willing to come and help to restore me to my kingdom, you will be at liberty to do whatever you like.

" Formerly I did not know God, but now I know the religion of Jesus Christ. Consider how Kalema has killed all my brothers and sisters ; he has killed my children, too, and now there remain only we two princes [Kalema and himself]. Mr. Mackay, do help me ; I have no strength, but if you are with me I shall be strong. Sir, do not imagine that if you restore Mwanga to Buganda he will become bad again. If you find me become bad, then you may drive me from the throne ; but I have given up my former ways, and I only wish now to follow your advice.

"I am your friend,

(*Signed*) " MWANGA."

In response to the appeal for missionaries, Messrs. Gordon and Walker left Usambiro on August 27th, *en route* to join Mwanga on Bulinguge Island. Mr. Stanley came into Usambiro with Emin Pasha the following day. As he journeyed from Kavalli's he had been met by Zakaria and Samwili, who had been sent by the fugitive Christians to ask his aid in restoring Mwanga, but Stanley had no great faith in Mwanga, and besides, it appeared to him that the Uganda question was rather too important a matter to enter upon as a parenthesis in his great feat of relieving Emin Pasha. He therefore felt obliged to refuse aid to the exiled Christians.

But to return to Uganda. Kalema, finding himself in difficulties as to water transport, attempted to obtain canoes from the island of Uvema, but unsuccessfully.

Meanwhile Kagwa Apolo and his following having somewhat recovered their spirits after the disaster which they had met, moved out of Kabula, and, marching by the little kingdom of Koki, on the western border of Budu, they made an alliance with Kamswaga, its king,

An Act of Christian Virtue!

and with him attacked Muguluma, the Muhammedan commander. Muguluma was killed, and his followers fled, and a vast number of women were captured.

MATAYO THE MUJASI.   REV. H. W. DUTA KITAKULE.

WASWA   KAGWA THE KATIKIRO
THE MUKWENDA.   WITH HIS WIFE AND SISTER.

These women were set free—all, I suppose, but some of the best of them. The Uganda commander speaks as if this were an act of Christian virtue; but there was a good deal of policy in it, since the army could not hamper itself with vast crowds of captives who required to be fed, and were always a tenfold source of danger. The Christians then advanced to a village called Nasenyi, where they were attacked in force by the enemy, and severely defeated, losing between two and three hundred men. Kagwa fled to a place called Jungo, and sent to call the fighting men to come to him there. He also sent to Mwanga for help. The king responded by sending him a thousand men with guns. With these Kagwa advanced to attack the Muhammedans at a place called Munkabira, which he reached at about three o'clock in the afternoon. Here a severe engagement was fought in which the Muhammedans were worsted, losing fully four hundred men. Kagwa followed them as far as the village of Kitebe, only a few miles from Mengo, where he slept. At dawn next day, October 5th, the battle was renewed, and again the Christians were victorious, inflicting severe loss upon the enemy, one or two important chiefs being among the killed. Kagwa then advanced on Mengo, which was quickly stormed and taken. The Muhammedans, under Kalema, retreated to a place about four hours' distance, called Kinakulya, where they formed a camp.

Mwanga, on hearing of this victory, came from Bulingugc to a place called Musambya, where he redistributed the chieftainships,* and six days later

---

* In this distribution the country was about equally divided between the two religious factions. How could this have happened if the Roman Catholics were numerically stronger and so much more powerful than the Protestants? It is a further entered Mengo in triumph, on October 11th, after an absence of some fourteen months.

The Muhammedans, though defeated, and though something like thirty Arabs had perished one way or another in the campaign, were by no means crushed ; and Kalema, having gathered another army quickly, advanced towards Mengo. Kagwa Apolo (now Katikiro) was appointed leader of the Christian army, and marched out to Kinakulia with two thousand six hundred guns and the usual complement of spearmen, who were not very particular which side they fought upon. Loot was their main object in following the more formidable fighting men of the religious factions. At first the Christians were successful, but unhappily their leader Kagwa was wounded, receiving a bullet in his armpit, whereupon his followers fell back. The Mukwenda Waswa (a Protestant) sustained the attack for some time, but he also fell back on the village of Kilangira, whither the wounded leader had preceded him.

When Kagwa found Waswa had been worsted he ran full speed to inform the king, and Mwanga and his court hurried off once more to Bulinguge Island.* The bulk of Mwanga's army now dispersed, part going to Kyagwe, on the east, and part going to Budu, to the south, of which province old Nikodemo was chief.

proof of what I have always maintained, that before the king became a positive partisan of one party there was little difference between the numbers of either faction.

* Bulinguge Island, in Murchison Bay, is about two miles in circumference, and has a hill some two or three hundred feet in the centre. It is about eight miles from Mengo.

The missionaries, Walker and Gordon, as well as Lourdel and another French priest, who had responded to the king's invitation, remained with Mwanga on the island.

At this time a very important event happened in the advent of messengers from Mr. Jackson of the Imperial British East Africa Company, who had found Mwanga's request for help awaiting him on his arrival at Kavirondo, November 7th, 1889. The object of his expedition was to make treaties with the chiefs *en route*, and to endeavour to procure news of Stanley. He had orders, however, not to enter Uganda.

He had five hundred Swahili porters, chiefly, if not wholly, Muhammedans, armed with Snider rifles. The men, however, were in a state of mutiny, and he had eventually to disarm a number of them.

Mr. Jackson, accordingly, wrote at once, explaining what his orders were, but saying that if help were urgently needed he would come, provided the missionaries would guarantee expenses, and that Mwanga would place his country under the Company's protection. Mwanga, as we have seen, had just suffered a reverse in November, and accordingly wrote on the 25th begging of Mr. Jackson to come; but the letter was written so guardedly that Jackson suspected some adverse influence. On December 1st, however, Mwanga's chief adviser, Père Lourdel, wrote to Mr. Jackson in the king's name, again imploring aid, and offering to accept the British flag, and to grant certain commercial advantages. He promised to provide food for Jackson's men and a large payment of ivory.

In reply to this Jackson wrote in a somewhat unsatisfactory manner, but sent one of the Company's flags as a guarantee of the Company's assistance. The flag reached Mwanga on December 15th. Jackson then went away towards Mont Elgon on an ivory hunting expedition, and was absent some three months.

He had not been gone very long, when Dr. Carl Peters, who was leading a German Emin relief expedition, marched into Jackson's camp in Kavirondo, and was politely received by the natives in charge, who, no doubt, accustomed only to the honourable dealings of Europeans as represented by Englishmen, handed him the letters addressed to Jackson. These Dr. Peters opened and read, and promptly acted upon, and determined to go himself to Uganda, steal a march on Jackson, and make a treaty for himself, thereby hoping to cut England out of Uganda—an audacious project, which the intrepid German imagined he had succeeded in carrying out, though the result of it did not turn out quite as he had anticipated. He therefore wrote to Uganda, and in reply received letters from Mwanga inviting him to enter the country.

But we must leave him, and return to consider the fortunes of Mwanga on his island encampment. The people were growing weary of the warfare, and both sides refrained for a time from renewing the attack. Early in January, however, it was arranged to gather an army from Chagwe and Budu. Old Nikodemo, the Pokino of Budu, showed some annoyance at receiving orders from Kagwa, since Kagwa was nothing in the

Church, where he himself was the principal man. Walker and Gordon felt that in showing this spirit he was quite wrong, though many of the Christians supported him ; when, however, he understood that the missionaries desired him to conform to some kind of discipline he gladly furnished his contingent. It was a matter for astonishment how anything was accomplished at all, so little discipline of any kind was there among the Christian faction. The same want of order doubtless obtained among the Muhammedan party, and this no doubt somewhat equalised the contending armies.

The arrival of Stokes' boat this month (January) with Halfan's fine, gave a great impetus to the preparations for war, which were pushed on apace, and the Chagwe contingent of some thousands was conveyed in canoes to the other side of the creek, *en route* to Jungo, the old rallying place, where the armies from Budu and Singo were to rendezvous. The thing was done quietly and quickly, and the junction was effected, while the Muhammedans were still encamped near Mengo.

On February 3rd, before Kagwa and his army finally started to attack Kalema, a solemn undertaking was drawn up between the Roman Catholic and Protestant chiefs, and a written promise signed between them, that if they obtained power they would not make war upon one another. This agreement had been brought about at the instance of the missionaries, who had over and over again used their influence in the interests of · peace between the factions, into which the Christians were unhappily divided.

A day or two before the final encounter with Kalema, for which the Christians were preparing, a blow fell upon the English Mission and the Christian cause more severe than even the loss of a battle. It was the death of Mackay. His manifold labours, the heavy work of fitting the machinery for his steamer in the pestilential climate of Usambiro, had proved too great for his strength, and just as his companion Deekes was on the point of leaving for the coast, on account of ill health, Mackay was struck down by his last fever. Deekes put off his journey and remained to nurse him, but was himself too ill to render any very efficient aid to his sick friend. After four days of fever and delirium Mackay fell asleep. A man whom some men blamed and some men praised, but a man who, whether praised or blamed, saw his duty and did it fearlessly; one who deserved the title King Mutesa once gave him, when, astonished at his young white guest's resolution, he cried, "Mackay, oli Musaja dala" ("Mackay, you are a *man*").

But to return to the war in Uganda. When all the preparations were complete Kagwa and his force marched to a point named Bulwanyi, where the Muhammedans met him, and on February 11th a great battle took place, in which the Muhammedans were utterly broken and driven in headlong flight to Kalema's enclosure of Nansana, near Mengo. And from there the Muhammedan Sultan fled with his following over the border into Bunyoro, where he set about attempting to reorganise his army.

He had had with him numbers of Kabarega's

people,* who were slaughtered in their flight owing to their ignorance of the roads, and thus fell victims to the Uganda spearmen.

After the battle of Bulwanyi the king and the missionaries moved to an island further up the creek, called Namalusu, while most of the people went to the mainland.

There now occurred what are the usual accompaniments of war—namely, both famine and plague, by which seven thousand persons were said to have perished.

When it became apparent that the Muhammedans, for the present, were completely crushed, Mwanga ventured back to his old capital of Mengo, in time to receive Dr. Carl Peters, who arrived on February 24th. Peters, with the aid of the French priests, concocted a treaty, which was brought before the king in the absence of the English missionaries, who had not been asked to be present. Nothing, under the circumstances, more clearly showed their hostility to the English Company than the action of Peters and the priests, and the attitude taken up by them towards the English missionaries. Surely it might have been thought, in a matter of this sort, the English missionaries might at least have been consulted. But, as we have seen, Peters and his co-helpers endeavoured to secure the treaty quite independently of the Protestant chiefs, who point

---

* Kabarega's main idea in helping Kalema seems to have been to please the Arabs, who were the chief means by which he was able to buy guns, ammunition, and other things which he desired. After Kalema's last defeat he sent an army to prevent his reentering Unyoro.

blank refused to have anything to say to it, on the ground that their missionaries had been excluded from the Baraza when it was brought forward. Things had now come to such a pass that both parties were rushing to arms to prepare for fighting ; so that for the sake of peace Walker and Gordon begged of the Protestant chiefs to sign the treaty. This is an admirable illustration of the usual manner in which treaties are made with African chiefs

The treaty was subsequently disavowed by the German Government, and was therefore harmless ; and it cannot be denied that Peters' coming had a good effect on the country. Peters, however, had an uneasy sense that Jackson might soon be on his heels to make trouble, so he did not stay long in Uganda. Meanwhile Jackson had returned to Sundu's in Kavirondo, and learnt that Peters had made very free in his camp, and had then proceeded to Uganda. Jackson therefore lost no time in hurrying to Uganda with his companion Gedge, and he reached Mengo in April with about one hundred and eighty Snider rifles. The treaty that Jackson now proposed was, one cannot but feel rightly, rejected by the king, for it was certainly unreasonable in its demands. The Protestants, however, were eager to obtain English protection at all costs ; but not so the Roman Catholics guided by Père Lourdel.

The controversy was strong. Walker had meanwhile left to go to the help of Deekes at Nassa, and it seemed that no settlement would be arrived at. The Protestants said they would leave the country, and Gedge appears to have encouraged them in this idea.

The Roman Catholics then said if the Protestants left they must likewise retire, since, by themselves, they could not hold Uganda against the Muhammedans. Wiser counsel, however, prevailed. Jackson ceased to press his obnoxious treaty, and offered to take back with him to the coast two of the chiefs, one a Romanist the other a Protestant, to find out what the intentions of the ruling European powers might really be; whether, in fact, Uganda was to be a British or French Protectorate. Jackson left in April, leaving Gedge in charge with as many Snider rifles as he could spare, and this was the *status quo* in Uganda till the end of this year.

But there was another event full of significance, which took place on March 11th, and this was the commencement of building the first Christian church in Uganda.

I cannot forbear to quote the words of one who witnessed the setting up the first palm trees which formed the pillars to support the roof.

"At last," writes Walker, "some of the very poles of Buganda * 'praise the Lord.' There they stand pointing up to the sky because man recognises the Creator. The branches of palm-trees once were strewed for the honour of Jerusalem's King; now palm trees again lift up their slender stems to support a house to the glory of the same King."

* These countries around the Nyanza are called by the Baganda Buganda, Busoga, Bunyoro, etc.

CHAPTER V

A NEST OF HORNETS

Uganda Problems—Interpretation of Instructions—A Quiet Young Scotchman—Captain Lugard's First Interview with Mwanga—Lugard's Manifesto—A perilous Negotiation—An unhappy Christmas—A simple Explanation—Exaggerated Rumours—Baseless Suspicions—Policy of the Priests—Policy of the English Mission—Policy of the Imperial British East Africa Company—The Question of the Sesse Islands—Changing Sides—A proposed Compromise—An intolerable Strain—The French Bishop—Mission Extension—An iniquitious Fine—Letters from the Coast—A Dictum discredited

CHAPTER V

A NEST OF HORNETS

A NEW actor now appeared on the scene in the person of Captain Lugard, D.S.O., who had been sent by the Imperial British East Africa Company to occupy Uganda, which the late Sir William Mackinnon had clearly seen was practically the key to the Nile Valley, and a place of the greatest strategic as well as of commercial importance. The instructions delivered to Captain Lugard were to the effect that he should offer Mwanga guarantees of peace in his kingdom, and impress him with a sense of the Company's power, that he should endeavour to secure the control of all white affairs in the country, and to exercise the strictest impartiality towards the three factions, Protestant, Roman Catholic, and Muhammedan, into which the nation was divided, assuring all of religious freedom and toleration. But if the other factions, however, proved intractable he was to "consolidate the Protestant party."

The framers of these instructions delivered to a military officer with an armed force did not apparently contemplate such a contingency as King Mwanga's refusing their agent admission to the country, yet something very like this happened; and Lugard, without permission from the king, and in spite of Mwanga's measures to prevent it, forced his way to the capital, and established an armed camp on Kampala Hill, within a rifle shot of Mwanga's enclosure. Lugard's orders were " Go to Uganda," and he went; though it is very questionable whether by his so doing the Company did not exceed the powers which their royal charter gave them.

His task in Uganda was, first, to offer guarantees of peace in Mwanga's kingdom, and to impress him with a sense of the Company's power—much the same thing, since both could only be accomplished by the presence of a strong force, which, as we shall see, Captain Lugard did not possess.

Next he was to aim at controlling all white affairs in the country,* the meaning of which I cannot pretend entirely to explain, since the only white affairs in the country were those of English and French missions and missionaries, and of the ex-missionary Stokes. The attempt to carry out this second instruction

* Those at whose instance such instructions were given were fully aware of the growing definiteness of aim displayed by France in its policy regarding an eastward movement towards the Nile. They were aware, moreover, that the French Government has never shrunk from making use of French missionaries in furthering its political aims where the missionaries are willing to lend themselves to its schemes. Moreover, the French Government had displayed an amount of interest in Roman Catholic missions in Uganda so little in accordance with their avowed indifference as to make its solicitude somewhat suspicious. I refer to the action of the French Government respecting Stanley's route, when he undertook the task of relieving Emin Pasha. It was the French who practically barred his approaching Wadelai by the route through Uganda. Reading this clause in the light

seems to have been beset with thorns, since before he left Uganda Captain Lugard had come into somewhat acrimonious controversy with all the " white affairs in the place." Then he was to exercise the strictest impartiality towards the factions, called respectively " English " and " French " and " Islamite." That the Directors of the Company could not, of course, have meant that he was to treat his warm supporters and his most hostile opponents exactly in the same manner is clear ; and in the next sentence he was directed, should the other factions prove intractable—that is, if they failed to accept his assurances of fair political and religious treatment at the hands of the Company—to consolidate the Protestant or English party, whose eager desire to accept the English flag was a guarantee that they would favour a British administration.*

The instructions were, in their very nature, alternative, and amounted to this : " If you can get hold of the country without the help of the English or Protestant faction do so ; but if not, make use of them."

of such knowledge, one can find a sufficient reason for the insistance with which the English Administration is urged to secure the control of all white affairs in the country, which might have meant, in other words, to make the political influence of England in the country stronger than that of France. If possible, this was to be accomplished by diplomacy and by keeping aloof from internal matters, religious or otherwise ; but failing this, then Captain Lugard was explicitly ordered to consolidate the Protestant-- *i.e.*, the English party.

* In their loyal acceptance of Sir Gerald Portal's decision, heaping honours and rewards on their rivals, who were so hostile to the English, the chiefs of the English faction have signally proved this assertion.

Captain Lugard entered Uganda with some two hundred and seventy porters, including about one hundred really good fighting men who were well armed. He had brought up a Maxim gun, on which he does not seem to have placed much reliance; but this gun was valuable, as its unknown powers were as likely to be exaggerated as not. News of the German machine guns further south had already reached Uganda. He had, moreover, fifty trained soldiers, consisting of Sudanese and Somalis, and best of all he had with him, besides young de Winton, whose courage and devotion were afterwards proved, a quiet young Scotchman named Grant, whose daring courage, quiet determination, and coolness in difficulties, would have made him no bad leader, where he was content to play the part of a loyal subordinate.

On reaching the Nile, Captain Lugard found his road practically blocked. Mwanga had ordered that no boats should be supplied; but Lugard overcame the difficulty by seizing one or two canoes, and with these he crossed his whole party, and came on by rapid marches to the capital, reaching Mengo on December 18th.

On December 19th he paid his first visit to Mwanga, with whom he was anxious to conclude a treaty, since he says he felt that "any action he took without such a treaty would have been mere filibustering." *

* What about crossing the Nile "*without waiting for permission,*" *marching rapidly on the capital, selecting his own camping ground?* See ("The Rise of our East African Empire," vol. ii., p. 21.) What were these preliminary proceedings but filibustering?

At this first interview with the King of Uganda two of the English missionaries, Messrs. Walker and Gordon, were present. The French priests had declined to attend, on the plea that they would take no further part in politics !

The English missionaries lent their services in translating the letters from the coast, which do not appear to have favourably impressed either the king or his Roman Catholic chiefs, who, somehow or other, were filled with the idea that Lugard had simply come to help the Protestants and to oust themselves. Captain Lugard, however, announced that all were alike in his eyes, Roman Catholics, Protestants,* and every one, and after saying that he hoped to arrange disputes satisfactorily, he took leave of the king and courtiers.

Captain Lugard next called on the French priests in order to try and enlist their sympathy and help in the treaty he hoped to conclude with Mwanga and the chiefs, but met with a disappointing reception.

So far Uganda had proved no bed of roses. The French party were sullenly hostile. The English party at first had received the captain with joyful acclamations, but had been somewhat coldly received by him, lest he should appear in the light of a religious partisan. They were now much crestfallen, while the captain, finding both parties difficult to deal with, threatened

* Roman Catholics and Protestants. The word Abaprotestanti (Protestants) was introduced by the Company. Until its arrival in Uganda this word was unknown. The parties were generally Bazungu or Bangereza ("English"), and Bafulasa or Bafransa ("French"). (*See* p. 68, vol. ii., "Rise of our East African Empire.")

to go to Kabarega, the bitter enemy of the whole nation, and form an alliance with him. Such was the condition of affairs when Captain Lugard attempted to force a treaty on the king.

The day before Christmas the question of a treaty was introduced before the king in open court, where a dangerous and excited crowd of chiefs had collected. All came armed with loaded rifles, the Roman Catholics to support the king against the English, and the Protestants to defend Captain Lugard. One angry partisan actually covered Captain Lugard with his gun, but the muzzle of the loaded weapon was instantly beaten down by one of the Protestant chiefs from Budu, the faithful Zakaria—then Kagolo, and now Kangao, Chief of Bulemezi. Twice de Winton— one of Lugard's companions—heard the click of a rifle being cocked, while the chiefs, seeing that a fight was imminent, quietly slipped their cartridges into their rifles. Lugard, however, was too absorbed to heed anything. The king was terrified and greatly excited, as the strange Englishman, heedless of his evident disinclination, insisted that he should sign the treaty. But at last, when the king seemed about to give way, such a clamour arose outside from the Roman Catholic party, that Captain Lugard felt it wiser not to face the rising storm, or to persist in a course which would presently transform Mengo into a bloody battle ground. He therefore returned to Kampala Fort to spend an anxious night. He could now realise something of the intense excitement which prevailed, as he listened to the shouting, drum-beating, and angry voices now and again crying out that the English should be killed.

Next day was Christmas. The other Englishmen, as the custom of Englishmen is, kept festival, but the anxious leader excused himself, for the extreme gravity of the situation oppressed his spirit. He determined to seek a private interview with the terrified king. But no sooner had he neared the gates of Mengo than the royal drums boomed out, and armed men with rifles ready came stealing up, and slipped in to guard the king. Some treachery was suspected on both sides it appears. Lugard then turned back amid the half-suppressed jeers and chuckling of the insolent rabble.

Next day, however, a wonder happened, for the treaty was signed by the recalcitrant Roman Catholics and king, and the storm was stilled. "We left the Baraza," writes Lugard, "to find there was perfect quiet outside, and not an angry and excited mob as I had expected." He need not have been astonished, for the explanation of the great change is simple enough. The French fathers bade their faction sign the treaty, an order which was immediately obeyed.

Next day, December 27th, the English bishop (Tucker) arrived at Mengo with several new missionaries, among them the brilliant young scholar, Pilkington. The bishop left in less than a month, apparently under the impression that he had been instrumental in effecting a settlement of the difficulties by a hurried conference with the French fathers, the result of which, however, as might have been expected, proved valueless. The arrangement arrived at was found to be unworkable, and was never kept to by either side.

The treaty had been signed, but there was no intention upon the part of the French priests of recognising the Company's flag as that of the English nation, much less of handing over the country to Captain Lugard. They were the guides of their converts. Every conversation and every word uttered to and by Captain Lugard were carefully reported to the priests. Every move was carefully considered at Rubaga (their mission station) before being taken. Lugard's pleasant and friendly manner, his gentlemanly feeling and sympathy with the natives, could not but make him deservedly popular with them ; but of real influence and weight of the kind which he aimed at he had none. His opinion was only valued when it agreed with the opinion of the missionaries. I do not doubt that by patience and in time he would have gained very much more power in the country ; but at this period his fighting force was not strong enough to enable him to stand alone, and the position was fast becoming intolerable to a man of his high and ardent spirit.

In January of this year (1891) news reached Mengo of the near approach of Captain (now Major) Williams, R.A., who had been sent to assist Lugard in his work in Uganda, and exaggerated stories were circulated as to his object in coming, while it was said that he was bringing flags to force on the chiefs. These reports about Williams, Mugwanya, the chief of the Roman Catholics, informed the Company's representative his party did not credit, and added further that they would not believe unpleasant reports from any source whatever about the Company, adding that they knew the captain was their friend ! This, Lugard tells us, was seriously said, and, he thinks, obviously meant ; yet this chief's subsequent actions all tended to show that he had no greater confidence in Captain Lugard than that entertained by Mugwanya's trusted fathers in God, the French priests.

With regard to the real feeling and position of the loyal Protestant and English faction, Captain Lugard from the first appears to have been in the strangest ignorance ; indeed, so little did he understand their true attitude, that he did not feel quite safe from an armed attack from them upon the Company's fort—a suspicion which would have been utterly ludicrous had it not been altogether lamentable. These Protestants up to this time had been almost entirely guided by the missionaries—that is to say, as long as the missionaries were in their midst—and were on terms the warmest and most affectionate with both Gordon and Walker. They would take no steps without consulting their revered white teachers. Over and over again they had submitted, as in the case of the Peters' treaty, to what they felt was a wrong on the earnest representations of the missionaries. Thus Captain Lugard's suspicions of these people were as baseless as it is possible to conceive. Had he really known the relationship existing between the English missionaries and their converts, he would no more have thought of suspecting an armed attack from the native Christians than from Messrs. Gordon and Walker themselves.*

I have spoken of this matter since the general reader may fail to grasp the situation unless he has some clear idea of the point of view of the various actors in this interesting passage of Central African history.

The policy of the French priests was partly based on the proposition, that, as an Anglo-German agreement did not affect their rights as Frenchmen if they could make their own possession of Uganda an accomplished fact, neither England nor Germany could oust them from it without having to reckon with the French nation.

This was surely no great enormity on their part. They had reason to believe they would soon be strong enough to seize and hold Uganda for themselves, and "a fair Catholic kingdom by the Nyanza" was an alluring dream which it may be presumed they hoped to realise by eventually fully arming their faction, and meanwhile keeping things balanced until they were ready for the final coup. Thus they supported Peters, and helped him with his treaty, and they gave Lugard a certain amount of support, since, as we have seen, they allowed him his treaty with Mwanga.

What, on the other hand, was the policy of the

* Captain Lugard writes as follows (*see* p. 42, vol. ii., " Rise of our East African Empire "): " I sent out Somalis as scouts, and presently they came back breathless to say the enemy was approaching. I did not know whether they would prove to be *the Protestants* or the Roman Catholics." He has just mentioned the anger of the English party at his not having identified himself with their faction, as they expected he would do.

English missionaries? It is hardly necessary to say that under the painful circumstances in which they had been placed by Mwanga's rapacity and cruelty, they would have gladly hailed the advent of any European power that would have guaranteed them liberty to preach and to teach. They never believed that Uganda could stand alone, rent and torn as it was by internal dissensions. Captain Lugard quotes the late General Gordon as saying "the Uganda mission, as it is composed, is more secular than spiritual," a statement which possibly its context would explain, in a sense less hostile to the English mission than it certainly appears; but if General Gordon did make such a statement one would like to hear the proof of its truth. Those specially qualified to form an opinion give a very different account.* I am necessarily out of court on such a question.† Lugard goes on to say, that on account of its being more secular than spiritual, General Gordon wrote to indicate the political attitude the mission should take. I never heard anything of these letters, though I was in Uganda when Gordon was last in England, and when he was killed at Khartoum; but it is perfectly true that Mackay and the missionary Gordon, and other English missionaries, did all in their power to

* *See* p. 86. Testimony of the missionary Gordon on first reaching Uganda as to spirituality of converts. It is needless to say General Gordon was never in Uganda.

† Captain Lugard is quoted by the *Record* newspaper as having borne testimony to the spiritual work of the Uganda mission while lecturing at Oxford in 1894. Similar testimony was borne by him when speaking at Norwich in 1893.

help forward English interests—not as opposed to French or German interests, for these were never presented to their view—but simply with the hope of securing a Government under which religious liberty should be guaranteed.

The above, I think, fairly represents the state of opinion and the aims of the respective missions at the time of Captain Lugard's arrival. He had decided— as I have mentioned—to endeavour to assume a perfectly neutral position, which, if the two factions had been merely religious, would have been excellent ; but when the question between them was the very existence of English interests in the country, a policy of political neutrality upon his part was in the very nature of things impossible.

The attempt to follow out such a policy very soon led him into a grave error of judgment, which served to deprive both factions of any confidence in his justice, and to throw a serious obstacle in the way of his obtaining influence over the leaders. In the difficult and intricate cases of disputed estates he permitted both parties to appeal to him, and undertook to adjudicate on the matters in question. That he committed the error of following the path of expediency rather than that of pure justice his own words unmistakably show. Here is his own account of his method. He writes : " Meanwhile, as far as I could judge from the inquiries I made, the Protestants appear to have had by far the greatest cause of complaint, and this seemed natural, as they were the weaker party. If, however, I should give case after case in favour of the Protestants purely because in each instance the evidence should point in their favour, I should undoubtedly alienate the Roman Catholics, who naturally viewed things from their own standpoint, and they would consider me partial however unbiassed I might really be. I therefore endeavoured to find two cases, one of which appeared to be clearly in favour of the Protestants, the other of the Roman Catholics, and thus, while deciding justly, to make the balance equal." He goes on to say: "This pairing off of cases has given umbrage to recent writers on the Roman Catholic side of the controversy."* How could it do otherwise than give umbrage to every right-minded person, on whatever side he might happen to be? A man who dispenses judgment in the way described above may command our amazement at his dexterity, but he will hardly win our respect for his sense of justice.

Another difficulty at this period was the question of dividing the Sesse Islands between the English and French factions. The owners of these islands practically held all the water communication on the Lake. It had been agreed that each faction should have a share; but so far the "French" had possessed themselves of the whole. Finally, however, the king agreed that the islands should be divided. Next came the great question of changing sides. It was the object of both factions to secure the person of the king, since whichever side held him gained the great mass of peasants, and of those who were indifferent to both the new religions, and who blindly followed the king. The

* "The Rise of our East African Empire," p. 70, vol. ii.

king, at the time we are speaking of, had nominally joined the "French" faction. There were not a few lukewarm "English chiefs" who would have gone over to his side, providing their changing their politics should not lose them their chieftainships. Now at the division of the country on Mwanga's return it had been expressly stipulated that a chief on either side abjuring his party or religion should lose his chieftainship. This was, from a religious point of view, not satisfactory, yet under the circumstances it was inevitable, and was, at any rate, fair, since it cut both ways as long as the king was neutral; but as soon as Mwanga came out clearly on the French side then it only cut one way, as the political temptation now was for chiefs to join the French side—that is, to forsake Protestantism and the English party. The English chiefs said to these turncoats, "By all means join the 'French'; but let them provide you with preferment." Captain Lugard tried to compromise the difficulty by proposing that the twelve* great chieftainships of Uganda should continue to be held equally by either faction; and if any of the chiefs holding these twelve should change his creed he must vacate his position. On March 5th of this year Captain Lugard

* Twelve great chieftainships. These are: (1) Katikiro (prime minister); (2) Kimbugwe (keeper of umbelical cord, with title of king); (3) Mukwenda of Singo; (4) Sekibobo of Kyagwe; (5) Pokino of Badu; (6) Kangao of Bulemezi; (7) Mugema (of the Enclosures or Busiro of the kings, is part of Kyagwe); (8) Kago of Kyadondo (also in Kyagwe); (9) Kayima; (10) Kitunzi; (11) Katambala; and (12) Kasuju. These last four are chiefs of portions of the great province of Singo.

took his statute book, in which the proposed compromise was written, to have the statute duly passed in the king's Baraza (Durbar*) and agreed to by the representatives of the two factions. The Protestants had only one amendment to make—namely, for "twelve chieftainships," to substitute the words "six hundred." The other side, not unnaturally under the circumstances, were in favour of complete freedom of creed! The English party now accused Captain Lugard of seeking to break his own treaty, since at the request of the French party he had agreed to the clause against changing sides, which they now wished to abrogate. The question was argued hotly, but the English chiefs stood firm, and it was finally agreed that the *status quo* should continue until the treaty itself expired two years later. Things were thus much where they were. Nightly war-drums were beaten, and daily excited crowds of either faction would collect armed for battle. The strain for all concerned was becoming intolerable.

Captain Lugard appears to have adopted a policy somewhat counter to that indicated by the Administrator of the Company, who told him that it was useless attempting to gain an influence with Mwanga. The predictions of the Administrator were remarkably fulfilled, since Mwanga could only be influenced by what appealed to his fears or what pointed to his own advantage. One thing his proud nature could not brook, and that was the want of respect for his kingly dignity with which he imagined the Company's officers

* Durbar, the Uganda word for which is Lukiko. Baraza is Swahili.

treated him. I have never been a very enthusiastic admirer of Mwanga's character, still a king is not like common men, for in him is summed up whatever of majesty there is in the people whose titular head he is ; and I can well understand how frequently the well-meaning Englishmen would cruelly tread on the corns of his kingly dignity while in the process of "gaining influence" over him. Monseigneur Hirth, the French bishop, much better understood his man, and treated the king with the deepest respect.

The French bishop and Lugard now began to come into somewhat pointed antagonism. The bishop accused the captain of making confusion worse confounded, and finally wrote a letter calling on Captain Lugard to do justice to the French faction if war were to be staved off. On this Lugard visited the king, and told him he thought it wrong for the people to consult their missionaries before going to the king or himself; that the missionaries were purely concerned with religion, and not with the affairs of the country.

His laying these views about European residents before the king was a little hard upon the missionaries, since no one has demonstrated more undeniably than Captain Lugard himself how inextricably politics and religion had become entangled in Uganda. In these complications Lugard was too weak to be cloud compeller ; but, like the rest, was swept along by the storm which none could completely control.

Another cause of friction between Lugard and the missions was the claim of the missionaries, both French and English, to occupy positions within the sphere of English influence without reference to the British administrator. Messrs. Gordon and Smith, English missionaries, had gone to Usoga to open a mission there. The French missionaries, desiring also to go to Usoga, politely appealed to Captain Lugard, who expressed disapproval of their going. They went, however, apparently in spite of his disapproval.

In " Two Kings of Uganda " I have expressed my views on the subject, which are quite in accordance with Captain Lugard's—that an administration must take cognisance of insults and injuries to Europeans, and that therefore it has the right to forbid their going to unsafe districts of the country administered. Strange to say, when the question arose the next year, while I was acting as secretary for the English Mission, I found myself obliged to ask Captain Lugard for an order in writing forbidding Mr. Roscoe and Mr. Smith to go to Usoga, whither it had been decided to send them. Though it appears the directors had given an explicit prohibition against mission extension without their Resident's sanction, Captain Lugard would not give any such prohibition, nor would he even ask, as a matter of courtesy, that they should defer going ; so they went.

The reason that we wished Mr. Roscoe to arrive at Luba's before any of the Company's agents was this. The Company had, with a cynical disregard of justice, determined to fine Luba for Bishop Hannington's murder—an outrage committed, be it observed, by Mwanga—hence we feared that Luba might think the question of his paying or not paying this fine would facilitate or the reverse his securing a white man to settle at his village.*

Things were in this extremely unpleasant state when in March a caravan arrived from the coast, under Martin, bringing cloth and stores, but no ammunition. The cloth was very necessary for clothing and for purchase of food. Captain Lugard had obtained a few loads of cloth from his friend, Dr. Stuhlmann, and the English missionaries in his extremity, which tided him over his difficulties till the caravan came in.† With this caravan arrived Dr. Macpherson and Mr. Bagge, whose sterling qualities soon won for them golden opinions.

Mr. Martin brought back with him also the two chiefs who had been sent to the coast to ascertain whether or not Uganda was in the English sphere. Letters also came from the Administrator and from the Consul-General, including one to the Katikiro (Prime Minister), advising them to go to the English bishop

* *See* pp. 520, 521, vol. ii., " Rise of our East African Empire."

† Captain Lugard writes (p. 47, vol. ii., " Rise of our East African Empire "): " The missions refused me the loan of their boat (to get the absolutely necessary cloth for food purchase from the south of the Lake), but I eventually bought a few loads from them and from Dr. Stuhlmann, at double their proper price, in my extremity." This remark displays Captain Lugard's strong prejudice against the mission. I have already mentioned that the English missionaries were kept waiting eighteen months for their necessary stores. So difficult was it to obtain boats that I myself, subsequently, was obliged to march round the Lake to Uganda. The cloth, however, was not sold at double the proper price to Captain Lugard in his extremity, but at the ordinary market value at that time, $20 per piece. It afterwards fell to $10 ; but I have known it as high as $40 in Uganda.

A Dictum Discredited

for advice in their disputes—that is to say, telling them to do what they were already doing, but what Lugard had told both king and chiefs was a very wrong course to pursue. This letter was rather unpleasant for Captain Lugard, since it was directly opposed to his constant dictum—viz., that the missionaries of both creeds were in the country to teach religion only, and not to intervene in political matters. The letter contained, moreover, what Lugard considered an unfortunate allusion to the flag.

The tension between the two Christian factions was at this time lessened by the arrival on the scene of their common enemy, the Muhammedans. But I must reserve an account of this for another chapter.

CHAPTER VI
BRINGING OF THE SUDANESE

A wise Stroke of Policy—A daring Scheme—"Knocked into a cocked Hat"—King Kabarega—Negotiations with Muhammedans—A quaint Flag—Uganda Diplomacy—Difficulties in Treating—A clever Manœuvre—The Victory of Kanagala—The Washenzi (Savages)—Clouds on the Northern Horizon—An erroneous Principle—The Start for Kavalli's—Beautiful Children—Kasagama reinstated—A hard Treaty—Selim Bey—Fadl Maula—Lugard at Kavalli's—A horrible Rabble—Devilish Deeds—Startling Communications.

CHAPTER VI

BRINGING OF THE SUDANESE

THE powerful Muhammedan faction, which had been driven out of Uganda by the united Christians, was becoming again exceedingly troublesome. They had laid waste the greater part of the province of Singo, the government of the Mukwenda, but for a short interval of time they had been unusually quiescent, owing to the death, by small-pox, of their cruel though valiant king, Kalema, and the important business of settling who should be his successor.

The choice eventually fell upon Kalema's and Mwanga's uncle, Embogo (Buffalo), the only surviving brother of the former King Mutesa. Embogo had been for many years a Muhammedan reader, but so quietly, that he had not drawn upon himself the wrath of his royal brother.

The Muhammedans, being now united under Embogo, made a raid into Uganda, and carried off fifty women. News of this calamity was carried to the capital, whereupon Mwanga beat his great war drums, apparently without any reference to the Imperial British East Africa Company's representative. This is a further proof that the Company were by no means looked upon as the paramount power in the country. It could only have become so, in its then weak condition, by coalescing with one of the three opposing factions.

Captain Lugard remonstrated with the king for beating his drum in this fashion, and requested that the drums should be beaten again in a formal manner in his own presence. The king acceded to this, and urged that no slight was intended towards the Company, and that the war drum was only beaten as a warning of the Muhammedans' threatened attack.

After consultation with the chiefs, Captain Lugard determined to march against the Muhammedans, in hope that having a common object before them, and a common foe to fight against, the opposing " English " and " French " factions might possibly be brought more into unison. It certainly was a very wise stroke of policy on Lugard's part, since it removed the rival factions for a time from the influence of their respective missionaries, and gave the Company's administrator a fair opportunity of gaining an independent influence of his own, and of proving his *bonâ fide* desire to act in the interests of the country. Captain Lugard had, moreover, much in his favour. A manner altogether pleasing and unaffected with the natives, undoubted ability, combined with the highest ideal of duty, and a large share of that personal daring and courage which characterises most British officers, and which gains the confidence, as well as the admiration, of all classes of natives. But to accomplish the desirable object of gaining that necessary influence and authority which should result in the healing of the party strife, time and patience were essential. But Captain Lugard, seeing a way by which he might make himself independent of either Christian party, abandoned the rival chiefs to their bitter dissensions, and left Uganda in charge of his second in command, having formed the daring scheme of getting hold of Emin Pasha's Sudanese troops, a number of whom were concentrated under Selim Bey at Kavalli's. But this plan was not yet ripe for putting into execution. The first thing to be done was to march against the Muhammedans, who had just made their presence felt by the robbery of the women, to which I have already alluded. The question of who was to command the Uganda army then arose, and a furious discussion immediately took place. It had been arranged that the Generals of the troops should be chosen alternately from the " French " and " English " factions ; and in the present instance the " English " claimed it to be their turn. The " French," in reply, asserted that the last war was not a proper war, and that the choice of leader lay with them. Under these difficult circumstances Captain Lugard hit upon the expedient of calling upon the king to lead his army in person, "Since," said the captain, " the present was too big a thing to relegate to any but the king of the country." " His majesty," to quote Captain Lugard, " was knocked into a cocked hat by this," having no stomach whatever for fighting. He therefore made all kinds of excuses. Then said Lugard, " If you refuse to go yourself you had better send the next biggest chief in the country." The king agreed to this with alacrity, and appointed Kagwa Apolo (the Prime Minister, or Katikiro), who was the head of the "English" party.

The expedition started at the beginning of April, and marched towards the frontier of Unyoro, whose king, Kabarega, was the ordinary type of African potentate, neither better nor worse than his fellows; yet on the whole an intelligent man, whom it might have been possible to bring to some sort of terms, had there been any kind of strong central government in Uganda. As it was, Kabarega adopted the policy of Mwanga, and endeavoured to steer his way through the stormy sea, clinging to whatever power seemed for the time being to offer any kind of stable support; hence, at the beginning, he had allied himself more or less with the Muhammedans. Not that he in the least cared for Muhammedans as such; but he found them useful as a kind of breakwater against the periodical tides of Uganda invasion.

Lugard was anxious, if possible, to come into communication with the Muhammedan party, but this was exceedingly difficult during a time of open war.

It was the custom of Kagwa to send out an advanced guard, or scouts, before the main body; and one day these men secured four women belonging to the enemy, whom they brought in to the general. Kagwa at once wrote a letter to the Muhammedans, which he sent by one of the captive women. The letter was to the effect that if the people of Islam did not wish to continue hostilities they might return to Mengo. The woman duly carried the letter, and the result of it was that some of the Muhammedans came into Kagwa's camp, and Kagwa sent them on to Captain Lugard. Lugard now proposed that the Muhammedans should return to Uganda ; but asked that they should give up their sultan, Embogo, whom he pledged himself to care for and treat with honour.

He also demanded that they should yield up their arms. On May 1st, as a result of a further interchange of messages, seven important chiefs of the Muhammedan faction came into the Company's camp to discuss the grave question of peace or war.

Meanwhile, a very important question had arisen between the Christian allies who were taking part in the expedition regarding the banner which should be displayed as the common flag beneath which they were marching to the war.

Kagwa Apolo, the general, reiterated the request that the Company's representative should give him the Company's flag. It appears that before Captain Lugard's arrival Kagwa had manufactured one of his own from a picture printed in colours on a treaty form which Jackson had left with him. This flag was so quaint that Captain Lugard had begged Kagwa for it, and had promised him a proper flag in exchange. This promise the Uganda general now called on Lugard to redeem.

Kagwa's idea may possibly have been to bring on a crisis which should display the loyalty of his own following to the English, and the open dislike of the French party to British influence—an idea, under the circumstances, not without wisdom, since it had the effect of raising the question of the acceptance or otherwise of the Company's flag. Captain Lugard accordingly assembled the chiefs of both factions, and proposed that from henceforth the designations of " French " and " English " should be abolished, and that both should accept the British flag as represented by the Company's emblem—a banner displaying a rising sun, with the Union Jack in the corner. Some of the " French " chiefs professed their willingness to accept the flag, but it is not unlikely they were merely exercising their diplomatic gift in forcing Lugard's hand, since, in spite of their expressed willingness to accept the flag, when it came to the point they refused to do so ; but they said they had no objection to the Katikiro's having one. The old Pokino Nikodemo, a brave old Protestant and out and out believer in the English, also succeeded in obtaining a flag, in his capacity of chief of Budu.

Both sides had thus obtained a diplomatic advantage. The Protestants now carried the Company's flag, were Company's men ; while the Roman Catholics could pose as patriots who had refused a foreign flag, and could urge with some apparent, though not real, reason the complaint that the Company's banner was merely the symbol of the Protestant party, which Captain Lugard had always taken pains to deny.

To return now to the negotiations with the Muhammedans. At first they consented to give up Embogo, but on second thoughts they refused to do so, asserting the while their unwillingness to fight with the English. They said they wanted to go to Zanzibar, and Lugard wrote a letter for them, asking the Germans at Bukoba to give them a road through German territory. The envoys then left. It is almost impossible to tell how far the negotiation on the part of the Muhammedans was, or was not, sheer deception. Lugard, at any rate, treated it as *bonâ fide*. The " French " chiefs scouted the idea of peace, and no doubt the Muhammedans saw that however friendly disposed the English leader appeared, his Christian allies were openly hostile. Kagwa, the general, evidently believed any settlement was impossible, and at all hazards determined to get as near the enemy as possible, and next day made a forced march, which brought the expedition close upon the hostile encampment.

The Christian army was now on the frontier of Unyoro, and by the banks of the Kanagala, a river, like many of the Uganda streams, running through deep papyrus swamps. Captain Lugard calls this river the Kanyangoro. While here, a messenger arrived from the Muhammedans to say they would neither give up Embogo, nor yet retire, as they had said they would do—in fact, bringing a declaration of war. It became, therefore, necessary to cross the river in order to attack them. They were said to possess between three and four thousand guns, while Kagwa's force, joined with that of Lugard's, reckoned over five thousand.

The question then arose how to cross the river. This was managed by a clever manœuvre of Captain Lugard, who, wherever hard marching, hard fighting, or hard work were to be done, was never found wanting. By his orders the drums for pitching camp were beaten ;

but a whispered order was given that when night fell the great body of rifles, spearmen, and others should cross the river. This was silently accomplished ; and as dawn broke Lugard himself, with his Maxim gun and soldiers, made the passage.

Thus the swamp, which might have proved an almost insurmountable obstacle to the advancing army, and which might have been easily defended against overwhelming numbers, was safely crossed without the firing of a single shot or the loss of a single man.

During the night following the Muhammedans, who seem to have been supported by some of Kabarega's people, gathered in great numbers, and next day the two hostile armies faced one another. The Muhammedan force was posted on the opposite hills. The signal was given, and Kagwa's followers rushed to the attack. The Uganda method of fighting is for the attacking party to run up to within a few yards of the enemy and discharge their guns. If any chief men fall on either side, then the side which has lost its leaders takes to flight, and the battle is won. Kagwa and his men were in advance of the Europeans, and when the latter came up they found, to their surprise, that the battle had already been won, and that the Muhammedans were in full flight. The Christians lost fifteen killed, while the Muhammedan loss was estimated at three hundred killed. Seventy wounded men in all were brought in, some of whom, doubtless, had been fighting on the Muhammedan side.

This battle of Kanagala was fought and won on May 11th. Captain Lugard now wished to march towards Kabarega's Kraal, but the Ba-ganda represented the swamps to be impassable, and showed little enthusiasm to advance. To make things worse smallpox broke out, and it was therefore decided that as enough had been done for honour, the victorious army should return to Mengo. Captain Lugard sent Captain Williams back to the capital with the Katikiro, while he himself, Mr. Grant, and Dr. Macpherson, marched with the greater portion of his fighting men in a southerly direction to Budu, where he intended to prepare for the important undertaking of enlisting the remnant of Emin Pasha's Sudanese soldiers, who had made their way down from Wadelai, and had established themselves under Selim Bey, in the neighbourhood of Kavalli's, on the Albert Nyanza. Budu, which Lugard had now made his headquarters, was the province of the old Protestant leader, Nikodemo Sebwato, who held the office of Pokino. He supplied the Company's soldiers with ample food without charge. Lugard's Muhammedan Swahilis and Sudanese looked upon the native Ba-ganda as Washenzi (pagan savages), and robbed them right and left. This Lugard put down with a strong hand. Speaking of the contempt displayed by the Zanzibari Muhammedans for natives, Captain Lugard once told me how one of his ignorant Swahili porters, a man who could neither read nor write, and who was probably a slave, spoke of the Uganda chiefs as "the Washenzi" (savages). These Washenzi reckoned among them some of the young men who had been carefully trained by the French fathers, and such men as Zakaria, of the English mission, of whom the late Sir Gerald Portal wrote : " His appearance was pleasing, his clothes the very ideal of whiteness ; while his manners were a type of politeness itself, and would have fitted him for a post in any European court."* But it is difficult to convey any adequate idea of the arrogant and overweening manner assumed by the Muhammedans to those who were not of Islam.

It was therefore a serious undertaking to introduce a large number of fanatical Muhammedans into Uganda, since the danger was always threatening of a coalition between those of the same religion against native Christians and Europeans alike. The knowledge of the vast hordes of Muhammedans in the Sudan had always hung as a dark cloud on the northern horizon, making thoughts of the future of Uganda gloomy in the extreme, since it seemed morally certain that, sooner or later, these hordes of Muhammedans would make their way southward to Uganda, and unless some stronger power than any at present on the Nyanza could be brought to meet them, would sweep away whatever of Christianity or civilisation had been established on the shores of the great Lake.

The Arabs were gradually and surely being driven out of the Nyassa region by the indomitable energy of Mr. Johnson, who took up the work as Government Commissioner, which Lugard, with an utterly insufficient force and inadequate support, had so gallantly and heroically initiated. The Germans also had declared war upon the Arab slavetraders, while the Congo Free State was operating against them from the west. So

* Pages 144, 145, " British Mission to Uganda in 1893."

that there was an increasing danger lest the various separate Muhammedan elements should coalesce into an overwhelming power, which should sweep everything before it. Under these circumstances it seemed, to both French and English missionaries, dangerous in the extreme to strengthen the Muhammedan cause by giving a large number of fighting men of the same creed a foothold in Uganda.

I am not aware, however, if this important decision to introduce Emin Pasha's Sudanese into Uganda was ever definitely communicated to the European missionaries in Uganda, or whether their advice was ever asked upon the subject, on the principle, I suppose, that their business was wholly of a religious nature. A principle which applied in so restricted a sense is entirely erroneous, since the European missionaries were most deeply concerned in every act of the Company's; for it is evident that any mistake on the Company's part might precipitate a crisis involving the gravest consequences to them, and the risk, if not actually the loss, of their lives. Eventually, as will be seen, they were actually called upon to take arms into their hands at the instance of the British Resident to oppose the Sudanese when the mutiny came. Hence the missionaries, as part of the little European band in the country, had the strongest possible claim, at any rate, to be heard before decisions were made which must so closely affect their nearest interests. This claim, however, was, I think, never allowed, nor was the political position of the missionaries considered until the arrival of the late Sir Gerald Portal in the country.

The important decision was, however, made, and Captain Lugard marched from Uganda on June 16th, being accompanied by Grant and Macpherson, two men that well supported the honour of Scotland, besides Zakaria, whose well-merited praises are in the mouths of all travellers who have met him, including Stanley and Portal. There also accompanied the expedition Kasagama and Bikwcamba Yafeti,* two young princes of the royal house of Unyoro, who were heirs to the throne of Toro. The boys had been brought to Uganda, and been given a small estate by Mutesa, Toro itself having been overrun by the Ba-nyoro. During my former sojourn in Uganda Yafeti used often to visit our mission with his sister, a handsome Muhuma princess, who came attended by two children, a boy and a girl, remarkable for their beauty. The boy Kibi-Kiriwo had one of the most perfect faces I have ever seen. When I last saw Yafeti, in 1892, I asked for his sister and the two children. He told me that the princess was dead, that the little girl had disappeared, and the boy Kibi-Kiriwo had died of the plague. Yafeti was one of those who, with his sister, was baptised at the time of the persecution of 1886. I do not remember Kasagama. He was probably living in the country estate when Yafeti was attending the mission classes. Lugard intended to reinstate his younger brother Kasagama as Mukama or King of Toro, and to make Yafeti his Katikiro or Chief Minister.

* Yafeti, the elder, was one of those who suffered mutilation by the orders of the late king on the advice of the vicious Arabs a that time at his court.

When his preparations were completed Lugard marched towards the Albert Lake, by way of Budu, passing Masaka, the Pokino's capital, where Walker (now Archdeacon) was established. He crossed the northern portion of the kingdom of Busagala or Enkore, whose Mukama (King) was Entare (Lion), and who, as we have seen, was the chief who had generously harboured the Christian refugees. From Entare's the expedition moved in a south-westerly direction till it reached the narrow water which connects Lake Albert Edward (discovered by Stanley in 1890) with the smaller Lake Lusango, both of which pour their waters northwards to the Albert Lake, through the Semliki River. Near this river is the small salt lake described by Captain Lugard. " Its water," he says, " is of a deep claret red. It is very shallow, and every stick and stone, and the banks on its margin, are encrusted with the crystal salt, exactly as you shall see a pond in England when a slight frost has fringed its edges with ice. The salt is excellent, white with a beautiful rose tint, and the natives come from great distances to barter goods and produce for it." *

Captain Lugard proceeded, in the first place, to establish Kasagama in his own country of Toro, which lies at the foot of Ruenzori, where he built a fort

* *Proceedings of the Royal Geographical Society*, December 1892. "Travels," etc., by Captain F. D. Lugard. These two lakes, Albert Edward and the Salt Lake, are in the neighbourhood of the great Ruenzori range, the highest point of which is snowclad, and attains a height of between sixteen and seventeen thousand feet. This mountain was also discovered by H. M. Stanley during the Emin Relief Expedition.

(Edward). He then made a treaty with his *protégé* the young king, who was forced to promise the Company a monopoly of all ivory (elephants swarmed in the district), and in "*all matters*" to obey the Resident at Mengo. This treaty is quite a model instrument. Insistence on obedience in all matters—after giving up the most valuable item of revenue—might appear even to the most cynical to be going too far; while to those who advocate fair treatment for native chiefs it will furnish a fresh argument against the system of chartered companies, a system analogous to the happily exploded iniquity of letters of marque.

Kasagama was gladly received by the people of Toro, and, to use the picturesque language of Lugard : " The fugitive Wahuma came out from their hiding among the mountains, escaped from their slavery among the Wanyoro, or bade farewell to Entare, who had sheltered them, and with great rejoicing recognised the boy Kasagama as their king." *

At the end of August Captain Lugard marched northward, and crossing the great Semliki River, finally, on September 7th, reached Kavalli's, where he came upon the Sudanese, who had made their way down from Emin's old province, and had established themselves in the neighbourhood of Kavalli, under Selim Bey. Selim himself was not present with them, having gone to meet the last and very large contingent of refugees from Wadelai. Four days later he came himself in person, having at first attempted to open negotiations

* *Proceedings of the Royal Geographical Society*, November 1892, p 837.

with Lugard by means of messengers. On the arrival of Selim the important object of the Englishman's coming was broached between the two African leaders.

Selim Bey seems to have been a man of some character, and, at any rate, had unbounded influence over his own people. In person he was enormously fat, and, I believe, dropsical. He could hardly walk, and was obliged to use a donkey in travelling. He was, I suppose, a Sudanese, though from what I recollect he was some shades lighter than the ordinary types of the people who are classed under this designation.

The Sudanese, much as I disliked them, and deeply as I regretted their introduction to Uganda, were yet not without sterling qualities, which, in some respects, made them superior to the pleasanter and more versatile inhabitants of Uganda. They were what the Scotch call "dour bodies"—scowling and sullen—but they were brave and industrious, and possessed a certain amount of dignity which commanded respect.

According to Selim's account, he had been given an impossible task when ordered by Stanley to collect the remaining garrisons of Equatoria in time to join the relief expedition on its coastward march, and he was especially bitter against Emin Pasha for having, as he said deserted him.

It is difficult really to thread one's way through the various narratives; but considering the extreme slowness with which people move in Central Africa, it is not impossible that Selim was really loyally endeavouring to carry out the evacuation, and Lugard, on the whole, seems to favour this view. A bitter opponent, however, of Selim's policy had appeared in the person of Fadl Maula Bey, who was in command at Wadelai. This man plotted with the troops, and suddenly seizing all the ammunition in the magazines, marched out of Wadelai. The garrisons whom Selim had been collecting flocked to Fadl Maula, who, however, was secretly plotting to place himself in the hands of the dervishes. Selim was thus left with a very small following, and with them he moved down to Kavalli's, with whom he was glad, after losing half his men in repelling attacks of hostile natives, to form an alliance. Meanwhile Fadl Maula was appointed Emir by the commander of the dervishes, but found it well to keep aloof from his own men, who would have nothing to say to the dervishes. Fadl Maula's soldiers then returned to Wadelai, and at that place awaited the coming of the dervishes. No sooner had the dervishes put in an appearance than these old troops of Emin attacked them fiercely, and defeated them with great loss. Fadl Maula Bey seems to have subsequently joined the dervishes, while his victorious soldiers, finding that their leader had betrayed them, now marched south to Kavalli's, to place themselves under the command of Selim Bey, and it was at this interesting juncture that Captain Lugard arrived.

Lugard at once proposed that Selim should, with his soldiers, enlist in the Company's service, on the condition that the Khedive's consent could be obtained, but that pending the arrival of letters permitting him to enlist with the English or otherwise, he should be under the orders of the British Company.

Selim at first agreed ; but next day he hung back, wishing to make his remaining in absolute control of his men a condition of joining Lugard, and also wishing to provide against the splitting up of his following. Selim's idea was rather of alliance than of enlistment; but partly by threats and partly by promises, Lugard obtained his consent to accompany him. Selim, however, stipulated that the Sudanese should retain the Egyptian flag, though in British territory, and that all orders should be given to the Sudanese through Selim himself.

Of Sudanese soldiers proper there were only a few hundreds, while women, children, slaves, camp followers, and hangers-on swelled the numbers up to some eight thousand souls. Thus, in order to obtain the doubtful services of a few hundred Sudanese soldiers, Captain Lugard was obliged to become responsible for this horrible riff-raff rabble of between seven and eight thousand persons. He recrossed the Semliki River with some nine thousand souls, and marching southward he built five forts in all between the Albert and Albert Edward Lakes, in which he stationed the bulk of the Sudanese refugees. These were placed under the surveillance of young Mr. de Winton, to whom was allotted the frightful task of endeavouring to keep them in order.

The task, as may be easily understood, was quite impossible for any one man short of a General Gordon, and this brave young Englishman died practically a prisoner in the hands of the Muhammedans. The boy chief, Kasagama, whom these wolves were placed to guard, very soon felt the sharpness of their fangs, while the unhappy people found to their cost that if Kabarega had scourged them with whips these ruthless strangers scourged them with scorpions. The frontier of Unyoro was laid waste by them, and it may be understood what just grounds Kabarega had for reprisals after these garrisons—left by the English—had been raiding, robbing, devastating, and doing in Unyoro such devilish deeds of hideous shame as one shrinks from writing down.

Poor young de Winton was not even nominally in control of the Sudanese, who were directly under Selim Bey and Captain Lugard—a position which must have been absolutely intolerable, and one in which he was practically powerless to be of any use or to gain any credit.

Lugard re-entered Uganda with some two or three hundred Sudanese soldiers and five or six hundred of the riff-raff before alluded to, having performed an incredible amount of hard work, and having concluded a task of almost overwhelming difficulty with triumphant success.

To my mind, however, the object attained was not a desirable object, for a most dangerous and disturbing element had now been introduced into the country, and the Sudanese afterwards became a sore thorn in the side of the English administration in Uganda.

On December 19th Lugard once more reached Masaka, the capital of Budu, where the Pokino Nikodemo happened to be, and where Walker was still stationed. But the events which had happened in Uganda during Lugard's absence, and the startling nature of the communications from England which awaited him on his arrival at Mengo, I must reserve for another chapter.

CHAPTER VII
UGANDA POLITICS

A reasonable Hope—An awkward Dilemma—English Missionaries support the Chiefs—A serious Breach—Inconsequent Reasoning—Williams secures the good Offices of Missionaries—Importance of the King—The King offers to join the English Faction—A neglected Opportunity—An unpardonable Vice!—Hostilities commenced—Importation of Arms—A solid Brick Fort—Arrival of new French Missionaries—A Bolt from the Blue—The Directors' Suggestion—Feeling of the Missionaries—Resolute Protestants—Failure of a Scheme—An Impregnable Island—A fair Catholic Kingdom—Uncertainty as to Withdrawal—A Match to the Powder.

CHAPTER VII

UGANDA POLITICS

IN my capacity of chronicler I feel it incumbent upon me to attempt some elucidation of the politics of this period, and to endeavour to show what were the main forces and influences at work. The French priests were the most active influence in the country, and were the backbone of the opposition to English political influence in Uganda as represented by the Imperial British East Africa Company. In spite of the somewhat pretentious claims of the Company, its influence was a good deal overrated by its representatives, and even after its victory over the Roman Catholic faction Sir Gerald Portal was able to write in 1893 : " The Company's influence here seems very small." It is true that the English missionaries had obtained great influence over their own converts, yet Bishop Tucker seems hardly to have realised the true attitude of Monseigneur Hirth (the French bishop), or had he done so I think he would not have told the late Sir Gerald Portal that, had he, Bishop Tucker, remained in Uganda, the arrangement between the political parties would not have broken down. I think the reader who has thus far followed me will see that unless the French priests had desired an arrangement, no arrangement with the " French " party under any circumstances was possible. The French priests had every reason to hope for the extinction of English interests, when they might step into supreme power, since British occupation depended upon the rapidly diminishing exchequer of a small trading company.

Captain Lugard has given it as his opinion that the priests were under the influence of a young Uganda chief named Mujasi, who had married the king's sister. Now, as this Mujasi had been bred and brought up in the French mission, it is evident that the influence was far less likely to be exercised by the young convert over men of the world (who had received a severe training with special reference to winning influence over men), than by the priests over the young convert.

During Captain Lugard's six months' absence on his expedition to Kavalli's he left Kampala in charge of his energetic colleague, Captain (now Major) Williams, R.A., whom he has described as a keen soldier, whose interests lay entirely in his profession.

There is every reason to believe that Captain Williams, like Lugard, was absolutely impartial on the religious question, and had the Englishman's characteristic desire for freedom in religious matters. But he fell into a not unnatural mistake in failing to see that the great question in Uganda was not so much religious as political, the point at issue really being the establishment or not of English influence in the country; unfortunately, also, religion and politics had become inextricably mingled, and could not, as things were, be disentangled. To support English influence it was necessary for the representative of the Company to become a partisan, for the time being, of that party which was nominally Protestant, while not to become partisans of the English party meant standing on one side to see English influence overthrown before the eyes of the men who had been sent to Uganda to make English influence paramount.

It was a very awkward dilemma, and one of which the clever French priests were not slow to take advantage; nor had they long to wait for the opportunity, which soon presented itself in the question already referred to, of changing from one political party to another, which involved also a nominal change of religion! The king was living openly as a heathen, but politically was French, and therefore the mass of heathen in the country were French. There were, naturally, out of the six hundred chiefs, great and small, of the English party, a large number who, if they might retain their positions, would go over to the strongest faction in the country—viz., that of the king, no matter what faction he favoured. Their doing so, of course, would weaken the fighting men on the English side, and the English chiefs naturally objected to their secession from the party.

The English missionaries supported the chiefs, since the question was very important. Their yielding the point might have meant the wreck of the Protestant cause in Uganda. Monseigneur Hirth, the French bishop, cleverly used the argument that to make a man vacate his post because he turned Roman Catholic was downright religious persecution. Whereupon Captain Williams consulted Captain Lugard's statute book, which he understood to contain nothing but binding agreements, and came upon the clause which declared every man free to join what religion or faction he pleased. This clause, however, it will be remembered, had not been agreed to by the Protestants (*see* pp. 162, 163).

This led to a serious breach between the English missionaries and the Company's representatives, and the missionaries sent Captain Williams a written protest. I have not myself seen the protest; but my readers will understand the strong sense of injustice under which the missionaries must have written when they saw so disastrous a policy being pursued, knowing the while that it was quite counter to the real agreement.

On Captain Lugard's arrival the mistake in the statute book was at once explained, and the *status quo* was restored. This of course was most annoying to the priests, and looked merely as if the Company had now oscillated back into the arms of the English missionaries.

By a curiously inconsequent reasoning Captain Lugard has taken the complaints made by both sides against Captain Williams' administration as a proof of its purity and impartiality, quite failing to see, that if the complaints in both cases happened to be well grounded, they would prove quite as conclusively the weakness and vacillation of the attempt to administer the country. I am not writing this to throw undue blame on the Company's officers regarding this particular matter, which was purely a mistake ; but to deprecate the conclusion that complaints as to the Company's failure to deal with the situation was a proof of narrow mindedness on the part of either English or French missionaries.

No one, for a moment, who knows anything of the circumstances in which Captain Williams found himself during Lugard's absence can fail to realise how difficult was his position. His resource and energy were sufficiently proved by the fact, that somehow or other during his administration the factions were kept from flying at one another's throats.

He adopted the policy of securing, as far as possible, the good offices of the missionaries in restraining the angry passions of their respective converts.*

* Extract from letter of Rev. R. H. Walker, July 14th, 1891, *Church Missionary Society's Intelligencer*, February 1892 : " Captain Williams has asked me to remain here for a few days to help him to arrange a few laws for the settling of the country. The Catholics and Protestants agreed that each of these religions should hold half the offices in the country ; the country has been so divided between the two parties. Now, many want to leave the Protestant party and to join that of the king, because they get more honour by doing so. The Protestants agree to their leaving and becoming Catholics, but say, of course, they leave their offices or territories behind them when they change parties. Some consider it unfair to make a man give up his position in the country because he changes his religion. The Catholics fall in with this, as it will increase the power of their

Without wearying the reader with details of endless quarrels about estates and gardens, I may now refer to one of the more important political accidents which occurred during this period; and first I may mention the offer of the king to join the Protestant party.

I have already spoken of the importance of the king as being the person who really drew in his train the great mass of heathen and those indifferent to the new religions, and the enormous advantage accruing to the party who obtained his support. It was the

party in the land. We, as missionaries, teach that political and temporal power are not aids to religion, and therefore advise our people to give them up. They say they are willing to do this, but then they will leave the country, as they do not care to remain in it just to be bullied by the Catholics. The Protestants say, ' We have bought half the power in the country with our blood, and it is as much ours as if we had bought it with money; therefore, if we wish to turn a man out of any of the offices or countries that have been allotted to us, we can do so, and the Catholics have no cause for complaint.' I have to go up to the camp every morning for four hours to meet the Roman Catholic priests and Catholic and Protestant chiefs."

Extract of letter from Mr. G. L. Pilkington, dated Namirembe, Uganda, August 11th, 1891, *Church Missionary Society's Intelligencer*, February 1892: " Now about things here. Politics, (how I hate them, but I suppose they are necessary evils!) hinder the work more than anything. When I came back from the island of Sesse, after a week's change to try to shake off fever, the country was terribly excited. We all of us (Walker and Baskerville were here then) really apprehended war, or at any rate, that the Protestants would leave the country. This was caused by a proposal from Captain Williams to abolish the agreement made between the two parties, and to permit chiefs (all of whom now hold office *qua* Protestant or Roman Catholic, appointed by one or other party) who change their religion to retain their chieftainships. We should, of course, be delighted possession of the king that gave the Roman Catholics such preponderant power in the country. This advantage was suddenly offered to the Company; and it came about in this way. The Roman Catholic chiefs, disgusted with the king's immoralities, had seized a number of the king's boy pages, and put them to death.

The king was furious, and at the same time terrified; and it was at this juncture he offered to join the Protestant English faction—not, it will be seen, from

to see full religious liberty, but the people do not understand it, and the Protestant party were very resolute against accepting the proposal. This was because, whereas the Roman Catholics in the choice of their chiefs had been guided by the priests, and had appointed consistently the most thorough-going Roman Catholics, our party, on the other hand, were guided by general, at least as much as by religious, considerations (*e.g.*, hereditary claims, fitness other than religious), Gordon and Walker refusing to choose the chiefs. Well, the other day, the Roman Catholic bishop claimed 'religious liberty' from Captain Williams, on the ground that the country was under the British flag. Our party answered that if that were the case, and we were really under British government, and therefore we could have British justice, let Captain Williams hoist the English flag, and let us follow British customs. He tried to do so, but the attempt did not succeed, the Roman Catholics and the king refusing point-blank.

"Well, this, and the division of the islands, and the innumerable cases of men turned out of gardens, houses destroyed, goods stolen, etc., etc., has occupied every one for weeks past.

"At first the church was empty on week-day mornings, but a day or two after Walker and Baskerville went I made a round of visits to various chiefs, urging them to be patient, and aim at 'peace at any price,' and to come and bring their people in the mornings. Since then we have always had fair, and sometimes very large (five or six hundred at least) congregations—on weekdays I mean. On Sundays the church is crowded out."

any love of English influence or Protestant Christianity, but merely from fear, and dislike of the faction he was now led by.

The Company's representative, however, did not venture to take the king at his word, but rather deprecated his joining the Protestant party, and advised him to wait until Lugard's return to Mengo. Thus a golden opportunity was neglected, and the king was lost to the English cause. The reason for refusing Mwanga's advances was apparently that the Company's officials hoped to get hold of the king apart from either of the two great factions, and by this means hold the balance between them—a clever enough policy had they been able to carry it out. The reader must not for a moment suppose that the present advances on the king's part were rejected on the ground that he was a man so evil, and such a disgrace to humanity, that no clean-handed person could make any agreement or have any dealings with him at all.

His character was well known before the arrival of the Company, who were well aware that he was grossly and disgracefully vicious, and that he had murdered Bishop Hannington and numbers of Christians, and yet they made overtures to him and concluded treaties with him; and therefore the omission to secure him absolutely on this occasion was due rather to the failure to grasp the situation, than to any feeling of shrinking from supporting so unsatisfactory a character as this unhappy king.

The king's sudden hostility to the French faction put a new complexion on political matters, and, at all hazards, the French missionaries felt they must in some way or other secure the king.

The king, according to one account, had become increasingly excited on the arrival of Martin's caravan with ammunition, etc., for the Company, and seeing that

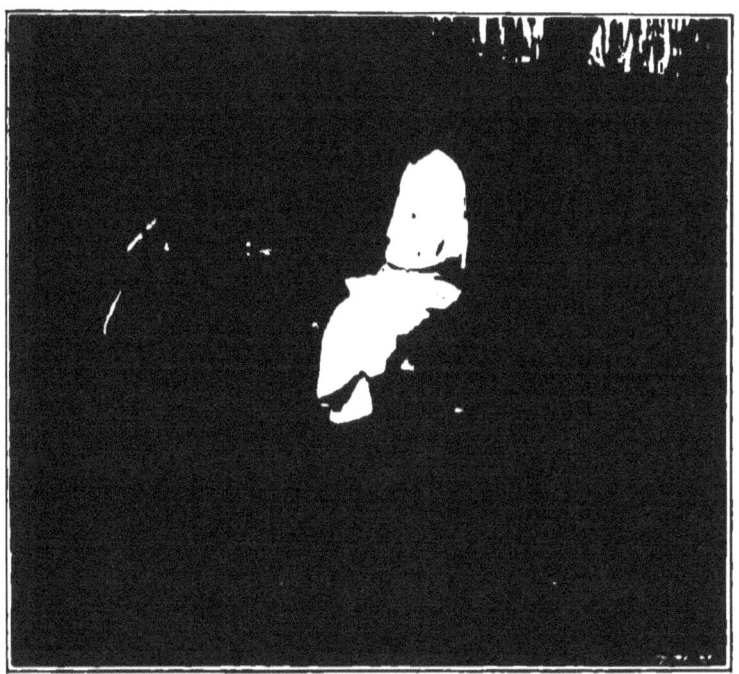

NIKODEMO POKINO, AFTERWARDS SEKIBOBO.

they were now exceedingly strong, he desired to join them, and in order to do so had now opened negotiations with the English party. This was met by a counter move of the "French," who suggested the deposition of Mwanga on the ground of his vices, the most unpardonable being his political leaning towards the English! They proposed to substitute one of

Mwanga's nephews, who was being educated by the priests at their station of Bukumbi, at the south of the Nyanza. The Protestant chiefs saw through this, and declined to assist in deposing the king, evil though he might be.

Soon after the murder of Mwanga's boys the French bishop interviewed the irate king, and subsequently a very large present of ivory was collected by the Catholic chiefs, and the murder was amply apologised for, and the king was once more won over to the French faction, and received the obnoxious French chiefs back into favour.

Having, for the time being, secured the adherence of Mwanga to their side, a bold provocative policy of aggression was now entered upon by the French party, and this policy resulted in what appeared like an organised attack upon the Protestants. There is little doubt that overtures were made to some of the neighbouring kings to support the King of Uganda in the attempted attack on the Protestant chiefs. Notably was this the case with the islanders of Uvuma, who were allies of Mwanga, and who received instructions to assemble their canoes, while Kamswaga of Koki, a semi-independent king, who possessed seven hundred guns, suddenly invaded Budu at the same time that a determined attack was made by the Roman Catholics upon their Protestant neighbours in that country. The English faction, however, under the old Pokino, who afterwards stood so staunchly by Captain Macdonald, met the attack with decision; and here, as well as on the islands and at every point where they attacked, they showed great courage, and, to quote Captain Lugard, "though greatly outnumbered, defeated their rivals, and were, in every instance, victorious." A more serious danger by far had threatened to the east in the province of Kyagwe, bordering on the Nile, where the French faction was especially strong. The arrival of Martin, however, with his large caravan, which took place about the same time as Captain Lugard's return to Kampala, for the time being averted a general outbreak.

The leaders of the French party had seen clearly that any hope of acquiring the country and defending it against Arab aggression (and this is a very important consideration, which must by no means be lost sight of as a strong justification for their action) must lie in arming the people themselves ; and with this object in view there is no doubt at all that the French missionaries endeavoured to import arms from the coast.* In considering the question whether there

* There is a most important statement on p. 130, "Notes on Uganda," by the Catholic Union of Great Britain, which admits that breech-loading rifles *were imported to the Nyanza by French priests concealed in other loads*. An explanation of this most extraordinary fact is given by Monseigneur Livinhac, who declares the rifles were duly declared in the ordinary course at the Custom Houses of Zanzibar and Bagamoyo, where authority to carry them into the interior was obtained. This is the more strange as that very same year the English missionaries had serious difficulty in getting the required permission to carry each a breech-loading gun. The Catholic Union adds that Monseigneur Livinhac says these rifles were required for the defence of the caravans and of the mission stations both in English and in German territory ; and he gives several examples to show that an escort of armed men is often necessary both for the security of

are any circumstances under which missionaries may import arms, or any motives which might justify their doing so, it is hardly fair to put missionaries into a different category from other Christians ; and as things were, the priests, if they were not justified in their action, were, at any rate, in so difficult a position that it is hard to see from their point of view what other course they could have taken.

The French missionaries, as a part of their plan, began to construct a solid brick fort on the very best strategic position at the capital. This fort, extra-

passage through the country as well as for the safety of the stations.

But if these rifles were needed for the protection of the caravans, it may well be asked, why should they be concealed inside bales, especially on an occasion when there was such real need of their being used that the whole caravan was looted for lack of these rifles, imported, as it is said, for the very purpose of defending caravans ? It seems to me that Monseigneur Livinhac brings rather a serious imputation against the German administration in asserting that it permits missionaries to import breech-loading rifles to protect their mission stations and caravans in such large quantities as stated. One feels that an authentic report, if it were possible to obtain it, as to the numbers of arms imported would be desirable ; but the secret importation of arms and ammunition has always been carried on by Arabs and others, and it is impossible to obtain accurate information.

But there is a further circumstance connected with these particular rifles which throws much light on the question of the French priests' desire for arms. It appears that the request for arms was made by the French missionaries in 1890, before the arrival of the Company, in view of aggression on the part of the Muhammedans.

In 1891 we are told that this danger was over ; but as a matter of fact this danger, as the whole tenor of Uganda history shows, was by no means over, nor was the permanent establishment of ordinary to say, was quietly built during the Imperial British East Africa Company's administration. When the war broke out two sides of the fortification were completed. After the fight I examined it with some care. It had a bastion at one corner, and loopholes were constructed so as to be invisible from the outside, but these loopholes, by knocking out a single thickness of bricks, could be made immediately available by those within.

Just before the close of 1891 a number of new French missionaries reached Uganda.

the English Company very likely to take place; yet Monseigneur Hirth wrote to Monseigneur Livinhac, on May 5th, begging him not to send the rifles to Uganda, and to cancel the application which he had made for them the year before. One would like to know the date of the first letter and the terms in which the order was cancelled. The letter cancelling the order, at any rate, came too late. The Catholic Union only quotes one passage of this letter, as follows: "These rifles are useless except in Bukumbi; they can be of no use to us in our stations in Uganda, as you know." Bukumbi is at the south of the Nyanza, and there is constant communication between Bukumbi and Uganda; but Bukumbi is also only a few hours from the Imperial German station of Muanza, on the Nyanza, so that one would imagine there was less need at Bukumbi than in unsettled Uganda for breech-loading arms, since the French mission was within easy reach of the German garrison.

The only puzzle in the whole matter is why the French priests or their defenders should be at such pains to make themselves appear as the hearty supporters of the Imperial British East Africa Company, contrary to all the plainest evidence on the subject that can be procured.

The best defence possible for their action is that they were under no obligation whatever to support an English trading company which came with doubtful authority, and without the intention of permanently remaining.

The Protestant missionaries now numbered five—
Pilkington, Baskerville, Roscoe, Wright, and Collins *—
while the Company's officers consisted of the two
captains, Dr. Macpherson, Bagge, Grant, and Wilson.
The arrival of Martin with the caravan meant a considerable access of fighting strength to the Company.
But the mail which Martin carried contained a letter
from the directors of the Company ordering Captain
Lugard to withdraw at once from Uganda. This was
a bolt from the blue. Whatever might be said of the
policy of the Imperial British East Africa Company in
sending their agents to Uganda, the order to withdraw
them at this juncture was a grave mistake; and though
it may have arisen from the cost involved to the
Company and the political exigencies of the then
government, yet it cannot be defended on any grounds
of the kind, since both the outlook as regards money
and politics was perfectly plain before the occupation
of Uganda was undertaken.

The directors of the Company, however, did suggest
a method of dealing with the country in case of withdrawal, which was to endeavour to get the missionaries
of both factions to agree upon some *modus vivendi*.
I do not know whether the priests would have been
willing to come to some agreement, or whether their
terms would have been so hard that, sooner than
agree, the Protestants would have preferred to undertake a complete exodus to some region nearer the
coast.

Captain Lugard has stated that it would not have

* Walker and I had not yet come up to the capital from Budu.

been possible to form a council of delegates of the missionaries, on account of the prejudice they entertained against one another. This is the purest assumption. And though I was acting secretary of the English mission at the time Lugard withdrew from Uganda, the first I ever heard of any such suggestion having been made by the Directors I learned from reading Captain Lugard's book more than two years afterwards. The French priests, I imagine, were much in the same position. They felt themselves not wanted at Kampala Fort, and studiously avoided going there except upon some urgent or pressing business.

My own feeling on reaching Mengo was—that as I had been told my business was not with any political matters, I would never go to Kampala to offer advice on the subject unless sent for by the Company's Resident. I particularly deprecated a general invitation " to chat " over political matters, as I considered the situation far too serious to be so dealt with.

Thus the missionaries, both Roman Catholic and Protestant, felt that they were studiously ignored by the Company's representatives; and speaking for the time I was in Uganda, no attempt at bringing the missionaries together was ever made by the Company's Resident.

There were of course the religious differences between the Roman and Anglican Churches which every one knows, but that there was any personal prejudice or animosity between the missionaries of the two Churches I can happily most unhesitatingly deny. The whole history of the mission, with the exception of the impulsive overzeal of Père Lourdel, which on his first arrival caused him for a moment to forget his native politeness, is a proof of the kindly dealings on all matters, save of religion, between the French and English missionaries.

It must be remembered that up to this time the relative strength of the two great opposing factions had really never been tested. There had indeed been more than the semblance of a general movement upon a large scale in the preconcerted attack already mentioned, the invasion of Uganda by Kamswaga on the south, and the concentration of the Uvuma canoes off the coast of Kyagwe, as well as the attack on the island by the French faction, and the important movement in Kyagwe. Thus it will be seen that only the courage and decision with which the English faction met the ill-directed attack saved that party from a disastrous defeat; since, had they been overwhelmed before the arrival of Lugard and Martin, it would have been a serious question whether the Imperial Company's troops could have opposed single-handed the victorious Roman Catholics. The directors of the French faction had certainly laid their plans with skill. They had obtained the promise of assistance from two powerful outside quarters—Koki and Uvuma; and had those intrusted with the execution of their scheme only acted with determination there is little doubt that the French faction would have been able

to dictate pretty much what terms they pleased—
terms, I have little doubt, that would have given
all the important posts to Roman Catholics, who
would have taken care that only Roman Catholic
teaching would be encouraged in their governments.

But the scheme had failed. Kamswaga was driven
back. The island of Kaganda had been stoutly
held, and the timely arrival of Martin with seven
hundred Zanzibaris had quashed the trouble in
Kyagwe. Now, it may be asked, why, if the French
faction were worsted before Lugard's arrival, did
the directors of it desire to force on a war at a time
when their enemies were so greatly strengthened?
The answer is very plain and perfectly clear. First,
the king had shown unmistakable signs of a desire
to go over to the Protestant party. They therefore
must force that party into taking up arms against
him when they would pose as his defenders and as
the patriotic upholders of Uganda against rebels
encouraged by the English foreigners. Secondly,
the directors of the French faction were well aware
that the representatives of the Company were under
orders to withdraw, and if they could weaken the
Protestant faction before that event happened they
would have the whole country in their hands. Thirdly,
there is little doubt that they hoped the Company
would hold aloof from actual fighting; but even if
the Company should fight they had every confidence
that they might hold their own. A sudden coup
might win them the game, and give them Kampala
Fort, and the whole stock of ammunition and rifles;

but even should the worst come to the worst, and they should meet with defeat at the outset, they might take to the islands, especially Bulinguge, which they believed impregnable, and where formerly Mwanga had held his court when Kalema actually possessed his capital. Here they would be safe from attack. They were strong in Kyagwe, and they owned nearly all the canoes; their Bavuma allies would help them; while the Muhammedans, hearing of the fight, would most likely swoop down on Mengo. There would doubtless be a desperate battle with them, in which the Muhammedans would probably be worsted. But the Protestant English would be greatly weakened and their ammunition spent, and they might then be attacked. At any rate, a few months must see the end of the Company's occupation, when they would be free to come forth from their island and reoccupy Uganda, and set up the fair Catholic kingdom by the Lake. Thus it will be seen that war was the easiest way out of their difficulties; they had much to gain by it even if temporarily defeated. Therefore, in view of the coming struggle. the king, and I believe the French missionaries, removed a large amount of their property to the islands.

The English party had thrown in their lot with the Company. They had hailed them eagerly on their arrival as co-religionists, as the fellow-countrymen of their teachers, and as friends. Their effusiveness, however, had been met with extreme coldness by the Englishman whom they had loyally welcomed, faithfully protected, and generously supported.

Lugard, since he had already taken the bull by the horns in his crossing the Nile, might well have insisted on the hoisting of the Company's flag as a purely political act. It would have been a bold stroke, but not bolder than his dash across the Nile and march to Mengo. It would have been in one sense indefensible, but not more so than what he had already done. It was indeed the only logical outcome of his previous action. He gave the flag to the king's chief minister and to the chief of Budu. Was not this really forcing it upon the King?

The other party, on the other hand, had opposed Captain Lugard bitterly, had scouted the idea of an English protectorate as represented by the Company's occupation, and with great ceremony had, subsequent to the arrival of the English officers, hoisted Mwanga's own flag. For this the priests were directly responsible. Thus the war against the Imperial British East Africa Company was a deliberate act of policy, and one which, though it is deeply to be regretted, may certainly be defended from the priests' point of view. Had the English Government said, "We will occupy Uganda, and be responsible for good government," or had they even said, "We will guarantee the permanency of the English occupation by the Company and religious toleration in Uganda," there is no reason to suppose the French fathers would have forced the issue to fighting. However that may have been, they had little to lose by fighting, and might have gained everything, and as it actually turned out they gained quite as much as they lost.

The position in the beginning of January 1892 was as follows :—

Captain Lugard's repeated assurances of religious neutrality appear to have led the Roman Catholics to believe that in case of their attacking the Protestants he would not interfere, but would leave the two factions to fight it out among themselves.

While things were in this state a system of gun snatching was set on foot between the retainers of the great chiefs on either side. This had been preceded by interminable quarrels as to country gardens, which, as we have seen, had in one or two instances led to severe fighting. But the stealing of a gun by a French partisan and the consequent shooting of a Protestant set a light to the mass of inflammable material in Uganda, which resulted in the deplorable war between the two factions, the French and English, an account of which I must give in the next chapter.

CHAPTER VIII

THE BATTLE OF MENGO

A scornful Challenge—Empty Excuses—Insolence of Kauta—Ill-timed Levity—The King's Decision—Dualla as Go-between—Rival Claims—Open Defiance—Alternatives—A middling Course—The King's Request—" Gwanga! Gwanga! muje"—Bible Reading under Difficulties—A doubtful Asylum—A clever Move—An African Ruse—The Four Hills—Christian Churches—Precursors of the Storm—Sembera's Death—Kagwa's Strategy—A masterly Retreat—Hoisting the Company's Flag—A fearful Predicament—Battle-field Vultures.

CHAPTER VIII

THE BATTLE OF MENGO

THINGS were in such a strained condition that the members of the hostile factions considered it to be their *devoir* to secure in any manner possible the guns of those of the opposite factions. It is not altogether easy to say how this gun snatching originated, since each party would doubtless lay the blame of it upon the other; but eventually a case was brought before Apolo Kagwa, the Prime Minister, by a French adherent, who accused one of the English party of having stolen his gun. The English chief adjourned the case, and the complainant, feeling that justice was being purposely delayed, determined to secure by a ruse a gun belonging to the opposite faction in lieu of that which he had lost. He therefore seated himself outside the enclosure of a sub-chief named Mugoloba, who was a party to the plot, and pretended to be selling a gourd full of Mwenge (banana cider), and in a little while, when a man of the English faction with his gun passed by with one or two of his friends he invited him to buy the cider. The unsuspecting buyer put his gun down in order to taste the liquor, when the pretended salesman immediately snatched it up and rushed inside the enclosure. Mugoloba was ready inside with a loaded gun. The man whose gun was stolen, followed by some of his companions, pursued the thief into the enclosure, but directly they entered the second gateway Mugoloba shot the foremost of the pursuers dead. The companion of the murdered man then fired his gun, and turned and made his escape. This incident took place on Friday, January 22nd.

The two men who had entered Mugoloba's enclosure, and of whom one had been murdered, were retainers of a chief named Mudima. Mudima, on hearing what had happened, went at once to the Katikiro Kagwa, who sent forthwith to Kampala to tell Captain Lugard of the outrage. The body of the murdered man lay where it had fallen, and the excitement grew intense, the French faction scornfully challenging their rivals to come and take away their dead.

Lugard, as soon as he heard of the fatal *fracas*, at once saw that it might mean a general outburst, and lost not a moment in hastening to the king. It is impossible to speak too highly of Lugard's earnest desire for peace, or of his patience and forbearance under the most trying circumstances; and I feel sure that had peace been possible no man that has ever entered Uganda was more fitted to secure it. He may, indeed, be criticised for having been too undecided, and for not having sooner seen what must be the inevitable outcome of the political troubles.

He had hitherto retained firm faith in his Roman Catholic friends, which, however, was shortly to receive a somewhat severe shock, for as soon as he reached Mengo he was received with studied disrespect.

First of all, he was kept waiting outside the king's enclosure in the broiling sun. Then the Kimbugwe came out to see him. This Kimbugwe was the ablest and cleverest chief of the French faction—a man entirely and wholly in the hands of the French fathers. He had been educated at their mission near Taborah, and was the greatest chief in the country after Kagwa the Prime Minister. He afterwards became the cause of a serious misunderstanding between Captain Lugard and his Protestant allies. Kimbugwe told Lugard that the king was dressing.

Presently another of Lugard's friends, also a Roman Catholic chief, came and saluted him; this was the Kauta (Chief Baker). He had professed the warmest friendship for Lugard, and appears to have been alienated from the Company in the matter of the scheme for deposing Mwanga, and making one of Kalema's boys king. Lugard asked him reproachfully why he never came to see him; formerly they had been on terms of greatest friendship. Kauta excused himself by saying his leg pained him, and to prove this he pointed to a pimple on his shin! Lugard now said he must see the king; but Kauta, not careful to make his excuse tally with Kimbugwe's, said that the king could not be found.

The king was really, of course, merely trying how

far the Englishman's patience would last. After
waiting a considerable time longer Lugard sent Dualla,
his Somal interpreter, to tell the chiefs or gate-keepers
that his master was going, and on receipt of this
message Lugard was at once ushered into the king's
presence. Mwanga received Lugard politely; and the
Englishman's first demand, when the subject of the
fatal incident was broached, was that the body of the
murdered man should be given to his friends for
burial. The king at once gave an order that the body
should be removed and buried. After some further
talk the king said the case should be at once dealt
with, and that the witnesses should now be called.
Lugard, overpowered with the fierce sun in which he
had been left to wait, and overcome by the heat of the
house in which the king received him, was now kept
indefinitely waiting for the witnesses, the king and the
French chiefs giggling and laughing the while, and no
doubt acting in such a manner as to make it unmistakable that the stranger Englishman was the subject
of their ill-timed levity. I, myself, have not unfrequently
been placed in a somewhat similar situation, and can
thoroughly understand how great the annoyance of
Lugard must have been under the circumstances. At
last he got up saying he felt unwell, and that he would
leave Dualla to hear the evidence. The king bade him
a courteous farewell, and promised that the important
chief Kimbugwe should come himself and tell Lugard
the result of the trial.

When the witnesses at last came the story was told
pretty much as I have related it; but the whole

question was made to hinge upon the legal right of a man to enter the enclosure of another. There is no doubt that the forcible entry of an enclosure at night would give the occupier the absolute right of killing a person so entering. But the question of the illegality of entering by day under the particular circumstances— namely, in the pursuit of a thief—is one which it may be imagined ought not to have the same answer; but though it is possible Uganda law might justify such an act, I understood from those of whom I carefully inquired that Mugoloba acted contrary to Uganda custom and law in shooting the Protestant. The king, however, unhesitatingly pronounced judgment, saying that the homicide was justifiable, since the slain man had entered by force another person's enclosure.

On hearing the decision Dualla remonstrated, and informed the king that Lugard would most strongly disapprove of it. The king replied that the decision was final, and could not be altered at Lugard's desire. Dualla then left.

The Protestants ably represented their case, and strenuously pleaded that the murderer should be given up. They themselves, in a similar case, had given up to their rivals a man named Omusamba, and also a man of the door-maker Mulamba's, who, it is stated, was put to death by the French faction. At any rate, the man was given up.

The understanding between the factions most clearly had been that the slayer of one of the opposite party should not be concealed or protected, and in carrying out this agreement two of the English party had already been given up, while a considerable fine had also been paid. The question with them was not one of abstract Uganda law—though in this they seem to have been in the right—but of the French party's keeping to an agreement which their rivals had loyally observed.

The king, however, remained obdurate, and refused to reverse his judgment or keep the agreement, and the baffled English leaders returned to discuss the next step.

Meanwhile Dualla had made his way back to Lugard and reported the king's decision, but Kimbugwe did not appear, as the king had promised. Dualla informed Lugard of how the king and French chiefs had laughed over his discomfiture. Lugard felt that no good purpose could be served by his returning to the king, so he wrote to Mwanga, sending his letter by Dualla, saying he greatly disapproved of the king's decision. Dualla had great difficulty in obtaining an audience, but eventually the letter was read ; but the king persisted in his first decision. Three of the " French " chiefs were present, the Mujasi, Musalosalo, and the Kauta. These added the most insolent remarks, and finally concluded by saying they would sack Kampalla Fort and massacre all its European defenders. Their manner was exulting and jubilant, and they evidently felt able to carry out their arrogant threats, since it appears that the Maxim guns had become discredited, for they had proved of little value in the late expedition against the Muhammedans, and were subsequently, as we shall see, used with the very greatest moral effect. At any rate,

Dualla's account of his interview clearly showed Lugard that the French party meant fighting. Lugard seems to have left no stone unturned in his efforts for peace. Nor in this serious emergency did he neglect to seek the assistance of Monseigneur Hirth, the French bishop. The bishop was the only person in the country indeed whose fiat could have averted war.

Lugard's letter to the bishop demands attention, as it is a document which sets forth what the representative of the Imperial Company held the position of the Company to be in Uganda. Speaking in this letter to the bishop of the murder of the Protestant he says : " I myself told the king that the murderer must be punished. Unless the leading Roman Catholics consent to justice being done in these matters the situation becomes impossible, as they have defied my authority." Now here it will be seen that he boldly claims an authority greater than that of the king and Roman Catholic chiefs. In other words, he claimed an authority equal, if not greater, than that wielded by the French bishop himself. He assumes, that is to say, the very point which was the true cause of contention between the French mission and the English Company. An appeal for help under such conditions could only have one reply.

Besides the general reasons already stated which make it unmistakably clear that the French faction had decided on war, and had determined, at all costs, to force it on, it may be noted that towards the end the nominal heads of the French faction refused to discuss the question with Captain Lugard, and, as we have seen, hurled open defiances against the English Company in the most insulting terms. Yet in spite of this, Captain Lugard appears to have laboured under a confused impression that, somehow or other, the war might have been avoided. He writes (p. 337 of his book): "Nevertheless, at the last moment, I am convinced, hostilities would have been avoided had not a spark led to a general engagement when already a *modus vivendi* had been almost arrived at." Yet nowhere does he give any indication of what the *modus vivendi* was to be, or how, or with whom, it had been almost arranged, while on the preceding page (336) he writes: "I gathered that the French party had definitely determined to fight, and had made all their preparations, and it mattered little what attitude I took." And a few lines lower down he acknowledges that the situation he had to deal with was quite apart from any tension created by any single petty incident.

Things had now come to such a pass that a fight was imminent, and a fight which the Company could not look upon with indifference, since the object of the attacking party was to overthrow English influence in Uganda. The case was full of difficulties; but the time for strong and decisive action had at last come. But Captain Lugard seems to have shrunk from the bold course of sending Mwanga an ultimatum demanding instant satisfaction for the insults to himself, thus avoiding any question of internal Uganda politics. This might possibly have brought Mwanga to his knees; but if Mwanga chose to fight the question would have been fought upon a very clear issue.

Again Lugard might have made a distinct and open alliance with the " English " party, demanding such conditions as would have left him free to administer the country in a large and liberal spirit regarding the opposing political factions. This would simply have been carrying out his instructions to consolidate the Protestant party. But Lugard, unhappily, as I think, chose a middle and more timid course. Secretly, and by night, the night of the 22nd, he issued to his supporters of the English party forty old muzzle-loading guns and five pounds of gunpowder, thus giving colour to the accusation that in secret he was supporting the Protestant cause, while openly professing to be neutral ; while the shabby amount of powder and the poor class of gun distributed cannot but have struck the loyal " English " leaders as a very grudging acknowledgment of their support, and as a miserly and poverty-stricken contribution from the military stores of Kampalla to the common cause. Though the distribution was made at night, the Kimbugwe (Mugwanya), the leader of the French faction, had his spies about, and this was met by a counter stroke by the king, who sent to the island of Bulinguge for a supply of gunpowder. Bulinguge, it will be remembered, was the island fastness which he had formerly defended when the powerful Muhammedan faction under Kalema had held Mengo. Some time previous to this he had removed the bulk of his possessions to Bulinguge in view of the coming fight. The same day, Friday, the 22nd, he sent a long letter to Lugard written in a haughty and uncompromising style, but, strange to say, ending up with an abject prayer that the Captain would give him time to tie up his goods and run away, clearly showing what his intention was—an intention, which, at all hazards, Lugard should have prevented him from carrying out. Lugard replied by simply affirming that it was his (Lugard's) duty to see justice done, and warning the king that if war should arise the responsibility would rest with him.

Saturday, the 23rd, was an anxious day. Reports of all kinds were rife, but in the evening a letter reached Kampala Fort, saying that the French faction meant to give up the idea of making their threatened attack; but almost simultaneously the war drums boomed out their call to gather for the battle—" Gwanga ! gwanga ! muje ju Junju !" (" Nation ! nation ! come for Junju !"*), a dismal comment upon the peaceable tone of the letter.

Next day, Sunday, the 24th, the whole of Mengo was in a state of the greatest excitement. All felt that the day of battle had come which was to decide the fate of the English Company and the Protestant faction. Captain Lugard now seeing that the " French " faction were collecting in large masses, issued three hundred muzzle-loading guns with ammunition, and one hundred and fifty Sniders to the chiefs of the English faction who were his own supporters. It must be remembered that Lugard had received an official intimation on the part of the king and French faction of their intention to sack Kampala Fort, and therefore his arming the party loyal to himself was an act necessary for the safe-guarding of English interests. It would have been an

* Junju was a former celebrated warrior king.

absurdity to leave the two parties to fight the quarrel out by themselves when that quarrel was, to a large extent, the question of an English protectorate. That he was tempted to do this would appear from his own account and that of the English missionaries. For he still seemed to cling to the assurances of their loyalty to himself expressed by the chiefs of the " French " faction—those very chiefs who, he tells us, were a parcel of liars, *par excellence*, and by whom their missionaries were continually duped.

All public religious services were out of the question. The English missionary, Roscoe, however, collected a few of the more earnest converts, notably Sembera— whose Christian name was Mackay—and began to have a Bible reading with them. Suddenly they were disturbed by hearing shots fired. These arose from the action of the Chief Cook Kauta, who had so grievously insulted Captain Lugard on the Friday previously, and whom Captain Lugard demanded to be sent into the fort as a prisoner, as well as Muguloba, the man who had killed the Protestant the same day. Kauta, seeing that he was personally involved in the trouble, found it convenient to precipitate matters, and was the most eager of all to begin the fray. His faction no doubt had given permission for what followed, which was a deliberate attack on the young chief Kibare.*

This attack happened at about 11 A.M., and resulted in the shooting of one of Kibare's men. The wounded

* In case the king should leave his capital for any reason, Kibare is the Regent during his absence, and Kibare's enclosure is next to the Kauta, or Chief Cook, or Baker.

man was taken at once to Kampala. The English party here showed great forbearance ; but so strongly had Lugard impressed upon them that they should not precipitate fighting by any rash action, that though they had the strongest provocation, and had arms in their hands, they took no action as yet in vindicating their rights or seeking to avenge their wrongs.

Meanwhile Lugard had thoughtfully sent to both French and English missions to offer the missionaries a temporary asylum at the Company's fort. The missionaries, however, in each case seemed to show very little eagerness to avail themselves of the proffered protection. The English missionaries, when Lugard sent forty porters to carry their goods, did eventually consent to go up to Kampala. The French priests, however, refused to leave their own brick fort, but asked for a guard of soldiers to protect them at their own place.

This was one of the cleverest moves in the whole game. If Lugard refused they had a specious grievance. It might well be urged that the first object of the Company should have been to protect life and property, and that the request for a guard under the circumstances was reasonable. But Rubaga was the very place where the hostile force was concentrated (and would be the first point of attack by the English party), that hostile force whose leaders had just threatened to sack Kampala ; but if Sudanese soldiers were in Rubaga, the English faction, in attacking this salient point of the enemy's position, would, in effect, be opposing themselves to the Company's soldiers. And this clever expedient would result in a conflict between the Company's troops and the English party, or, at any rate, would involve a frightful risk of such a contingency. Lugard has not referred to this in his account; he has, indeed, given other reasons for his action; but this, in my mind, fully justified him in refusing to put his own troops at the mercy of the enemy, or in such a position that they might have to fire upon the leaders' own allies.

Thus it will be seen that many things occupied Lugard's mind—the negotiations with the king concerning Friday's outrage and the insults to himself; the safety of the two sets of European missionaries, both French and English, when this new difficulty arose in the incident related above of the shooting of Kibare's man. Messengers had been continually coming and going between Lugard and the king. Lugard now sent off to demand that the man who had wounded Kibare's follower should also be given up. On this the king's party adopted a common African ruse; they seized and tied up a poor peasant, and presently the messengers arrived, bringing a man bound hand and foot, whom they asserted to be the culprit. This unhappy man had in no way been concerned in the outrage, and piteously pleaded his innocence, and the wounded men and other witnesses bore out his statements. Lugard, however, considered the sending of any prisoner as a sign of yielding on the part of the king's party, and sent down to say that the original culprit need only be given up.

There were four chief points in the capital where

the hostile factions were now massed, each of them a well-known hill—first, Kampala, on which stood the Company's fort, where all the Englishmen in the country were collected; second, the low hill of Mengo, on which Mwanga's enclosure was built, which was distant about a mile from Kampala; between Mengo and Kampala was the Kimbagwe's enclosure and those of several other chiefs; a broad road ran past Kampala to Mengo, each side of which were the banana plantations belonging to various chiefs; third, Rubaga Hill, opposite Kampala and distant about two miles, but between Kampala and Rubaga rose the lower slope of Namirembe, or Market Hill, conspicuous by the great tree which overshadowed the market-place. Rubaga was crowned by the French fort and partially completed church—the latter a great reed-built structure, which might have held from 2,500 to 3,000 people closely packed; and lastly, there was the lofty hill of Namirembe, crowned by the new Protestant church, also nearing completion. Rubaga was distant less than a mile from Mengo. A person standing on Mengo, the king's hill, and looking north, would face the wide road leading up to the market about a mile distant, and would see Kampala to the east of the market, and Rubaga to the west, whilst the new Protestant church on Namirembe rose up behind the market-place a little to the right. The English mission was behind the market-place at the base of Namirembe to the left.

At these four points, then, the contending parties were massed. Messengers, as we have seen, were coming and going between the king and the fort, when an incident occurred which precipitated the fight. The forcible entry of Kibare's place and the shooting of the "English adherent" not having resulted in reprisals, the French faction now attacked the Katikiro's people (the Katikiro was chief of the English faction), and forcibly seized some clothes which they were carrying. In doing this they fired a gun; the Katikiro's men replied, firing two guns. Just as things, in Lugard's opinion, seemed to be assuming a more hopeful aspect, and while Captain Williams was telling one of the English missionaries that there would be no fight, these three shots, precursors of the coming storm, broke the stillness. The two shots fired by the Katikiro's men were at once replied to by a volley from the French side, and in another moment the whole of Mengo became a battlefield. The main strength of the English faction was posted on Namirembe. All their best fighting men were there except the Katikiro, who, with a very small following, had to bear the brunt of the attack of the force, occupying Mengo, where the chief strength of the French faction was posted, strongly supported in their rear by a mass of men stationed on Rubaga. Part of the English force now descended the broad road towards Mengo to support the Katikiro, while the main body made straight for Rubaga. The party, however, who had gone to assist the Katikiro met with a stubborn resistance from the chiefs whose places lined the broad road— namely, the Kangao, Musoloza, and others. Musoloza, an important French chief, however, was killed, and the French faction at this point driven back; but before this happened the English party had lost one of their best and bravest adherents, Sembera, called Mackay, after his friend and teacher. Sembera, with a small following, was endeavouring to make a *détour* and attack the enemy on their flank, but was shot by some of them lurking in Musoloza's banana plantation. Sembera fired his rifle and then sank to the ground, mortally wounded. He bade his boys carry him to the side of the path, and then told them to leave him and go to the help of their fellows, since every gun was needed in the fray. They pulled down some banana leaves and covered him, and leaving this simple saint and hero, they followed the main body, who were near the top of Rubaga. Here the French fathers were gathered within the fort, while their adherents defended the approaches. But it appears that the French party, seeing that the chief point of battle would be Mengo Hill and Kampala, had quickly concentrated the greater part of their force there, leaving Rubaga comparatively weakly defended. This was a fatal error. The hill was carried in a few minutes by the English faction, and soon, alas! the grand new French church went up in flames.

The English faction were now on three sides of Mengo. Meanwhile, the small English force under the Katikiro had been driven back, and naturally it was the policy of their prudent leader to put Kampala Fort between the enemy and himself, especially as Captain Lugard had shown signs of not interfering more actively than by arming the Protestant faction. The Katikiro's retreat was followed by a forward movement of the French partisans. All this happened in a few minutes, and soon a mass of French adherents came charging down from Mengo, as Lugard thought, to attack Kampala Fort. In a moment he had swung the Maxim into position, and opened fire upon the advancing mass. The rain of bullets told on their ranks, but they still advanced. Lugard, shooting at a very long range, now moved the gun so as to cover an open space over which the advancing body must pass. The gun was well aimed and steadily handled. As the enemy appeared in the open the horrible sound of the rapidly fired Maxim rang out, and a hailstorm of bullets from the gun played for a few moments on the deadly spot. The moral effect of the gun was instantaneous. The French faction broke, and fled in all directions. Williams was now sent with a few Sudanese in the direction of Mengo.

Mwanga, as soon as the fighting began, followed the dictates of one of his ruling passions—namely, that of terror, and fled towards the Nyanza. As soon as the Maxim opened fire the French leaders—two of whom, Kimbugwe and Kauta, were slightly wounded—drew off their following, and, under the courageous young chief, Mujasi, executed a masterly retreat towards the Lake—a retreat which was not interfered with in any way.

As soon as the Company had taken an active part in the fight the conduct of the battle lay with them. But no orders of any kind seem to have been issued by the Company's officer, and after a desultory pursuit the victorious English faction returned to Mengo ; for the setting of the sun means in African warfare the cessation of hostilities. Captain Lugard attempted no pursuit, and apparently ordered none, and this in spite of his own dictum, which he has laid down referring to another occasion. He writes : " The whole moral effect of a victory lies in the rout and in the pursuit. Where this has been neglected, as at Macneil's Zeriba, the result has been a demoralisation of the victorious side, and an access of confidence leading to a renewal of fighting on the part of the vanquished. The use of arms of precision, of a Maxim, etc., and a bold pursuit, are the main factors in securing a moral effect ; and a moral effect in its results is to save life by putting an end to the war." Captain Lugard's dictum has a further illustration in this present case, for things turned out precisely as stated. The enemy retreated safely with the king to the small and, what they considered, impregnable island of Bulinguge, where they gained such an access of confidence as to lead them to reject scornfully all overtures of peace, and to prepare for further fighting.

However, let us leave the enemy to retreat, and return to Mengo. Captain Williams and his Sudanese marched up to Mwanga's deserted reed-built palace and hauled down the king's flag, which, it will be remembered, had been hoisted with great ceremony as a sign that the French party rejected English occupation, and at last the Company's flag floated over Mengo. Williams then marched on to Rubaga, where the

French priests were shut up. Their bishop has most graphically described the incidents which befell them, and of the valour of their lads, and how, as the French faction, supplemented by the little band of boy soldiers, under Francis Goge—a *Hausa* doctor—one of the mission staff, defended the fort outside, the fathers were administering the rites of their religion to those within. I cannot forbear to quote almost verbatim the bishop's own words. "Our children," he writes, "defended themselves bravely. They were alone, for all the Catholics were attacked on other points. Francis Goge, our doctor, received a ball in his heart, and fell like a stone; another, Cyprian, had his head broken, and the others were scattered. In a moment all Rubaga was in flames, and—what contributed not a little to fill our Christians with terror—they believed their fathers dead. In fact, we were bombarded on two sides in our poor mud house, and we were bound to be burnt alive. Some catechumens were there who had not yet been regenerated. These were the young children who, after seeing their master fall, had been able, through fire and flame, to reach our house. They were all cleansed in the saving waters, and I gave last absolution to all the Christians and to the missioners, and received it myself from the father superior. It only remained to die. Our aggressors, meanwhile, haply ignorant of our retreat amid the flames, withdrew to pursue our Christians. The firing altogether ceased. What would become of us in our prison? The first plunderers, an immense band of vultures, that descend upon the battlefields of Uganda, approached. We were discovered, but our numbers terrified them. They withdrew, doubtless to seek reinforcement. Through the black smoke which covered the capital reduced to ashes two of our children volunteered to go in order to carry to the fort a note, in which I made a last appeal to the humanity of Captain Lugard. An hour afterwards the captain arrived himself with a strong force. Our lives were saved. We had passed two mortal hours surrounded by the flames. In passing out we found everything burnt around us. We buried our poor Francis, despoiled and half burnt, and by his side Luekula, another Catholic chief, while the soldiers ate the cooked flesh of our animals burnt in our stables. The captain left a guard to protect our few effects rescued from the magazine, and the missioners sadly took the road for the English fort."

Thus ended the eventful day. The wounded of both sides were carefully collected by the victorious Protestants and carried to the fort, where they were tenderly cared for by the two excellent and able doctors, Macpherson of the Company, and Wright of the Church Missionary Society.

CHAPTER IX

THE TRAGEDY OF BULINGUGE

Captain Lugard urges Mwanga to return—The French Bishop determines to join the King—The French Bishop's Statements—The Way the French Bishop's Influence was used—Negotiations continued—Stokes' Men as Envoys—The King's Value to the Propaganda—The Satisfaction demanded by the Company's Representative—Undesirable Objects accomplished—Kisule attacks Protestant Canoes—War continued by the King's Party—Captain Williams arrives at Bulinguge—A heart-breaking Scene—Rescue of Kisule by the Protestant Chiefs—A Night and a Day in the Deep—An English Officer's Opinion—A quiet Shot at the Bicycle—Escape of the " French " Chiefs—Mistake of sending Dualla in charge of Sudanese—A young German on the Scene—Shaky hostile Witnesses.

CHAPTER IX

THE TRAGEDY OF BULINGUGE

THE battle of Mengo had taken place on January 21st, and the same evening Lugard discussed the situation with the French bishop, who suggested a division of the country between the two factions. The position of the French faction, in spite of their defeat on the battlefield, was really politically stronger than ever. They had met the whole force of the Protestants and the Company as well. True the Company did little or no fighting, with the exception of firing the Maxim behind their walls. But the people of the country would believe that they had done their very best, and that all they could do merely resulted in killing a dozen of the side opposed to them, while the French party had retreated in good order carrying off the king.

Buganda was where the king was, and after the battle of Mengo the French party held Buganda. Thus the priests might well feel that the king was hopelessly committed to their cause.

On the other hand, as a result of the battle, the Company had possessed themselves of the empty enclosure of the king, containing a few of the royal huts, which were of no value, since it is the person, not the place, which Uganda loyalty associates with the glory of their nation. The royal enclosure and royal buildings were but the mushroom growth of a day, whereas Mwanga was the descendant of an unbroken line of at least thirty kings.

Lugard, as soon as he had lost the head of the nation, seemed to awake up to his real value, and at once sent off letters urging the king to return from the island. He also wrote to two important chiefs, Sekibobo* and Kago,† inviting them both to remain in their offices. The result of these letters was that the king sent Kago to tell Lugard that he was willing to return in two days. There is little doubt that Mwanga had chafed under the severe tutelage of the earnest and austere prelate who was ruling his country, and the awful sound of the Maxim had helped to evaporate the little courage which he possessed; besides, he had a shrewd guess that when it came to fighting the English party seemed more successful in the field than the side which he was now supporting. The king cared nothing for Popery nor for French politics, and had not the slightest desire to suffer the smallest in-

* Sekibobo, of Kyagwe, has under him more than thirty important chiefs.

† Kago is the Ruler of Kyadondo and Sebadu of Uganda, the person whose duty it is to consult the Mandwa or priest on behalf of the king. Under him are Sebalija, keeper of the king's cattle, who in turn has under him Mutamanyang'amba, the executioner and Sengoba, who has under him Musigula. Both these executioners are important sub-chiefs.

convenience for the sake of these institutions, much less to pose as a martyr in their behalf.

There is little doubt that Mwanga was sincere in his desire to return. His French allies and teachers were at Mengo in the hands of the English, and for aught he knew prisoners in the stocks.

Kago, however, had an interview with the French bishop, who at once expressed his intention of repairing to the king. It is interesting to have the French bishop's own view of the negotiations which were now held with Mwanga. He wrote : " The Company wished to restore him (Mwanga) to his throne, on condition that he would accept the Company's flag, now the Protestant flag, and that he would yield to these last the chief Catholic charges. On the 26th the missioners themselves received permission to quit the fort, in order to go and persuade the king to return. An escort accompanied us to Munyonyo. We found the country a desert. What a welcome when our dear faithful saw us saved! The king meantime would not hear of returning to Mengo ; he would have been the slave of the Protestants. For the Catholics there was this sole choice between apostacy, death, or exile."

Now there are certain points in this statement that deserve attention.

First, that the Company's flag meant the Protestant flag. When Captain Williams had by mistake conceded the point as to allowing the turncoat chiefs of the English faction to retain their offices on joining the French faction, even then the French faction would not hoist the Company's flag, but ostentatiously hoisted the king's own flag. This clearly showed that the concession asked for would not cause the priests to accept the Company as a valid representative of English protection. There was now no change as regards the flag, and the French bishop is still prepared to refuse the protectorate of which the flag is a symbol, and which the Protestant or English faction had loyally accepted from the first. The Union Jack was objected to because it signified British ascendency.

Next, the bishop says that Lugard demanded that the king should yield to the Protestants the chief Catholic charges. But so far from this having been the case, Lugard had actually offered to reinstate in their offices *all* the " French " chiefs. Again, the bishop states that the king would not hear of returning to Mengo. This is quite contrary to what the king had said, and to what he afterwards did—namely, by running away from the French faction, and making his escape to Kampala. It was evidently the bishop's view that the chiefs returning meant apostacy. But why? The chiefs appear not to have thought so till they were assured by their spiritual ruler that such was the case.

And finally, I cannot but think the words used of the permission to leave the fort, " in order to persuade the king to return," must be half ironical. How could he, who believed that the king's return meant apostacy, persuade the king to return?

The English chiefs declared to Captain Lugard that if the French bishop was allowed to go to Mwanga all hopes of a peaceful solution of the difficulty were at an end. The bishop, however, determined on going, in spite of Lugard's polite protestations to the contrary. Here was a case in which Lugard might have used his discretion by forbidding these missionaries to risk their lives during the very progress of the war; but Lugard gave way. And the bishop went "to persuade Mwanga to return"!

But the bishop must have done, as those who heard him declared that he did, use all his influence and all his persuasions to urge the king NOT to return. His assurance to Lugard that he would influence the king to return can only have been a diplomatic ruse to obtain his own liberty and that of his *confrères*. Though his conduct may have been in some measure blamable, yet it must be remembered that he did not view this Imperial Chartered Trading Company as representing England authoritatively; and in spite of the protestations of the Company's officers to the contrary he was quite right, since Sir Gerald Portal subsequently seems to have explained that the Company did not represent the Government. Anything more humiliating than the position in respect to the Company and to the people of Uganda which the late Sir Gerald Portal felt it his duty to take up can hardly be imagined. The Company held a royal charter, and was allowed to fly the Union Jack, and actually coin money, and yet Sir Gerald took the position that the Government was not responsible for the Company's actions—that is, to black chiefs.

The French Government, however, told our own in the plainest terms that it held the English

Government responsible for the acts of the Company, and perfectly rightly so. My earnest hope is that our Government will come to see how thoroughly wrong in principle Imperial Charters are, and that it will for the future abstain from granting them. Where there are trading companies let there be British consuls, and where there is British commerce to protect by land, let there be British soldiers to protect it, as there are British sailors to protect it by sea. In the long run it is cheaper. Men in Government service are in a far more assured position of both authority and subordination than those under the committee of a trading company.

But to return to the negotiations. The next day the French bishop showed his real view, for he wrote to Lugard expressing his regret at not having been able to transmit Captain Lugard's request to the king, adding that, perhaps, he might have been able to influence him somewhat, leaving Captain Lugard to infer that this influence had not yet been employed, nor would be unless certain concessions which he would demand were granted by Captain Lugard. And then, as if to show that he wished negotiations to be opened, he continued, " Let us not despair, however, of seeing him quit his island."

The next day, January 28th, Lugard sent two men to the king. He could not, or would not, see that it was the bishop, and not the king, who was the actual head of the French faction. The bishop had requested Lugard, as the latter says, somewhat brusquely to send all messengers and letters through the fathers, giving, as an excuse, that the Captain's messengers had been insulted by the orders of the king, as they had not been introduced by the French priests. Could anything have been plainer than this insistence that negotiations should be conducted through the medium of the priests? Yet Lugard persisted in ignoring the very people through whom alone it was now possible to come to an understanding with either the king or the French faction. Far otherwise would it have been if he had kept the French fathers under his own protection at Kampala till the war was ended by the return of the king.

Captain Lugard's messengers were two of Stokes' head men—Muftahaa, who was buying ivory in Uganda for his employer, and the Captain, or Nahotha, of Stokes' boat. These men were both Muhammedans, and were absolutely neutral, and were the negotiations to have been conducted with the king alone, no better choice of envoys could have been made. They saw the king, who told them that he was exceedingly anxious to return, but that he was a prisoner in the hands of the French party. The bishop, according to Muftahaa's account, asked the latter if he had been sent from Lugard, and whether he thought it good first to expel the king, and then to invite him to return.

"If Captain Lugard wants the king," he added bitterly, "he had better bring his cannon and kill us all here." Some of the great chiefs appear to have desired to return; but they were quickly overruled by the bishop, who was warmly supported by Gabrieli, the fiery young Mujasi, and Kisule,* the clever blacksmith. The position was very strong. Once let the king be established in Budu, negotiations could be opened up with every prospect of success ; but if the king should return at once to Kampala, then all the advantages which the possession of his person carried with it would be lost. No one seems to have realised more clearly than Monseigneur Hirth the value of the king as regards the propaganda, for he says, referring to Mwanga's open profession of Roman Catholicism : " The number of our catechumens who come to the mission has almost doubled in eight days. Some four thousand to five thousand men come to us on ordinary days." † Hence his vehement objection to the king's return to Kampala.

On the 29th Lugard held a long discussion with the Protestant chiefs, who appear to have behaved with much moderation, and consented to invite the king and all the " French " chiefs back to their former positions and office. They hoped that the battle of Mengo would be a lesson to them, which would put a stop to those insolent acts of aggressive violence which had

* Kisule is an intelligent and far from narrow-minded man. In our old days at Natete a constant visitor and friend. He gained much of his knowledge in iron working from Mackay; and so skilful was he, that it was said he was able to turn muzzle-loading guns into breech loaders. At any rate, he could fit springs, new nipples, etc., into broken guns. Strange to say, this man's skill was animadverted upon by one of the Imperial British East Africa Co.'s officers, as one of the deplorable results of missionary effort, merely because the man used it for mending guns. A Christian captain or general may use and break guns, but a Christian blacksmith must not mend them !

† Quoted p. 59, in " Notes on Uganda." (Waterlow & Sons.)

forced on the war. But Captain Lugard went further than this. He wrote in a sense which seemed very like a confession of being in fault, since he dropped entirely the question of the outrages which had led to the war, while he made the paltry personal insults cast at himself through Dualla the only injury from which he demanded any redress.

Though one may feel that, as the representative of English prestige, he could hardly ignore the insults, one cannot but regret that the original demand that the Roman Catholic faction should give up the first culprit should not have been made a *sine quâ non* before permitting the king and chiefs to return, since if the question were worth fighting about it was worth representing diplomatically after the fight. Again, the method Lugard used in demanding reparation for the personal insult, can hardly commend itself to a sense of abstract justice. In giving an account of the satisfaction he demanded he writes : " As to the three chiefs present in the Baraza when the insults were offered I would forgive the Mujasi since he spared the life of one of my men who fell into his hands. The Kauta must lose his place, but should be reinstated if he behaved well. Salo Salo (Musalo-salo), who is a *very* petty chief, and generally disliked, being a thoroughly bad man, must be degraded."

Thus considerations quite outside the offence were allowed to influence his demands. It would seem also that to be in a humble position, or to have the misfortune to be unpopular, was part of the reason for being degraded, as well as for being very bad. What

Musalo-salo's badness consisted in Captain Lugard does not say. Unpopular he may have been, but at the same time he was an important chief, since he was in the closest attendance on the king.

Thus it appears that no indemnity was asked, the question of giving up the men who had shot the two English adherents was dropped, the offer to reinstate everybody was made, and the promise to blot out the memory of the whole affair was made.

It must have looked to the king and his advisers as if Lugard was now repentant, and terrified at what he had done. He had really effected nothing but the driving out of the king and the French missionaries, and destroying their mission buildings and church, the very objects which were furthest from his desires. At diplomacy he was no match for the priest, while the cunning of the natives overmatched his *finesse*. The priests at once saw their advantage, and, as I have shown, exhorted the king not to return.*

The negotiations seem to have been rather one-sided, and no written answer was returned by the king. Meanwhile the French faction was gathering in Budu, and the chief of Chagwe was preparing to march there with the whole " French " population. Thus all Uganda was in movement. Some ten thousand men, women,

* I think native evidence here, since it agrees perfectly with what actually happened, may be set against the priests' promise while prisoners to carry the invitation to Mwanga to return and to persuade him to do so. We are not told in what terms they promised to influence the king's return, and I have seen no categorical statement upon their part that they ever did promise to persuade the king to return unconditionally.

and children of the Protestant population of Budu were making their way towards Mengo, while the Catholic populations—including, of course, the heathen adherents of the king—were moving towards Budu, coming from all parts.

Sesse Island, with its people, were loyal to the king. Koki, with his seven hundred guns, was also on Mwanga's side, and the king's allies, the brave Buvama islanders, at Mwanga's call were preparing to help, so that the French faction were very strong indeed. It must be remembered, also, that their loss at the battle of Mengo had been trifling. They were therefore fully determined to renew the struggle, and accordingly, on the evening of the 29th, a party in canoes, under Kisule the blacksmith, attacked the canoes of a Protestant chief named Muwambi, which were bringing food from the island of Komi to the mainland. Kisule captured some of these boats, and, it is said, sank two of them; at any rate, he returned in triumph, bringing his prisoners and booty. Muwambi immediately sent word to Mengo. Lugard for five days had laboured for peace, with no result but this violent act of aggression by the king's party; and so Lugard determined to send Captain Williams to attack Bulinguge the next day.

Meanwhile, he received a verbal message from the king agreeing to return if the English faction would pay a fine to the king, and deliver up to him all the guns which Lugard had lent them. One would like to know more details as to this demand, and whether it was made by a messenger from the king duly accredited. At any rate, it was a demand which Lugard viewed as a mere insult, and so he agreed that the English faction should attack the island in conjunction with Captain Williams, who took with him Dualla, the interpreter, a hundred Sudanese soldiers, and a Maxim gun. The use of undisciplined native allies in African warfare is deeply to be deplored, since they cannot be kept in hand. There may be occasions which seem to justify it, and it has been largely practised, not in Uganda only, but throughout Africa, and by other nations as well as the English. In this case, however, the precaution was taken to secure a steady leader, and an important Protestant chief, and a consistent Christian man named Paulo, was selected as commander of the Protestant contingent. At that time Paulo held the important chieftainship of Kitunzi.

It will be seen that the king's party, in the face of Lugard's earnest endeavours for peace, continued to prosecute the war. The attack on Muwambi's was planned and carried out from the armed camp on Bulinguge Island, and was therefore totally different from mere local and unauthorised pillaging.

Lugard was therefore most certainly justified in attacking Bulinguge. The only question which might occur is why he should not have selected some one or two hundred of the best men of the English faction of the rank of chiefs and sub-chiefs, of whom he tells us there were six hundred, and over whom he might have exercised something like strict discipline. It was not apparently the policy of the Company nor of the Government to enrol the Baganda of either faction as English soldiers; yet neither one nor the other shrank from employing undisciplined mobs of these people in the prosecution of their wars.

On the morning of the 30th Captain Williams arrived at the shore of the Lake, opposite the King's Island, which was some four hundred yards from the mainland. His men found two women who had crossed over to collect grass for thatching. These women tried to escape to their canoe, but were secured. The canoe got off, and the men in it reported the capture of the women by the Protestants. Toli, an old Madagascar man, was with the king, and he, with the caution of his nation, advised the king not to fight. The fiery young Gabrielli Mujasi, however, buckled on his cartridge belt, as also the valiant blacksmith Kisule, and, followed by a number of boys, ran down to the beach, and it is said fired a few shots. Williams was meanwhile getting the Maxim into position, while his men, under Dualla, and a number of Protestants, crowded into fifteen canoes, and paddled rapidly towards the island. It was now about two o'clock in the afternoon, and the French bishop has thus graphically described what took place.* "I saw," he writes, "fifteen boats rapidly approach the island. All of a sudden the bullets began to rain upon the royal hut, making a terrible noise in the copse that surrounded us. It was the Maxim mitrailleuse, which joined its fire

* The extracts from Monseigneur Hirth's letter are taken from the July number, 1892, of the *Church Missionary Society's Intelligencer*, which copied it from the Roman Catholic paper, the *Tablet*, of June 4th, 1892, which says that it amounts to a full translation of the very important document, etc.

to that of the boats loaded with soldiers. The king seized me by the hand and dragged me away. If we were not riddled it was the Lord who shielded us. A crowd of women and children fled with us. How many fell! We had soon gained the other shore of the island; the bullets could no longer reach us. But what a sight! Just a few canoes and a crowd of three or four thousand throwing themselves into the water to cling to them; it was heart-breaking. What shrieks! what a fusilade! what deaths by drowning! The king was pushed into a boat; I had to follow him in without even thinking of my six colleagues I was leaving behind. We were soon in open water, whence we saw the flames that marked the presence of the enemy in the island. It was disputed foot by foot. Gabriel (Mujasi) and all the rest of our bravest—Fundi (Kisule), Kangao, Kaggo—were there.

"And the fathers! I have not seen them since. I am told that at the first firing they also rushed for the boats; one only remained. They leapt inside, and filled it with Christians until the boat broke at the side. Once more they resigned themselves to death. I am told that they themselves went first, avoiding a *mêlée* with the fighters. They were able to surrender to the Ba-gandas without being wounded."

Lugard describes these Protestants as having shown no pluck whatever. This is so contrary to their invariable behaviour in the field, as described by Captain Lugard himself, that one cannot but feel that some other explanation is necessary. I think it is not far to seek. The Protestants acted with reluctance, and saw, I believe with disgust, the ruthlessness of Dualla's Muhammedan Sudanese, who, let loose on the island, perpetrated, as I have been given to understand, not a few atrocious murders. Père Gaudibert himself told me he witnessed the shooting dead of a boy; a Protestant chief who was present corroborated the statement that unarmed people were massacred, a woman being among those killed. Kisule, the Fundi, and Sensalira, an old heathen sub-chief, were rescued from the hands of the Sudanese and from death by the Protestant chiefs. It is impossible to say what the utterly heathen adherents of either party might be capable of; but that the well-instructed chiefs of either creed would commit the atrocities charged against the Protestant leaders I feel sure is contrary to the whole tenor of their actions. For when the Protestants made their exodus from Budu, and were attacked by the Roman Catholics, a boy belonging to Kajerero, who commanded the enemy, was made prisoner. This boy was an intelligent Roman Catholic. He was treated with the greatest kindness by Thomas Mukisi, the Protestant leader, and when I asked what he meant to do with him he said, " I will send him back to Monseigneur, the French bishop."

One must read accounts written under a strong sense of wrong and with evident anguish of heart with a sympathetic caution.

Monseigneur Hirth continues his graphic story as follows : " For my part, I rowed sadly, very sadly, on the Lake, withdrawing slowly, for our overcharged boat threatened even to capsize, engulphing thereby the last hope of Uganda, its king and its bishop." (Another undesigned coincidence showing Monseigneur's appreciation of the paramount importance of the king.) He goes on : " With difficulty we emerged from the creek, leaving Uganda all around us in flames.

"After a whole night and day on the water, without repose, without nourishment, we landed at Sesse. I had to leave the king to continue his course alone towards the south of Budu, in order to take counsel on my own part, to save the last colleagues that remained to me in Sesse itself, or in Budu.

"All of us then slowly proceeded to the Kagera and the German frontier. It is not exile but rather new fatherland for us, for an immense immigration, beginning from the frontier of Unyoro and the banks of the Nile, has followed us for several days. The whole of Budu has become a Catholic province. The Protestants, though ten times more numerous, have been driven out. God only knows how this terrible trial will end for us. I have trust in Him, and in the holy martyrs of Uganda. Humanly speaking, all our hopes seem destroyed.

" Nevertheless, I trust that God will awaken faith on the Nyanza in spite of the endeavours of the East African Company to bring us under the Mussulman yoke. The last letters from Captain Lugard threatened to surrender Uganda to Embogo, King of the Mussulman Baganda. If Mwanga had for one year been free to act as he liked there would at present have been no Mussulman state here, and no more slave trade." Another statement bearing out my view of Monseigneur's most strong belief in the value of Mwanga in

KING MWANGA'S FLIGHT.

carrying out any policy which Monseigneur favoured. He continues: "But that is not what the officers of the Company look to. One of them lately said to me, 'Among the three sects known in Uganda, Protestants, Catholics, and Mussulmans, I like the last much best.'

Indeed, he has built for the last a school in the fort, and a mosque. It is infatuation which makes him speak against the Catholics ; but he seems to do justice to the Protestants, whose morality is as bad as that of the Mussulmans ; besides, they all smoke hemp furiously."*

The letter ends by a request for the sympathy of the writer's European co-religionist. He says : " Deign especially to beg for us the compassion of the faithful, for we have lost much. We ask neither for bicycles nor for champagne, but let them not refuse what is needful. It is three weeks since I have been able to say either mass or office."

The letter is of thrilling interest throughout, often pathetic, and the quiet shot at the bicycle shows that the writer was not without a sense of humour. The poor man's horse must be sneered at even in Central Africa. I was the only person who had a bicycle, but for a time I was puzzled as to how champagne should have been associated with bicycles. Mr Roscoe, one of our missionaries, was able, however, to explain the mystery. Among the boxes which I left at Bukoba, and which were looted, as well as the bicycle, by the French

* Here, I think, is a statement which requires to be read with caution. The sweeping assertion as to morality is made without any realisation of the character of Christian Protestantism in Uganda, while the entirely false assertion that the Protestants all smoke bhang furiously plainly betrays its untruth by the absurdly unguarded nature of the accusation. The unfairness of classing the bhang-smoking Pagans with the Protestants in this instance is quite obvious, since Monseigneur and his *confrères* knew that they were a quite distinct faction, with leaders of their own. They had nothing whatever to do with the Protestants except on the field of battle, when the Protestants fought with them.

faction, was a case containing a few bottles of champagne, which Mr. Roscoe was bringing up for medical use.

This, in brief, is the French bishop's account of the affair at Bulinguge.

It will be evident from Monseigneur Hirth's letter that the French faction showed much courage, and Lugard says they fought with great gallantry. The Protestants seem to have busied themselves on this occasion chiefly with looting the huts and stores containing the property of the king and the defeated chiefs. There seems to have been again no pursuit, and Captain Lugard, writing of it, says, had these chiefs been captured it would have ended the war. He blames his Protestant allies for their escape. I think, however, that the blame rests rather with his own lieutenant, who was commanding the expedition. With reference to the numbers killed, two accounts, those of Père Guillermain and Rev. R. H. Walker (who follows Toli's account of the matter), give the number of canoes sunk by the Maxim as six. Baskerville, who is not always careful to note that his statements are not his own observations at first hand, gives the number sunk by the gun as eleven. Another informant, Namenyeka, a Protestant chief, gives the number as two or three. Captain Williams admits that some sixty men were killed in the boats. This must have been on the side of the island facing the mainland at Munyonoyo, since the Maxim was not, I understand, landed upon the island. The deplorable loss of life on the other side arose from overcrowding the canoes.

Those actually killed in the fighting, according to Captain Lugard's information, amounted to eighty-five persons ; but how Captain Williams could estimate the number of those killed in the canoes at sixty is not made quite clear. At any rate, it is much to be feared that in this deplorable affair some hundreds of people perished, either under fire, or by the overcrowding of canoes, and that among them was a large number of women and children. The statement that Captain Williams purposely fired upon women and children cannot for a moment be entertained, nor can it be substantiated ; but that there were women in some of those canoes sunk is very possible.

If Captain Williams were to blame I should say it was rather that he did not send one or two of his European companions in charge of the Sudanese soldiers instead of Dualla, who, it seems, was the person in charge of the Company's landing force. Captain Williams has been blamed by the Catholic Union for confiding the priests to the care of the Pokino Nikodemo, whom he had described in one of his letters as a " rabid and cantankerous Protestant " ;but Captain Williams knew that he could not have chosen any one in the whole of Uganda who would have been more tender or more courteous to the European strangers than the kindly old Pokino. But that there should be no ground for complaint, they were escorted back to the Company's fort by Dr. Macpherson, where they were politely received by Captain Lugard, who says that they were utterly done up and exhausted ; and when he offered them his own clothes they were apparently too polite to accept them, and consequently spent a miserable night in a very damp condition. If they met with but poor fare and poor treatment at the Imperial British East Africa's headquarters in Uganda it was because Lugard and his subordinate officers had no better to offer. The fault lies rather with the failure of the Company to supply its officers with necessaries than with any lack of hospitality on the part of those gentlemen themselves. Thus ended the most unhappy incident of the war. Something had indeed been accomplished since the king now saw that he was fighting with the English Company rather than with the Protestant Ba-ganda, but the French faction had once more been allowed to carry off the king. The Protestants, according to Père Coullaud, who wrote February 16th, 1892, made an effort to capture the canoe in which the king was escaping; but strange to say, at this juncture a young German non-commissioned officer appeared on the scene, and took the French bishop and king under his protection. I shall have occasion again to mention this young man, whose former kindly relation with myself I have already referred to. I have now given what I believe to be a fairly accurate account of this period. But I must here deprecate evidence hostile to the English Company and the Protestant faction, given by a number of persons, all of whom had some motive in taking a more or less hostile view, and none of whom were within hundreds of miles of Uganda at the time of the occurrence.

Among hostile witnesses are Herr Stuhlmann, who, when the fighting took place, was making his way from somewhere in the neighbourhood of Kavalli's, and was naturally more or less hostile to the Company after the

Peters' treaty and its resultant *fiasco*. Herr Wolf, when a thousand miles off, had swallowed whole the *ex-parte* statements which he received from the French priests, and had committed himself to the view that the Protestant missionaries and English Company and English faction were to blame—and this before he set foot in Uganda. Then we have Mr. Muxworthy, who was intimately connected in business relations with the important trader Stokes, with whom Lugard had a serious misunderstanding, and Muxworthy, though an excellent man, was nevertheless likely to be prejudiced against the Company and those who supported it; besides—and this vitiates his testimony—he was two hundred miles from Uganda at the time of the war. Then we have Dr. Maloney giving his opinion. Dr. Maloney knew nothing whatever about Uganda, had never been within two months' journey of it; besides, he was a Roman Catholic, and this perhaps accounts for his bias. Sergeant Robinson, Captain Stair's attendant, who also was quoted as saying the Protestants were in the wrong, was in company with Dr. Maloney, and, like Dr. Maloney, knew nothing whatever about the affairs of Uganda. They happened both to have been in *Africa*, and, except for this, had no other claim to speak on Uganda.

On the evidence of such witnesses as these serious and unfounded charges against innocent men have been supported, and hostile judgments formed of the Protestant Christians of Uganda, who, whatever their faults may be, have given irrefragible proof of possessing many noble Christian qualities.

BOOK III

UGANDA REVISITED

CHAPTER I

THE FLIGHT FROM BUDU

Walker's House—Uganda Implements, etc.—A Munificent Present—Disquieting Tidings—News of the Fight—We abandon Masaka—Pursued by former Friends—Our Pursuers defeated—A disturbed Night—A Herd of Eleven Elephants—We send urgent Letters—A disappointing Communication—A vast Host of Fugitives—An unsatisfactory Interview—Grounds for Misunderstanding—I avoid Kampala.

CHAPTER I

THE FLIGHT FROM BUDU

I NOW take up the story of what occurred in the province of Budu, on which the Roman Catholic or French faction was now concentrating its whole force under the king. As I have already stated, I had passed the mouth of the Kagera River on my journey to Uganda, and had reached Budu on January 13th; and the following day I reached Bali, the nearest landing-place for Masaka, where Walker's mission was established. Immediately on landing I sent messengers to tell Walker of my arrival; and he came himself the next day to meet me, bringing a number of porters to carry my luggage. Walker and I had parted at the south of the Lake in 1888, four years before, and much of what I have related in the former chapters had taken place during that period. Walker was accompanied by several friends of mine, especially my old boys, Timoteo Kaima and Jimmy Kangiri. My camp was pitched upon a stretch of sand and coarse grass just above the beach.* Soon we were having tea together, the *pièce de resistance* being a duck, which

* I have made use of my friend Walker's letters describing this period, especially those in the *Church Missionary Society's Intelligencer.*

I had had the good fortune to shoot with a rifle. After tea we started for Masaka, the capital of Budu, and the headquarters of the Pokino, known in former days as Sebwato. We rested a day on our journey, Sunday, January 24th, the same day that the battle was taking place at Mengo. When we finally reached Masaka we found the house all ready for us. Walker possessed but few European articles of furniture, and did not disdain to use things of native manufacture; and the accompanying illustration will give some idea of African skill in its various departments. Zakaria (now Kangao) was occupying the house in Walker's absence, and he had most thoughtfully seen that boiling water was ready for tea, and had filled a large wooden trough,* used by Walker as a bath, with water. Zakaria would have accompanied Walker to meet me, only he was suffering from a thorn in his foot.

I was soon shown to my quarters, two magnificent rooms. The house was divided into six rooms, and was the largest building I had yet come across in Uganda, with the exception of some of the great royal houses which I had seen in years past at Mutesa's court. Walker and I had much to talk of, and I was naturally interested to hear how my old school-fellow and friend, Captain Lugard, was getting on with the people of Uganda. I had met him at occasional intervals during his active career: after his return from Afghanistan, where he had done good service, and amply fulfilled the promise of his younger days; also

* Wooden trough called Lyato (canoe), used for making banana cider.

UGANDA IMPLEMENTS, UTENSILS, ETC.
(*For description, see p. 265.*)

on his return from Nyassa, where he had been only partially successful in his campaign against the Arabs, owing to his weakness in fighting men, an ill-fortune which pursued him to Uganda, where the same

---

DESCRIPTION OF ARTICLES ON PREVIOUS PAGE.

1. Uganda tobacco pipe, black polished clay bowl, with white wood stem. The hole is pierced through the stem by means of a hot iron. Some pipe stems are three feet or more long.

The pipe below not numbered should be also numbered "1."

2. Uganda knife of smaller size, used as a razor by the women, who do the shaving. All the Ba-ganda men, women, and children are shaved entirely about once a month. The blade is not steel, but only fine iron.

3. A small charm, entirely covered with bead work, in blue, black, and white.

4. A round bracelet, hollow slit all round the outer side, made partly of silver from Nubian dollars, and partly from copper exquisitely soldered together.

5. A suction tube, covered with plaited grass in various colours, having a strainer worked in grass at the thicker end. Used for drinking strong plantain cider from the bottle gourd (seen at No. 19, below).

6. An ivory bracelet, about 2½ inches wide. The larger ones are worn on the ankles also.

7, 8. Solid brass neck ornaments, worn by king's messengers to indicate their office.

9. Another variety of Uganda tobacco pipe, with large ornamented clay head and short white wood stem.

10. A woman's neck ornament, made of grass, and entirely covered with beads of various colours in accurately worked patterns.

11. A roughly made iron cowbell, with a thong of otter's fur.

12. A very old "Lubare shield," used in the ancient witchcraft of Uganda. This was given by Nikodemo Sebwato, a Christian chief, as a specimen of what once was believed in by those of the old heathen religion.

13. A small coffee berry basket, as used by a princess, exquisitely made of plaited grass of various colours. A few raw dried coffee berries are used as a sign of good will on greeting a friend. The berries are chewed. The ordinary use of coffee is not understood by the Ba-ganda.

14. A strap or belt of ornamented leather. The pattern is worked on with a tool, and coloured in black, red, and white.

15. A chief's stick or club, about 2 feet long, made of fine white wood. Worked smooth by means of a leaf, which acts like sandpaper.

16. The iron blade of a spade or hoe. This variety is intended to fit through a hole in a thick wooden handle or shaft, in a slanting position.

17. A polished clay bottle or jug.

18. A small drinking cup, 3½ inches high, of the same material. Used for extra strong banana cider which has been made with grain in it.

19. An elegant bottle for fermented drink. It is simply a gourd of natural shape, with a ring of blue glass beads for ornament.

20. A drinking vessel made from a similar gourd.

21. A chief's shoe or sandal of ornamented buffalo hide.

22. A low stool, cut from one piece of hard wood, brought from Kavirondo.

23. A string of Cowrie shells. A hundred are in a string, and equal sixpence in value.

24. A mallet cut from a single piece of very hard wood. It is used in the

weakness marred his success in the somewhat ambitious projects which he entertained.

The news of my arrival spread through the district, and, though the kind old Pokino was not at his capital —he was at Mengo in attendance on the king—many of the smaller chiefs came to see me, bringing presents of bananas and goats. It was pleasant to meet many familiar faces of men, now in high positions, who formerly had been nothing esteemed in the old heathen days of Mutesa and Mwanga. One of these kind friends determined to present me with a hundred parcels of food, each carried by one person, so that there was a time of great plenty for the newly arrived guests.

At Masaka I had the pleasure of seeing an ideal

---

manufacture of the native bark cloth, and the ridges and grooves of the mallet cause the peculiar markings on the bark cloth.

25. A milk bowl, as used by the Wahuma or cattle-herding people of Uganda. A single piece of wood hollowed out quite thin by means of an iron scoop. The deep groove round it is coloured black, the rest is smeared for daily use with grey clay. This vessel is held between the knees as the man milks into its small opening with both hands at once. Burnt grass is put inside before milking, so as to give a smoky flavour to the milk, which is moreover never used till it has turned sour.

26. A waist circlet, for young unmarried girls, the only covering used at this age. This is made of plaited palm leaf, but the upper classes would have them entirely covered with ornamental beadwork.

27. Is a waist girdle, as worn by baby girls. It is made of pieces of round wood, strung together and stained black.

28. A white wood hand drum.

29. A large drinking cup cut out of wood. This was used as the cup in the administration of the Lord's Supper.

30. A small square of plaited palm leaf, used to place over drinking vessels in order to keep the flies and dust out. These are made of all sizes, according to the vessels they belong to.

31. The mat on the ground is one made in Uganda, and used in the chiefs' houses. Narrow strips of palm leaf are plaited into bands of about an inch wide, at times in excellent pattern. These bands are carried in a spiral fashion, and in a definite pattern round and round a framework, and the edges of the bands are sewn together till a sort of cylinder is made on the framework. This is then cut down length ways, and the whole opened out flat, and bound with a plaited binding all round the edge of the mat.

B. W. W.

mission station, and, in Walker, a missionary who, in a most remarkable degree, seemed to have grasped, and to be carrying out, the true functions of his calling.

I had succeeded in bringing the bicycle to Masaka, and it proved a source of great astonishment to the people, who never tired of looking at this new piece of European magezi (cleverness).

A few days after my arrival, Mr. F. C. Smith, of the Church Missionary Society, came in on his way to Kyango, Zakaria's chieftainship, which was some sixteen miles distant from Masaka, and where Zakaria, like the Pokino, had built a nice house and church. Mr. Smith hoped to remain with Zakaria to carry on missionary work with him. Smith left us on Monday, the 25th.

We were some ninety miles distant from Mengo, and no rumours of the war had as yet reached us; but on the evening of Monday, January 25th, messengers arrived from the capital with a letter from the Katikiro to Zakaria, stating that they were expecting the French party to attack every moment, and saying that Lugard wanted him to come to Mengo. The messengers also brought a hurriedly written note from Baskerville to Walker, in which he said that war was imminent, and that the Roman Catholics were expected to take to the islands. But there was no communication whatever from Captain Lugard.*

* In referring to this crisis ("The Rise of our East African Empire," vol. ii., p. 131), Captain Lugard states that he had *ordered* messengers to be sent to Mr. Walker, in Budu, to warn

Next day, the 26th, I had intended to start for Mengo, and Walker was hoping to set me on my way. Some men, who were going to carry my loads, had arrived, when a man came who brought news from Mengo of the fighting which had taken place. This upset our plans, and we waited, expecting messengers every moment from Captain Lugard. Walker sent a verbal message to the Company's garrison at Bujaju, on the Lake, asking the soldiers to come and help us. They sent back to say they dare not leave their fort without orders. At eight o'clock the same evening a number of sub-chiefs and church elders came in to say that the situation was very serious, that the whole

him; but in the next paragraph he excuses his own neglect of sending any warning by saying it would have been worse than folly on each occasion of such crises to have sent alarming messages to Budu. But if so, why did he order messengers to be sent to warn Mr. Walker?

His omitting to send any warning himself to his countrymen in Budu was the more notable since he had already gone so far as to begin arming the English faction in view of the imminent war—a step which he had never even contemplated in the former crises, while a month before he had repudiated such a possibility as monstrous. His action at this time showed clearly that he viewed the present crisis in a very different light from any of the former troubles. Though no doubt strain and worry may be pleaded as an excuse, his further omission to warn his own garrison of Sudanese in Budu, under Ferag Effendi, was a serious omission of a similar kind, which, but for the courage and devotion shown by these men, would have resulted in their annihilation. Their soldierly instincts and high ideal of discipline forbade their joining Walker and me at Masaka, or even evacuating the station, without orders from their superior officer, till absolutely forced to do so by the enemy. These orders were never sent, and it was only by their valour that they fought their way up to Mengo through the hostile host of the French faction.

defeated Roman Catholic faction intended to occupy Budu, and that we stood in the very gravest danger of being caught between the French party already in Budu and the main party, who were coming to occupy the whole country, and that we had better leave Masaka at once and make our escape. We therefore packed up a few things, and made ready for an early start next morning. At 11 P.M. the same night Walker wrote to the soldiers at Bujaju, telling them of the war, and that Captain Lugard had armed the English faction, and was therefore fighting against the French faction, and again asking them to come to our assistance.

Next morning we left Masaka, abandoning all our belongings, and marched some dozen miles to the place of a chief called Kalunda, where next day Zakaria joined us, with Smith. Zakaria brought on a bale or two of cloth and a few other things, but most of our possessions remained behind, and were quickly looted by the French faction, who were up in arms. As we slowly withdrew from a province which had now become wholly "French," we were followed by a vast host of people, including women, children, sick folk, and blind people. We were being pursued by the Roman Catholics, who had drawn to a head, and who intended to attack us in the rear. The chiefs, Katabalwa, Kajarero, and Mubinge, were the principal "French" leaders in Budu. Ordinarily Budu was the stronghold of the English faction; but the absence of the Pokino at the capital had greatly weakened its fighting strength. Kajerero, whose name was Nantinda, was a man greatly liked and respected by the Protestant chiefs. He, with Mika Sematimba, a Protestant, had frequently been a king's messenger, appointed to take charge of Europeans either leaving or arriving at Uganda in canoes. In this capacity I had made his acquaintance some years before, while Mubinge had only a few days previously come to see me at Masaka, bringing me a present. He had been an old pupil of mine, but had received an office which brought him under the influence of the Roman Catholic Katikiro, the young Confessor Honorat, who had been killed fighting against the Muhammedans. Mubinge had welcomed me most kindly, and it was a melancholy reflection that this miserable outbreak had made it necessary for these kindly friends to follow us now with arms in their hands. We had left Masaka on Wednesday, and on Friday the enemy came upon our rear. Walker and Smith and I were well in front of the host of fugitives. Our way lay through a rich country, rising here and there into hills, at the base of which were swamps. There had been a great deal of rain this year—much more than usual—which had made the swamps particularly unpleasant. At about 10 A.M. the word was passed along that there was firing in the rear, and we heard the distant report of guns. Zakaria, Mubanda, and Thomas Mukisi, who was head of the Baganda soldiers of Budu, with some two hundred guns, many of them breech-loaders, were guarding the rear of the retreating Protestants. As soon as they heard the firing, many of the terrified women, in order to expedite their movements, threw down their goods, which were immediately looted by some more courageous and less burdened wayfarers.

We went on a little further and then halted, in order to help our brave rear-guard in case they were obliged to retire before the enemy. But there seemed to be no signs of people in flight, so, after waiting more than an hour on the *qui vive*, we retired to a house, and lay down to rest. At about 4 P.M. Zakaria came in to tell us that the Roman Catholics, under the chiefs Kajerero and Mubinge, had made a determined attack. There had been a sharp fight, but Kajerero himself had been killed, with ten of his followers, and the rest had then taken to flight. Two prisoners were taken. One of our men was shot in the arm, but the wound was trifling. We learnt afterwards that Nantinda Kajerero had been very much averse to making the attack, but that his people had accused him of cowardice. The death of Kajerero, however, seems to have averted further fighting, for we now heard that Katabalwa, the second chief in Budu,* who had been coming to attack us on another road, hearing of the defeat of Kajerero, had abandoned the enterprise, and quietly went to conduct the obsequies of the fallen chief with due honour. I think they did not care to try conclusions with the enemy who had so gallantly repulsed the first attack.

The night after this engagement, while we were still expecting Katabalwa's attack, we received a fright

* The inferior chief in most cases is said to be the Mumyuka of the man directly above him. Thus Pokino was the Mutuba Muto of Uganda, Katabalwa Mumyuka, Kalunda, the third chief, was Mumyuka of Katabalwa, and a Protestant. The fourth chief was Kajerero, whose Mumyuka was Kagoro Zakaria.

which I think we shall not soon forget. Walker and Smith and I, and some of our immediate friends and followers, were sleeping in a house where the camp for the night was pitched. We were all asleep, when suddenly Walker was awakened by hearing a shrill cry which swelled into the hum of many voices shouting. Then he heard the people who were camped in the vicinity of our hut buckling on their cartridge belts. Walker immediately began to dress himself, and as he was doing so he heard a gun go off. He at once shouted to me, so I hurriedly put on my clothes and Smith did the same, while Mika Sematimba went out to see what was the matter. He soon returned to tell us it was only a leopard. I gathered afterwards that, in reality, the disturbance had been caused by a dog which came sniffing round one of the huts, and that a man, mistaking it for a leopard, fired his gun, but killed his wife who was sleeping near. I never saw the man; but in such a vast host, and at a time like that, such an incident does not make a very deep impression, especially if one only hears about it and does not see the dead body or the unhappy author of the tragedy. At any rate, whatever caused the commotion, it was not the enemy, so we all lay down to resume our sleep so rudely broken.

We had not been quiet very long when we were awakened by the door of the hut being suddenly dashed inwards, and by the sudden rush into our sleeping place of what we supposed was Katabalwa's hostile followers, who must have crept up unseen to the house where the English missionaries were collected. We were caught in a trap, and escape seemed hopeless. These thoughts flashed through my mind. I was up in an instant, groping for my rifle, and expecting every second to see the flash of a dozen guns fired by our foes. There was nothing of the kind. The mystery was explained next moment by one of the boys, who said " Emboozi " (" It's the goats "). I struck a match, and found it was even so. Walker and Smith had both jumped out of bed as soon as they heard the scuffling and bumping in the hut. The goats were always accustomed to sleep at night in the houses, and not liking to be left outside, had taken the matter into their own heads, and butted open the door of the hut where we were, and had knocked down a chair against which my rifle was leaning. Once more we resumed our efforts at sleeping; but were not sorry when daylight broke, when at least we should be able to see the disturbers of our peace, in whatever shape they appeared.

This day we had to cross the Katonga, which is merely one of the river swamps not uncommon in Uganda. That is to say, a swamp with a slow current. On reaching the bank of the river or swamp we saw a herd of eleven elephants, the first I had ever seen in Africa. We were warned not to fire at them, as the shots would mislead our friends in the rear into supposing that we were engaging the enemy. The young chief, Samwili Mwemba, who had come as far as Masaka to meet me, now took some men to reconnoitre the path in front. Finding no trace of the opposing faction we then advanced, and slept that night in what had formerly been a flourishing village and plantation; but it had been raided by the Muhammedans, and what the Muhammedans had spared the elephants had finished. It was an extraordinary sight to see the havoc these mighty creatures had made, uprooting trees of considerable size in their rude gambols.

The chiefs always built a large and commodious hut for Walker and Smith and me when we came to any place where there were no houses. At this camp, on January 30th, we sent off most urgent letters to Captain Lugard, telling him of our critical position, and of our being on the road to Mengo, and asking for help. Captain Lugard received these letters on February 3rd, but before the receipt of our first letter of January 28th, he had written on the 27th of the same month saying he feared we should be overpowered in Budu, as the Roman Catholics were going down that way. This shows that he thoroughly realised our dangerous position, yet he did not see his way to send any of his officers or men to our assistance.

On Monday, February 1st, we received Lugard's letter of January 27th. It was of the most disappointing character. Walker, in referring to it, wrote, " He sent us no help, not even a box of caps."

He did, however, make some tardy endeavour to render assistance to his own garrison at Bujaju. This garrison, I may mention, would not follow Walker's suggestion that they should join us, but preferred to wait for orders from headquarters. The difficulty of communication does not seem to have been so great as Lugard imagined, since the Pokino sent messengers, who had reached us the day after we left Masaka, carrying letters to the Protestant chiefs bidding them take the greatest care of the missionaries, and to regard nothing in comparison of our lives.

The result of the Pokino's letter was that our willing offer to assist in guarding the rear was utterly scouted by our faithful friends, who would not hear of our doing so. We came on slowly towards Mengo, passing, in the distance, the Mukwenda's headquarters at Singo and the picturesque lakelet on the shores of which his capital is situated.

As we drew nearer the capital we made shorter marches ; for the people were worn out and weary with the fatigues of the long journey, and they were often walking knee deep in swamp. On February 2nd we were momentarily, until we had opened it, cheered by again receiving a letter from Lugard. It was a long letter, principally taken up with blaming Walker for his message to Ferag Effendi and his garrison at Bujaju, though Walker's proposal that the garrison should effect a junction with us at Masaka was the very wisest possible. Lugard, in excusing his failure to assist us, has argued that he could not pass the army of the hostile French fraction concentrated between Mengo and Masaka ; but this is not sound, since sixty rifles under a European officer and three or four small boxes of ammunition could easily have reached us, and would have made us strong enough to meet the hostile army, encumbered as it was with women and children, had it fallen in with us. As it was, however, we had providentially avoided the main body ; but that same evening we heard firing, which turned out to be the end of a desultory attack made by the Protestant Chief Mulondo on the retreating rear-guard of an exodus of Roman Catholics similar to our own, which had taken place from the Roman Catholic province of Kyagwe, under the Sekibobo, a chief of the French faction. We were encamped on the summit of some low hills while the vast host of the retreating fugitives wound their way through the valley in the dark. At intervals, people carried flaring torches to show the path. Though they had more guns than our rear-guard they never thought of attacking us, being only anxious to put as great a distance between themselves and Mulondo's rifles as was posssible. Walker and I, with our friends about us and rifles in hand, waited outside the house where we were staying until the hum of the receding host became silent and the flashing torches disappeared in the distance. Next day we saw the wide pathway which the retreating Roman Catholics had trampled out in the grass. A wounded man lying in a house near at hand gave us an account of the yesterday's fight, which led us to infer that the Protestants had been several times repulsed.

On February 4th we reached the Pokino's camp. He and the Kitunzi and some others had come out thus far in order to settle the fugitives in places where they might obtain food and cultivate the ground. There was one circumstance which mitigated in a great degree the sufferings of those compelled to take part in these migrations of which I am speaking, and that was, the extraordinary amount of food in the country owing to the quantity of rain which had fallen this year.*

All fear of attack was now at an end, and Walker, Smith, and I continued our journey to Mengo, which we reached on February 8th. I have not mentioned what was perhaps one of the most serious dangers which threatened us, and which, by the good hand of God upon us, we entirely escaped ; and this was an attack from the hostile Muhammedan faction, which was expected every day to appear upon the frontiers of Uganda. Our fellow-missionaries gave us a warm welcome, and we were accommodated in a house lately vacated by a chief of the French faction.

Next day we visited Captain Lugard ; but the interview was not satisfactory. I complained that we had received from him neither information nor help. He excused his action on the ground of the difficulty of his own position, but expressed sympathy with us in the loss of our goods, and promised to do all in his power to obtain compensation for us from the Company.†

* In Egypt in 1892 the Nile was unusually high.

† Captain Lugard's subsequent statements upon the action of the Church Missionary Society's Mission in reference to the question of compensation are hardly correct (*see* p. 36, vol. ii., line 4), the only action taken by the missionaries being to send home a statement of losses, leaving it with their agents to consult with the Church Missionary Society Committee whether any claim should be submitted to the Company. Captain Lugard subsequently, quite spontaneously, asked for a statement of the losses, and himself submitted them to the Directors of the Company, who entirely refused to compensate the missionaries for their personal losses. This Company had nevertheless received £16,000 from the supporters of missions to help its finances.

My communications with the Company's representative were established, from the very beginning, on an unsatisfactory basis ; but it is not unlikely that a good deal of the misunderstanding that followed arose from Lugard's theory as to the position in the country of the missionaries, and his dislike of in any way admitting them to his counsels. The reasons for this he has specifically stated. (1) He asserts that the missionaries were completely *ex-parte* advocates, and vehemently prejudiced against the opposite faction. (2) Such a course would have lent some grounds for the assertion made by the French bishop, that the Company was under the influence of the English mission. (3) He did not consider that the duties of missionaries included political action.

With regard to number one, it is obvious that the missionaries were never credited with the smallest desire of looking at the question in any but the most bigoted and illiberal manner. The Catholic Union is more just in dealing with this matter than was the Protestant Captain Lugard, for on p. 27 of " Notes on Uganda " it draws attention to the fact that there were in Uganda educated European gentlemen, missionaries of either creed, who had influence over their followers, and deprecates the fact that the reports of the Company do not show any real attempt was ever made to bring these gentlemen together under the auspices of the Company.

And with regard to the second point, Captain Lugard had no scruples of the kind when he found it convenient to officially employ the French missionaries as envoys to the king—a course of action which would have been quite unobjectionable *per se* had it not been so entirely opposed to his own views of what his duty was, and inconsistent with the somewhat narrow theories he so dogmatically lays down.

The result of this was, that I never went to Kampala Fort to discuss any matter connected with politics unless by invitation. Captain Lugard was well aware that the chiefs of both factions discussed every matter with the missionaries. I told him this in the most explicit terms, and assured him of the influence that the missionaries held. I told him that whenever he wished to see us we would most gladly place our time at his disposal, and use our influence as far as possible to further his plans. If he consistently kept us in the completest ignorance of what these plans were, it is no wonder that he wofully diminished our power of being useful to him.

CHAPTER II

ENGLISH INTERESTS AND GERMAN OFFICIALS

Kühne causes the Retirement of English Canoes—The German plays a double Game—The Reason for Bagge's Hosts hurrying his Departure—Reason for the German Officer's Position—Lugard questions us as to our Conversation with the Priests—Valuable Caravan left with the Germans—Mr. Kühne gives the Loads to irresponsible Natives—Mr. Kühne's Failure to ascertain their Bond-fides—The Company fine their own Ally—Kühne secures the complete Failure of Captain Williams' Mission—Langheld suddenly ceases to check Import of Guns—Cumulative Evidence of German Hostility.

CHAPTER II

ENGLISH INTERESTS AND GERMAN OFFICIALS

AFTER his flight from Bulinguge, Mwanga, as we have seen, made his way south in company with Monseigneur Hirth. They appear to have been pursued by Protestant canoes, and were nearly captured, until saved by M. Kühne, a German officer, who suddenly appeared on the scene as a *deus ex machina* to snatch Mwanga from the hands of the Protestants, and to cause all the canoes in the service of the English Company to retire. Mwanga's life was in no kind of danger from his pursuers, for they were most keenly anxious to catch him alive and to restore him to his kingdom. The Ba-ganda do not kill their kings. And Mwanga himself formerly, when Kiwewa was made king, was allowed to escape unscathed. It is extremely interesting to trace the action of this German non-commissioned officer all through, and to notice his attitude towards the English. According to Lugard's account he had been sent by his superior officer, Captain Langheld, with Mr. Bagge, one of the Company's agents, to see the representative of the English Company on some matters. But his whole action points to some other motive than a visit on business to the English Company—a motive which may be judged by his consistent hostility to English interests. They travelled together, Mr. Bagge in the Company's steel boat, which he commanded, and M. Kühne in canoes, with a number of soldiers. They reached the coast of Uganda at Luwambu, the straits between Sesse Island and the mainland, the very day Mwanga fled from Bulinguge.

It is to be presumed that it was on this occasion that Kühne effected the rescue of the king and Bishop Hirth, and caused "all the canoes in the service of the English Company to retire."* He was able to do this without Bagge's knowledge, since the German's canoes travelled much faster than Bagge's boat, and the Englishman was therefore far behind.

As soon as Bagge came up it was arranged that the German should land on the north-west shore of Sesse Island where the *king and French bishop now were*.† Kühne accordingly landed, but came back secretly at night, and told Bagge to return to Bukoba as fast as possible, as his life was in danger. He tells Bagge nothing, be it observed, about the presence of the French bishop, or, as far as one can gather

---

* Père Couillard, writing on February 16th, mentions Kühne's meeting with Mwanga and Monseigneur Hirth, but Lugard knows nothing of any such meeting between the two. Mr. Bagge evidently knew nothing of it, and, as Lugard's account makes it very evident, *was not told of it*.

† See the bishop's letter in *Tablet*, June 4th, 1892, stating that he had reached *Sesse* with the king.

from Lugard's account, of the king. Bagge accordingly hurried back to Bukoba, leaving Kühne behind.

At this juncture Stokes' boat happened to pass by on her way to Uganda, and the captain, seeing Kühne's German flag on Sesse, put into the island, when the boat was instantly seized by Mwanga's people. Kühne stated that he had saved it from being burnt by the king, who, by the way, had everything to lose by quarrelling with Stokes, from whom he hoped to buy ammunition. The saving of the boat for any other purpose than because the Germans happened to want it is most doubtful. At any rate, they kept it for a considerable time, and Stokes had some little difficulty in recovering it. Captain Lugard's own account of Bagge's adventure is remarkable, since it displays the completest confidence in the German, who was all the time playing a diplomatic and double game. Thus Lugard tells us that on this occasion Kühne "himself ran a considerable risk. The feeling against Europeans ran so high that he saw it was best to clear out as quickly as possible, and this even though Mwanga looks to the Germans to help him and lend him a cannon" (Diary).* Lugard evidently knew nothing of the coincidence of Mwanga's sudden hope in the Germans with his meeting Kühne.

But to continue Bagge's adventures. He reached Bukoba again on February 5th, and was warmly welcomed by the Germans. Kühne, he found, had already come in, having passed him in his swift canoes. Three days later the French bishop arrived

* "Rise of our East African Empire," vol. ii., p. 373.

From him, however, Bagge learned little. But " the Germans, on the ground of their deep distrust of the French bishop, after dinner that evening of February 8th, advised Bagge to start off at once by night, and escape, lest any harm should be done to him." *

Bagge took the advice, and left without opportunity for conversing with any of the Baganda or for his men to gossip. It is evident that Bagge could not have been in any great danger from the bishop; he was the guest of the Germans, who had a very strong fort, two machine guns, and plenty of repeating rifles. It seems strange indeed that Bagge should have been hurried off because he was in danger. The reason for his hosts hurrying his departure is probably what I have stated, that he might not hear the explanation of Mwanga's looking to the Germans to help him and lend him a cannon, or of any negotiations between the Germans on the one side, and the French bishop and king on the other. Mwanga, at this time, was at Mutatembwa's, the chief mentioned at p. 45, as an honoured guest. The Germans were hated and disliked by Mutatembwa, with whom they had lately fought. This chief had fully three thousand fighting men, but the Germans' machine gun and repeating rifles had indeed given them victory; but if Mwanga formed an alliance with him backed up with the moral support of a dozen Europeans and two thousand rifles, and reckoning Kamswaga of Koki's nearer three thousand, it might cause the utter overthrow of German influence on the Nyanza.

* " Rise of our East African Empire," vol. iv., p. 374.

No doubt this question had been carefully considered by the Germans. The whole of that western part of the Nyanza owned Mwanga as over-lord, and it was with the greatest difficulty the Germans could prevent its paying tribute. Mutatembwa, Mukotanyi, Nyalubamba, Kahigi, might all be likely to join against the hated Badaki (Germans) if Mwanga were to fight against them. It is not inconceivable that some six to ten thousand men armed with guns could have been put into the field, besides many thousands of spear-men.

It is therefore not at all unlikely that the German officers considered it to their own interest not to offend Mwanga, while they wished to keep at the same time on good terms with the English.

The fact that the question of German help was seriously considered by Mwanga's advisers gains further curious confirmation from a conversation which the English missionaries held with the French fathers during a visit which the latter paid them, and when, over a friendly cup of coffee, the events which had just taken place, and which so deeply interested us all, were discussed.

We spoke together in Swahili quite unreservedly. Both the French and English missionaries had grievances against the Company's representatives which it is needless to particularise. And both highly disapproved of the vacillation of their policy. In the course of conversation, however, the fathers astonished us by saying that Mwanga would probably go to Bukoba and offer his kingdom to the Germans. Walker said he thought these latter could not take Uganda—meaning that by the Anglo-German agreement Uganda had fallen to the English sphere. The reply given was that the Germans had one hundred and thirty magazine rifles, and that if they succeeded in taking the country the home government would applaud them. Roscoe, Walker, and I understood this as being the tenor of what was said. It appears that the father superior, Père Guillermain, has since denied that this was the sense of what was said. The Catholic Union omits, however, to supply an alternative version of what passed. I have therefore retained my own report of the conversation as I wrote it down at the time.

The visit from the French Pères took place on the 11th. The next day I went up to see Captain Lugard on the question of a mission being opened in Usoga, but did not speak of the conversation with the priests. It was Dr. Wright who happened to mention something of what had passed when he went up to Kampala to attend the wounded men. The same night a note came down from Lugard asking us to go up and explain what Dr. Wright had said. So next morning Walker, Roscoe, and I took our way to Kampala to see Captain Lugard. We said that what I have written above was to the best of our recollection what the priests had asserted, and it had caused us unfeigned astonishment. "Would I write it down?" he asked. I demurred to this; but in the end Roscoe said he had no objection to doing so. I felt it was not fair to make an official report of what was merely a friendly conversation. Lugard, however, then said that the statement had so dwindled down from what he had imagined, that it was not worth putting on paper, There was no particular harm in the statement, and perhaps not an unnatural one to make, and therefore I have little doubt in my own mind that something very similar to it was really said. Indeed, what we reported has further confirmation from Lugard himself, who describes himself as saying to Père Guillermain, " I pointed out to the father superior, in conversation, that it was unlikely that the Germans would be anxious to afford an asylum (as they seemed to take for granted) to several thousand armed men who had risen against the British." *

I must now relate another incident which has never been explained, and in which Mr. Kühne again had a prominent share. I mentioned that I left the valuable Church Missionary Society's caravan at Bukoba, under the kind care of Captain Langheld. That officer generously undertook to store the loads until I should be able to send for them. The caravan was in charge of two responsible head men, Mnubi and Hamisi, the latter a man who could both read and write in the Arabic character. The outbreak of the war, however, prevented me from sending carriers from Budu or canoes, since the whole Protestant party had left Budu, and all the coast was in the hands of the king's faction. In the first week in April, however, Captain Williams, on his return from Bukoba, mentioned to me that he had been unable to procure some cloth from the bales left there, and which I had authorised him to take, saying that the whole caravan had been removed

* " Rise of our East African Empire," vol ii., p. 393.

from Bukoba. He added that he thought it strange that we should have been able to send for the things during a time of war. Captain Lugard, in giving an account of the affair, says : " Canoes had come to Bukoba with the English flag bearing letters from Ashe, and had removed all the property there." It transpired that the letter was a forgery. The forged letter, said to have been presented by the chief in charge of the canoes, which the French faction sent to Bukoba for the things, has never been produced, and I have a shrewd suspicion never existed. Captain Langheld happened to be absent from Bukoba at the time, leaving Mr. Kühne in charge of the station. When these canoes arrived Mr. Kühne knew all about the war, and that the whole of Budu was in the hands of the Roman Catholics, that it was so unsafe for the English faction to appear at Bukoba, that Mr. Bagge had been advised to fly at midnight to escape the French bishop. And yet we are told that Mr. Kühne believed a number of canoes of the English faction dare venture into Bukoba, which was completely cut off by the Catholic faction, and this, moreover, at the very time when the dreaded bishop was actually at that place !

It is, I may mention, quite an unprecedented thing for a European in Africa to deliver up property to a native without a written order from the persons responsible for it. But it is said there was a letter from *me*, which, indeed, proved to be a forgery ; but Mr. Kühne *believed me to be dead*, and had actually sent the report of my death to Mr. Muxworthy, and the report was duly telegraphed home, and appeared in the papers. But even granting that there was some kind of letter, could not Mr. Kühne have ascertained the *bonâ fides* of the persons coming with the canoes, by asking Monseigneur Hirth whether they were people of the English or French faction ; for surely had he done so, the French bishop and the French *père*, his companion, who were sojourning in the fort, could most easily have enlightened him. With the exception of ten loads of heavy iron goods, Mr. Kühne handed over to these irresponsible natives of the French faction the whole of the valuable property, which was immediately taken into Budu, and looted in the presence of the French fathers, one of whom was called by Mwanga to explain what certain of the chemicals contained in a box of medicines were. It must, however, be borne in mind that there was war between the factions, and much of the French priests' property had been looted by the Protestants ; and though never in the presence of English missionaries, yet in expeditions under the guidance of English military officers. As soon as I heard of the robbery I at once wrote to Captain Langheld ; but he had not yet returned to Bukoba, and Dr. Stuhlmann replied to my letter. But he also had not been at Bukoba at the time of the robbery, and Mr. Kühne, the person who had placed the property in the hands of the fraudulent natives, had left for the coast. Captain Langheld subsequently wrote to me on the subject from Berlin,* calling the incident a dark adventure, and saying he had given my letter to the German

* Letter dated from Berlin, October 18th, 1892, *Brunken Allu*, No. 40.

Foreign Office. I myself laid the matter before our own Consul, but I have not heard the final result of the inquiries which no doubt were set on foot.

Captain Lugard promised to look into the matter, but kept putting it off until he left for the coast. He has curiously blundered in speaking of the affair by saying that the mission claimed £2,000 from the Company for this robbery, and that I called upon him to exact reprisals from the Roman Catholics. I merely asked that he would obtain some restitution or compensation from the chiefs who had received the property. The Company admitted that what I asked was fair and right, for they promised to make Mwanga pay £200 worth of ivory for his share in the business; but this only when Mwanga had joined the English faction and become their own ally! And I believe this ivory was actually paid; but whether the Church Missionary Society has yet received the amount I do not know.

The two head men, Mnubi and Hamisi, were dismissed by the Germans, who told them that I was dead, and a Snider rifle which belonged to the Church Missionary Society, and which Mnubi was carrying, was rendered useless by having the firing pin extracted. These men were not sent on to Uganda to give an account of the goods with which they had been entrusted, and I never saw them again.

We now come to the last occasion on which Mr. Kühne, the German official, figures in connection with English affairs. Captain Williams had been sent by Lugard to Bukoba to endeavour to prevail upon the Germans to make the French priests at Bukumbi hand over Mwanga's nephews and Kalema's children, in order that if Mwanga remained obdurate Lugard might place one of Kalema's boys upon the throne. The Germans were most polite, and promised to do all in their power to promote his interests. The Catholic Union (" Notes on Uganda," p. 102) relates how they carried this out. Here is Père Hauttecoeur's account : " Captain Williams reached Bukumbi on March 23rd ; and having produced authority from M. Langheld (the German Administrator), proceeded to endeavour to persuade the widows of Karema and Kiwewa and their infants to leave this Catholic mission. Mr. Kühne, who was present, interpreted M. Langheld's order (sanctioning their departure) only to apply if the women showed a desire to comply with Captain Williams' request ; but as they expressed the greatest repugnance to be placed under his protection, he was obliged to go away without the princes, and his mission was a complete failure." Thus we have the young German, Sergeant Kühne, appearing for the last time in his favourite character of *deus ex machina* to thwart English and to serve French interests. It is a curious coincidence that after his secret visit to Sesse, whither Monseigneur Hirth had come, he is always found actively hostile to English interests ; but in such a manner as entirely to blind Captain Lugard and Captain Williams to his real attitude.

It must be remembered that Monseigneur Hirth was a German subject, and therefore had his nationality in his favour in winning the good offices of the young soldier-printer. Poor young Kühne, as I mentioned, was afterwards killed, so that he, too, has carried to his grave whatever he might have been able to tell of these matters.

The facts here mentioned are valuable, since they are chiefly gleaned from Lugard's and the priests' accounts, who seem quite unconscious of their bearing ; in fact, so little did Lugard suspect any hostility to his plans from the Germans, that he writes as follows : " On April 14th Williams returned, accompanied by the German official Captain Langheld, whose courtesy and kindness nothing could exceed. He had been to the south of the Lake," etc.

We now come to another very significant piece of news brought to Uganda on this occasion by Captain Williams. Lugard writes : * " Williams brought news that the Germans, finding that arms and powder were pouring in from the west, through the Congo State, had withdrawn their prohibition of the import of munitions, except so far as breech-loading arms and ammunition were concerned, and that Langheld could no longer check the import of guns and powder to Uganda, as he had hitherto so kindly exerted himself to do. This news, together with reports brought me by the men who had conveyed my mails, that powder was already coming in, and being bought by the French faction, was of very serious importance." The coincidence that Langheld should suddenly find himself unable to stop the import of guns and powder to Uganda at this particular juncture was certainly very strange.

* " Rise of our East African Empire " p. 443, vol. ii.

The various circumstances already mentioned, though no single one of them affords conclusive evidence of hostility on the part of the German officials, yet taken together, form a mass of cumulative evidence of a strong kind, which justifies the suspicion that such hostility really existed. But I must leave the reader to judge for himself whether the grounds stated are a sufficient justification for suspecting opposition to English interests on the part of German officials.

CHAPTER III

THE KING'S RETURN

Lugard resumes his First Position—Lugard at Loggerheads with the Protestant Chiefs—Good Character of the Chiefs of the English Faction—The Whereabouts of the Factions—The Company and the French Priests—Arguments that appealed to Mwanga—Attack on Sesse—Lugard and Williams distrust their Supporters—The Vacant Chieftainships are filled up—Negotiations for Mwanga's Return—A hasty Plan of Escape—The King running away—Mwanga returns once more to Mengo—English Influence an established Fact.

CHAPTER III

THE KING'S RETURN

MWANGA having again made his escape, negotiations for his return were at once set on foot. The representatives of the Imperial Company do not seem to have quite decided what their exact position was. Lugard had made a treaty with the king and chiefs, which, he believed, gave him an acknowledged and legal status in the country, and by which Mwanga accepted the suzerainty of the Imperial Chartered Company. Yet the king and certain of the chiefs had set aside the treaty, and refused its obligations in such a manner as even to engage in warlike operations against the Company. Lugard, in consequence, had been compelled to drive out the disloyal king and his rebellious chiefs, with the assistance of the chiefs who remained loyal to the terms of the treaty and to the Imperial Company. This appears to have been the position that Lugard had taken up, when he armed the chiefs who were loyal to the treaty.

But, as we have seen, he suddenly receded from this position, and implored the disloyal king and rebel chiefs to return, and practically asked them to forgive him for

his action in driving them out. It was here that
Lugard betrayed an obvious weakness, with, as we have
seen, the worst results. His action amounted to the
virtual confession that he had been wrong, an admission that those who guided the French faction
were not slow to take advantage of, and the king and
" French " chiefs then posed as persons who had
suffered wrong at Lugard's hands, and who smarted
under it. Hence they would not come to terms with
him unless he paid compensation.

Then we had Bulinguge, when Lugard resumed his
first position of a British representative, whose treaty
rights had been outraged by a disloyal king and rebel
chiefs. The loyal chiefs were naturally averse to the
terms which offered to restore to their former positions
the offending king and chiefs, without their yielding
one jot or tittle of the matter in dispute, since, it might
be presumed, a further course of aggression would be
put in operation against the loyal English faction.

Mwanga's household and large numbers of captives
had been taken on the island. The king's household was sent to Mengo, and a responsible chief,
Mulamba, was appointed to guard them. The other
prisoners were set free, but I have no doubt some of
the rabble who had landed on the island carried off a
number of the French faction as slaves. This was one
of the most deplorable features of the fighting, that it
let loose mobs of people on both sides who had no
religion whatever, and who rejoiced in anarchy and
war, which meant ample opportunity to plunder.

I think the numbers said to have been enslaved were

grossly exaggerated on both sides. But that certain of the French faction did sell a number of captives from Protestant Budu for the gunpowder which their Baziba neighbours were vending with the connivance of Germany, I have no doubt. And though I never heard—as it was not likely I should—that the rabble of the Protestant faction had enslaved people of the other faction, it is probable in the highest degree that they did so.

Mwanga had continued his journey southward until he came to Mutatembwa's, on the other side of the Kagera River, my visit to whom I have described. Mutatembwa received him and his following (which was very numerous) with all hospitality.

Lugard, meanwhile, had come to loggerheads with the Protestant chiefs, who had stood by him. He had showed cynical indifference to them by his intention of putting back into power their enemies, with whom he had just fought, and by so doing proved that he knew them to be the aggressors in the late war. The foremost of these chiefs were Apolo Kagwa the Katikiro, or Prime Minister ; Zakaria Kizito ; Sebwato Nikodemo ; Waswa the Mukwenda ; Paulo Bakunga the Kitunzi ; Henry Wright Duta Kitakule ; Samwili Naganafa (the envoy who had been sent to Zanzibar). Tomas Semfuma ; Tomasi Mukisi ; Wakirenzi the Mulondo ; Mika Sematimba ; Mattayo ; Sila ; Stefano ; Yosua, the Mugema ; and others. Not a few of these were the very highest type of this nation, and, I venture to assert, were consistent Christian men. The praises of some of them have been sounded in turn by every

European who has had any dealings with them. Such sweeping statements as that they were a parcel of liars and traitors will not be hastily accepted by thoughtful persons. It will not do to give them their full mead of praise in one place and in another to blacken them, when they are opposing some view the writer objects to. They were intelligent men, naturally greatly dependent for knowledge of European affairs upon the English missionaries, as the French converts were dependent on the priests.

Slanders have been published on these men, I regret to say, bearing the name of Monseigneur Hirth, which, I feel sure, in his cooler moments he would never have written—slanders which were written in ignorance of the men whose characters he traduced. Among the Roman Catholic converts were men also of good report, some few of whom I had the pleasure of knowing a good deal of. But of these men mentioned above, I will ask the reader to believe that some were actuated by noble motives, and had far other views than merely greedy desire of power and self-aggrandisement, and that all were respectable men, who were shrewd enough to see that loyalty to the English Company was not only good for the country at large, but wholly to their own private interests. They were, however, jealous of making Captain Lugard or any one else an absolute autocrat. I believe that a great deal of the influence with them possessed by the missionaries lay in the fact that the latter never attempted to exert any secular authority over them, nor even ventured to advise them, unless they came to seek counsel, which they frequently did. I was most careful to tell Captain Lugard this fact, and also to inform him that I felt it within the right of a missionary to advise any one or every one who chose to ask his advice. This advice, however much or little it was worth, was open to him as to any one else. Captain Lugard himself has shown how inextricably politics and religion were mixed up, and his asking, or expecting, the missionaries to take no part in politics was much the same as asking them to take no part in religion. These men I have mentioned above were in constant daily communication with the missionaries. Not a few of them were being prepared for Holy Orders. All were engaged in learning and teaching, so that naturally the serious condition of the country could hardly fail to be discussed.

The war had left the Protestants masters of the whole of Uganda except the province of Budu, south of the Katonga River, which was held by the king and rebel chiefs. A freebooter, who was a daring elephant hunter named Namutegere, had obtained a considerable following in Chagwe, the province bordering on the Nile, but was never a very serious menace to the peace of the country. The Muhammedans were in the country lying between Lugard's line of forts and the frontier of Uganda, Bulemezi and Singo being the provinces nearest the place where they were concentrated. It was now arranged that Waswa, the chief of Singo, who with his fighting men had reached Mengo the day after the fight, and too late to take part in it,* should return to guard

* Many important chiefs of the English faction were absent from Mengo when the Roman Catholic attack was made.

his frontier, and that another force under Mugema Joshua should attack the Abanywa-enjai or bhang-smokers under Namutegere. Yosua did so, and succeeded in dispersing them.

The Protestant chiefs now wrote begging Mwanga to return, sending their letters by a man named Nzitiza, who duly delivered them to the king at Mutatembwa's. Meanwhile reports came in that the French faction were concentrating in force on the Budu side of the Katonga River, while another band was preparing to attack the island of Namuimba, a chief of the English faction. The Company, it might be supposed, had by this time learned a lesson as to the real attitude of the French priests. The bishop, according to their account of the matter, had on the last occasion, so far from urging Mwaga to return, counselled him to refuse to do so. But the Company's representative, I understand, on this occasion accepted the proposal of the priests that they should be the bearers of messages to Mwanga. The matter is important, and is dealt with on p. 285, vol. ii., of the " Rise of our East African Empire." Here Lugard speaks of the proposed Embassy as merely a suggestion. The fathers, however, seemed to think the matter had been finally arranged, and actually set about making ready for the journey, which they were to take the day after the affair (as they supposed) was settled. But when Captain Lugard consulted the Protestant chiefs they brought grave reasons against employing the priests as intermediaries They knew Mwanga well, and they knew best how to get hold of him.

They had seen that Mwanga had found the dictation of the priests and "French" party very irksome, and was like a man carrying a heavy weight, who, though he cannot get rid of it, likes to shift it from shoulder to shoulder. And Mwanga was now desirous of a change of masters. The English, he knew, had control of Zanzibar, and might really be the stronger power, and might also stay in Uganda, as the Company's representatives assured him they would ; but if English control were withdrawn he could easily return again to the French faction. The Protestants knew also that they could put the screw on Mwanga by threatening to put his uncle, the Muhammedan Embogo, on the throne. But besides this they had other arguments, and could urge what Mwanga was well aware of, that the French faction had his two nephews in their hands, whom they might easily put on the throne in case of their growing weary of him ; his death might also be compassed. And Mwanga knew that African kings are sometimes poisoned, though usually they are said to die of small-pox. The Protestants were able to show Lugard that there was every likelihood of securing Mwanga, and this, taken with the continued hostility of the Roman Catholic faction—the threatened attack on Namuimba's Island had just been reported—and the purport of what our English missionaries understood to be the remarks of the French *pères apropos* of German aid for Mwanga, were considerations which caused Lugard to change his mind about sending to ask Mwanga to come to terms, and made him hold to the demand that until the king was safe back in Mengo he would discuss no terms with the hostile party.

Lugard sent Captain Williams with eighty men and a Maxim gun and six hundred Ba-ganda in canoes to occupy Sesse. The use of these auxiliaries without discipline and with arms in their hands could only have one result; and there is little doubt that they would have committed much violence had it not been that most of the people in Sesse cleared out. As it was, the chiefs, Semugala and Sewaya, were driven out, and a large number of cattle were looted—I have mentioned the fact that the plague had not reached the islands in the Nyanza—and no doubt also a quantity of stores.

Nikodemo had been sent overland towards the frontier of Budu with six hundred guns. Captain Williams having now occupied Sesse, desired to advance into Budu and endeavour to seize the king. But the Mudima and Wakibi, two fighting chiefs who were with him, absolutely refused. Mulondo, the native commander, apparently acquiesced in Captain Williams' wish, but there is little doubt that he felt they were too weak for the effort. If, as they feared, Mwanga had obtained the help of the Germans, or even of Koki and Mutatembwa, they, with their twelve hundred guns, could do very little. If they were to carry the war into Budu it must be with an expedition organised on a much larger scale than the present. They, therefore, not unwisely returned to Mengo, much to the disgust of Captain Williams, who was ready for any amount of fighting.

Captain Williams then went to Bukoba, and from thence to Bukumbi, on what, as we have seen, was an utterly futile mission, since the Germans were quietly determined that he should not, at this particular juncture of affairs, secure the two young nephews of Mwanga. Meanwhile Nzitiza had returned from Mwanga, bringing a request that Namagambe and Nabisubi, two of his female favourites, should be sent to him. These ladies were duly despatched to the king with instructions to assure him how earnestly the English faction and the Company's officers desired his return. Captain Lugard at this time tells us that he and Williams had lost confidence in the English faction, and made up their minds that they were not to be relied upon,* though he does not state why. Possibly the semi-independent position they took up, and which the Company's own action had made almost inevitable, was distasteful to the officers in command at Kampala.

Meanwhile, at Mwanga's orders, the people of Uvuma, it is said, prepared to attack Muwambi, the chief whose being attacked by Mwanga's faction had led to Bulinguge. Luba, who had imprisoned Bishop Hannington, had much influence with the Bavuma Islanders, and Mwanga persuaded Luba, as his own advisers were always assuring him, that the English meant to take vengeance for Hannington's murder by killing the King of Uganda and Luba of Busoga. The Bavuma, therefore, as has been stated, attacked Muwambi, and were met by a strong force of the English faction, who appear to have had a hundred

* " Rise of our East African Empire," vol. ii., p. 381.

rifles, and were able to repulse the attacking party, and inflicted upon them the loss of about one hundred men."*

To come back now to the question of Mwanga's restoration. The embassy of the ladies, Namagambe and Nabisubi, was much more successful than that of Monseigneur Hirth had proved; and the king sent his man Senkoma, on March 5th, to say he was anxious to return. The country was meanwhile in a state of disorganisation; for no one cared to cultivate what they felt they might be turned out of next day. Lugard had no other course open to him but to fill up the vacant chieftainship provisionally. They were already occupied, and Lugard felt it to be a politic measure to ratify the appointments—his so doing gave him a status in the country that nothing else could have given—so on March 12th the vacant offices, with the consent of the Imperial British East Africa Company's officer, were duly filled up with the loyal English chiefs. The province of Kyagwe, which was abandoned by the French faction, was given to Nikodemo, who had lost Budu, and who now became the Sekibobo. The faithful Zakaria became Kangao, chief of Bulemezi, while Paulo became Kago, and the great fighting chief Mulondo became Kimbugwe. It must be remembered that the Protestants before the war held large numbers of minor chieftainships in these provinces, so that these appointments did not mean that they had gained some enormous advantage. They had entirely lost the

* This is extracted from "The Wars of the Ba-ganda." I never heard particulars of it while in Uganda.

whole of their chieftainships in the great province of Budu, which is the richest part of Uganda.

Mwanga had now been absent from his capital forty-nine days, when he sent Mugwanya, the former Kimbugwe, a clever man, though entirely in the hands of the priests, to open negotiations with the Company. With him came Seboa, the former Sekibobo, a really nice man, though a little too fond of his banana cider —a failing which, though it could not be called a monopoly of either faction, was, on the whole, creditably absent from the chiefs of both parties. Mugwanya and Seboa then said, "Let the land be divided, and we will restore the king to Mengo." The Protestant chiefs were willing to agree, but Lugard remained firm in his decision that before he would come to any terms the king must be given up. He had now serious thoughts of accepting Embogo, the leader of the Muhammedan faction, as king.

It was finally arranged that Seboa should return to Mwanga, while Mugwanya should remain behind. Mugwanya was easily the foremost man of the "French" faction. I suppose he remained as a guarantee of the good faith of his party. The "English" chiefs selected two of their number, Stefano Kalibwani and Bartolomayo Musoke, to accompany Seboa back to Mwanga. The Protestants were wise in sending two of their number who had acquired more influence over Mwanga than any other of their party. Stefano especially, who had all his wits about him, seems to have acquired an extraordinary hold over the weak king.

These three made their way to the king; and the two "English" envoys found that Mwanga was being watched, as a mouse is watched by a cat, by his Roman Catholic subjects, who were now really his gaolers. The truth is that the king was thoroughly sick of being a fugitive in his own kingdom, and had a growing distrust of the French bishop. He had, moreover, a wholesome horror of the deadly music of the Maxim gun, which had deprived him of any little courage which he remained possessed of. But no chance, for a time, did Stefano obtain of a private word with the king. It had been arranged that Mwanga should come to the frontier of Budu, and that from there envoys should be sent to make some definite arrangement as to the division of the country before the king should be given up.

At last Stefano one evening managed to have a few moments with Mwanga in a banana grove, and a hasty plan of escape was arranged. The king so managed it that Stefano, Bartolomayo, and Lutaya a favourite Muhammedan, and one or two of his trusted pages, should be together in the same canoe, and on the day that they neared the last camp from where the negotiations were to take place, the king's flight was accomplished. On this very day, March 29th, the French *pères*, Brard and Roche, actually arrived at Mengo, in order, it was said, to arrange the terms of peace; but Lugard again refused to enter into any discussion before the arrival of the king himself.

But to return to the seafarers on the Nyanza. The canoes, as evening drew on, were slowly making their way to the last camping ground in Budu, when the king, whose skill with the paddle was well known, said he would take the place of the Mugoba, the man who sits at the pointed stern of the canoe, and who, by placing his paddle against the boat, can thus use it as a rudder, and can vary the angle at which he holds it, so as to alter the course of the canoe. The king gradually kept the boat more and more out to sea. It was a grand canoe, and the men very soon saw what was in the wind. The other canoes had meanwhile headed in for shore, except one, which was occupied by some of the chiefs, who were jealously watching the king. The canoe swept on, its consort following at racing speed. Then at last all reserve was flung aside, and it was evident the king was running away. But the race was not for long. The other canoes were far behind, and the king and his guards were armed with rifles, even had the French chiefs been successful in overhauling the flying canoe; and very soon the baffled chiefs gave the word to 'bout boat, and sadly they rowed ashore with the disheartening news that Mwanga had at last given them the slip. The king held on, but with many misgivings, for he was haunted by the ever-present fear that the English, when once they had him in their power, would avenge on him the death of Bishop Hannington. I did not realise till some time afterwards how strongly that terror influenced him, nor how his evil deed seemed always to be meeting him and crying vengeance. I do not think there was the least touch of remorse much less repentance. He had ordered the murder with the idea that he was putting out of the way his country's enemy. The fear was simply craven dread of punishment. Early on March 30th news came that the king was rapidly journeying towards Mengo, and then was heard a sound that had not echoed in Uganda for sixty-one days. The great drums boomed out the king's beat without ceasing from morning till night, that note which told that there was once more a king in Uganda. Towards evening Stefano arrived at Kampala to say the king was close at hand, and in great fear. Lugard sent one of his own men to convey polite messages, and as the sun went down Mwanga appeared on Mengo Hill once more. The Katikiro Apolo was there to welcome him, and the king caught him in his arms, and embraced him in Uganda fashion. Mwanga first came to the Wankaki (great gate of his own enclosure), and then, as Lugard had requested, he made his way to Kampala Fort. The captain came out on a horse to meet him. Mwanga was dressed in a loin cloth and dirty white coat, a piece of calico was wound round his head as a turban. Weary, travel stained, dirty, and unshorn, he presented a very different appearance from the sleek and smooth Kabaka who had left Mengo some two months before.

Mwanga was being carried on the shoulders of one of his men. Lugard advanced to meet him, and the two shook hands over the heads of the people, and then, followed by a surging crowd who had assembled to welcome back their king, the procession slowly wound its way to Kampala. The Sudanese soldiers were drawn up ready; and as the king and representative of England passed through the ranks they presented arms. Lugard led the king into his house, and gave him a little present, and then the king returned once more to Mengo after his third flight from that place. The Company's flag at last floated over the king's enclosure as well as over that of the chief minister, and English influence was an established fact in Uganda.

CHAPTER IV

THE MUHAMMEDAN QUESTION

Muhammedanism—Reasons for fighting with Arabs not Religious—Unwisdom of bringing into Uganda organised Fanatics—Arrival of important Muhammedan Chiefs—Diplomatising with the Muhammedans—Understanding between Muhammedan Ba-ganda and Sudanese—Death of de Winton—A disastrous Blunder—Position of the Muhammedans an Anomaly—Two Sultans in Uganda.

CHAPTER IV

THE MUHAMMEDAN QUESTION

AS soon as Mwanga returned Captain Lugard set himself to endeavour to solve the great question of how to deal with the Muhammedan faction. The number of true believers or of those who had some intelligent understanding of the religion of Islam was exceedingly limited. The great mass of Muhammedan adherents consisted of people who had somehow or other been drawn into that faction from far other than religious motives. As we have seen in the case of the Roman Catholics (or Bafransa French) and Protestants (or Bangereza English), a great deal of the differences were political. Religion had supplied a good rallying or party cry. One can understand how a cry was a political necessity from the fact that Namutegere, the freebooter, called his followers the " Smokers of Bhang." His people might smoke the bhang forbidden by the other religious sects, and drink the banana cider refused by the Muhammedans, and marry many women disallowed by the Christians. Moreover, Muhammedanism was a religion which granted much and demanded little. The outward mark gave its votaries whereof to glory in the flesh. A religion which had its ordinances, washings, prayers ; and above all that short and musical formula, " La illāha ill' Allah Muhammedu rasul Allah " (" God is God, and Muhammed is His prophet "). The stereotyped confession of the faith, which supplied a noble rallying cry, a splendid battle shout. A religion which reckoned among its votaries numbers of constant martyrs, and a glorious roll of devoted warriors, the heroes of some of the most brilliant battlefields the world has ever seen. Here was a religion which offered a magnificent ground on which to form a strong political party. Blind indeed must the man be who does not see clearly the tremendous power of the organisation which Muhammed called into existence—a glorious truth linked to a daring lie ; a heresy armed with weapons forged in the armouries of God ; a power which has shaken the world to its centre, and which, before the callous Christians of the West had awakened to the fact that there was a continent waiting for Christ, had darkened half Africa with its baleful shadow, and converted millions to its cynical creed. Muhammedanism had become a political power in Uganda, and as such could boast a strong organisation well abreast of the other factions, and stronger possibly than either of them singly. True, Christianity calm in the possession of the Light of the World, will patiently await its final triumph. But Muhammedanism will not brook any rival religion, and therefore must either conquer or be strongly held down. It must of necessity try conclusions with the sword. It takes the sword, and must either triumph or perish with the sword.

The policy that the Imperial British East Africa Company's representative attempted to carry out in the present instance could only end in disastrous failure. His attitude hitherto in Africa had always been one of strenuous hostility to Arab influence. He had fought with the Arabs for four years on Nyassa with varying success, and had been on one occasion seriously wounded by them. Now no one for a moment could suspect Captain Lugard of being a fanatical bigot, who was fighting against the *religion* which certain people held. He was not fighting Arabs because they were followers of the prophet, but because they were bidding politically for the region of Africa, which he had been sent to secure. But we find him in Uganda reversing his own policy, and instead of endeavouring to crush the political organisation which was at deadly enmity to English influence we find him taking the strongest means at his disposal to consolidate it and to give it an organised position in the country. His defence of his action on the ground of his religious toleration does not touch the question. No one in Uganda objected to the repatriation of the Muhammedans when they came back in a private capacity as natives of the country; no one objected to their having their mosques and attending them; but many saw that to introduce them as a strongly equipped political organisation was a proceeding which could only end in disaster.

It was strange that the broad general question of the march of Islam in Africa did not arrest the attention of the Imperial Company's representative, that he did not see that the inevitable tendency must be for the members of a common religion, when their worldly interests also appear to be identical, sooner or later to coalesce together in political action. A Madagascar waiting boy, a Muhammedan, in Zanzibar, speaking of the high-handed action of the Germans and of their insolent contempt for the people whose country they were occupying, confidently expressed the hope that his co-religionists throughout the world would come to the help of Zanzibar—an idea though not feasible as things were, yet not without reason. Islam is somewhat on the wane in Europe; but in Africa it has not yet been discounted. And therefore one must condemn the policy of bringing into Uganda an organised host of ignorant fanatics, whose folly must sooner or later lead to violence, and when once blood is shed—the sacred blood of the followers of the prophet—however loyal some may desire to be, or however much it is to the pecuniary interest of others, the likelihood of their joining hands with their co-religionists against the "hated Kafir" (infidel) is too great to be lightly risked.

Early in March of this year, while the question of Mwanga's return was still a subject of negotiation, two messengers arrived from the Muhammedans, Kajubi and Nanyumba, saying the Muhammedans desired to return to Uganda. Lugard had openly discussed the question of accepting Embogo as king of the whole country. The Muhammedans had received news of this, and thereupon hastily gathered up their belongings, and moved towards the province of Singo, on the frontier of Uganda, of which district the Mukwenda is chief. They then sent messengers to Waswa, the Mukwenda, a capable man in his way, who had visited Zanzibar in former days, to inform him that the whole Muhammedan faction was on its way to Uganda. Waswa sent back to say they must not advance until their messengers had been sent on to Mengo. They therefore agreed to remain, while their envoys, Kajubi and Nanyumba, should proceed to the capital to find out how matters really stood. On their arrival at Kampala Lugard received them, and temporised with them, in order to gain delay, alleging that he must have some of the most responsible of their faction to confer with. But when these eventually arrived, appropriately enough on April 1st, they found that Mwanga was back again once more. He had come two days previously, and therefore all their hopes of seeing Embogo Sultan of Uganda were somewhat rudely dispelled.

The second envoys from the Muhammedans who had now come were considerable chiefs, Nabugo and Magato. They stated plainly that they had come to Uganda, bringing Embogo with them, on the clear understanding, as they considered it, that Embogo should be made king in place of Mwanga.

Lugard explained that he had replaced Mwanga because he was the rightful king, and the only surviving son of Mutesa; and said that failing Mwanga Kalema's son, and not Embogo, would be heir; that Mwanga's past history did not indeed warrant their placing great confidence in him; but it was the duty of the British Resident to see that justice was done, and that about that they need have no fear! The envoys replied that they fully trusted Lugard; that from all sides they had heard confirmation of the Company's impartiality and justice!* Such statements on either side meant nothing, as both sides very well knew. The Muhammedans knew very well that the Englishman was diplomatising with them; while it is to be presumed Lugard could not have believed that the envoys accepted as gospel all he said. The Muhammedans believed, and rightly believed, that the whole question with Lugard was one of expediency rather than of abstract justice; for Lugard had stated again and again to the Protestants, and to the French fathers, and to the king and Roman Catholic chiefs in his letters, that if the Muhammedans came in force with their king, and Mwanga either could not or would not return, then he must accept Embogo; and the Muhammedans, hearing of this, had actually brought Embogo to the frontier of Uganda.† Hence Lugard's saying now that he restored Mwanga because he was rightful king was, as his own words proved, merely a diplomatic ruse.

But, it may be asked, why then did the Muhammedans, almost immediately afterwards, accept his terms, and eventually hand over their Sultan Embogo? The answer is that they must have had an understanding with the Sudanese. That some such understanding existed becomes more and more undeniable the more

* "Rise of our East African Empire," vol. ii., p 437.
† *Ibid.*, p. 383.

we study the evidence at our disposal. There appears to be an axiom current in many quarters that the evidence of a black man, however respectable he may be, is absolutely unreliable ; but fortunately we have testimony of white men which leads to the strongest presumption that an understanding had already been come to between the Sudanese and Muhammedan Baganda.

As early as 1891 vague reports had reached Lugard that the Muhammedan Ba-ganda had tried to tempt the Sudanese to coalesce with them as being their co-religionists ;* but at the beginning of 1892 things had taken more shape, for early this year Lugard sent urgent messages to the Sudanese to order them to be ready with a powerful fighting force, to watch the Muhammedans ; and if they saw they were advancing into Uganda to attack them in the rear. On March 26th he received a letter from young Mr. de Winton to say *he had not got the force together to wait on the flank of the Muhammedans, as Lugard had directed him.* The Sudanese, it will be remembered, were left to raid and ravage King Kabarega of Unyoro on the ground that he had given countenance and help to the Muhammedan Ba-ganda. On March 9th news reached Lugard that the *Muhammedan Ba-ganda had finally broken with Kabarega*, and had declined to fight against their co-religionists, the Sudanese. Kabarega's people therefore attacked the Sudanese without their Uganda allies, and received a severe defeat at their hands. Then the Muhammedan Ba-ganda turned round on Kabarega,

* " Rise of our East African Empire," vol. ii., p. 381.

seized large numbers of the people of Unyoro, and plundered and looted the country before leaving it on the way to Uganda.* Thus it will be seen that Lugard's order to the Sudanese to check the Muhammedan advance on Uganda was disregarded, while we now find the Muhammedan Ba-ganda fighting on the same side as the Sudanese against their old ally Kabarega. This, in my mind, is convincing and overwhelming testimony to the categorical statements of natives that there did exist a complete understanding between the Sudanese garrisons and the Muhammedan Ba-ganda.

To make this more clear than ever is the fact that the Muhammedans had written to young Mr. de Winton begging him in the most friendly manner to come to their camp, and that he actually did so, accompanied, or rather carried, by the Sudanese themselves—a clever policy, which placed an important Englishman as a helpless prisoner in the hands of that faction whose one aim was to obtain a firm foothold in Uganda, in order to carry out further schemes as occasion might offer. De Winton died on March 20th, and thus passed out of the hands of the faction hostile to English rule. With him died out the last spark of light in Toro. And Kasagama and his unhappy Katikiro now felt the weight of the fell Sudanese, who, armed as they were with Remington rifles, were the real masters of the country. The horrors and atrocities which they then perpetrated upon the people of Toro and the natives of Unyoro is one

* "Rise of our East African Empire," vol. ii, p. 400.

of the darkest pages of the book of Africa's story, that roll written within and without with lamentation and mourning and woe.

However, the negotiations proceeded, and Lugard asked the Muhammedan envoys what they would be satisfied with; and it was finally arranged that they should receive the three provinces of Kitunzi, Katambala, and Kasuju. This was done against the strong remonstrances of the chiefs and king, who, according to Captain Lugard, would listen to neither justice, fair play, nor common sense. In other words, they could not adopt his views since his arguments did not convince them, though they gave way to the vehemence he displayed. It was then settled that Lugard should go himself, in order to arrange the matter of Embogo's return.

There are very few passages of African history more interesting than Captain Lugard's fine description of his interview with Embogo, the Muhammedan Sultan, and of the manner in which the various difficulties were overcome. There is little doubt that the presence of Selim Bey, and the advantage Lugard possessed in having a faithful Muhammedan adherent in Duala, made it possible for him actually to return with Embogo and his Muhammedan adherents to Kampala. It was a brilliant feat, and Captain Lugard's fellow-countrymen might well be proud of the courage and resource he had displayed; but viewed in its merely political light it was a disastrous blunder.

First of all, it meant the eviction from their homes and exodus from their province of a large number of persons who had settled in the three districts now handed over to the Muhammedans, and who had built houses and cultivated land. They had to leave everything, and fly for their lives before this marauding host of fanatical freebooters, suddenly introduced into their country.

Secondly, these Muhammedans came back to Uganda in the proud position of those who were conferring a favour upon the patient British Resident, who had come himself to invite, nay, to implore their return, and who had, moreover, bribed them by yielding up to them a large territory.

Thus this Muhammedan faction, which had been driven out of the country when it came to a matter of fighting, now returned with all the arrogance and pride which one may imagine was the bearing of the followers of the first conquering Caliphs.

Their position in Uganda was an anomaly. They were not the conquerors, as are the Muhammedans in Turkish dependencies; nor the members of a vanquished race, as in India.

Their entrance into Uganda meant a new era of crime, while it was evident to all observers that Lugard's settlement was merely the calling of an armed truce. Outwardly it looked well to see Mwanga and Embogo embrace, and for the moment appear as if the Muhammedan Sultan recognised his weak nephew as his king and superior. Nothing, moreover, was further from the proud hearts of these haughty followers of the prophet. They loathed their lawful king, and studiously kept away from him, and very soon there were two Barazas held—one of Sultan Mwanga's on Mengo, the other of Sultan Embogo's at the base of Kampala Hill, and under the shadow of Kampala Fort, garrisoned as it was with Muhammedan Sudanese soldiers.

CHAPTER V

THE RAILWAY SURVEY

A sleeping Man carried off by a Leopard—Discovering the Dead Body of a Companion—Steady Advance of Missionary Work—Earnest Desire of Ba-ganda to obtain Books—Arrival of the Railway Survey—Regret of all at Lugard's Departure—Departure of Walker.

CHAPTER V

THE RAILWAY SURVEY

WHILE the state of the country was, as may be imagined, the all-absorbing interest, sometimes a diversion from politics would occur in the excitement of a leopard hunt.

The place where Walker and I were established was about half a mile away from the quarters of the other missionaries, and facing the large house which Walker and I occupied was a long, low, square-built hut, divided into compartments, in one of which our boys slept, the other being occupied by some goats. One night a leopard broke through the reed-built wall of the house, and carried off a fine goat, though providentially the boys escaped, a good fortune which by no means always attended human sleepers on the occasion of a leopard's visit. At the very same time another leopard paid a visit to the house of the other missionaries, and carried off a large native dog which belonged to one of them. Next day a grand hunt was announced by the Katikiro, and all the chiefs beat their drums and collected their fighting men to seek the leopards. They arrived only with sticks and spears, no guns being allowed. The warriors now formed a vast circle, and began beating inwards and advancing towards the centre. Two fine leopards were eventually found at the base of Namirembe Hill and at the foot of Pilkington's Garden. The partly devoured bodies of the dog and goat were discovered; the leopards were lurking hard by. They were soon despatched by the yelling mob without doing more damage than inflicting a scratch or two on the more daring. The failure of any chief to attend a leopard hunt is very severely visited, and a heavy fine is usually inflicted upon an absentee.

Some time afterwards an incident happened with a more terrible ending. One of our native teachers who is now ordained, Jonathan Kaidzi, came to me in the greatest grief and even in tears, and told me the following story. The night before his only brother, he said, had been carried off bodily by a leopard. It appeared that at Jonathan's country place, some miles distant from Mengo, a number of people were asleep in the house, the door of which had been secured merely by tying. The doors in Uganda are made of reed canes laced on both sides of several cross sticks, and form a substantial barrier. The leopard, however had forced its way in, awaking no one, and had pounced on the sleeping man, who was lying on a bed, and had carried him off. The other inmates of the house immediately arose, blew the embers on the hearth into a flame, and saw that their companion was missing. They ventured out

1892] *Discovering Dead Body of a Companion* 333

and heard the horrible growling of the fierce brute in the long grass as he was devouring his unhappy victim. They were too frightened to venture into the reed canes. Probably the other inmates of the

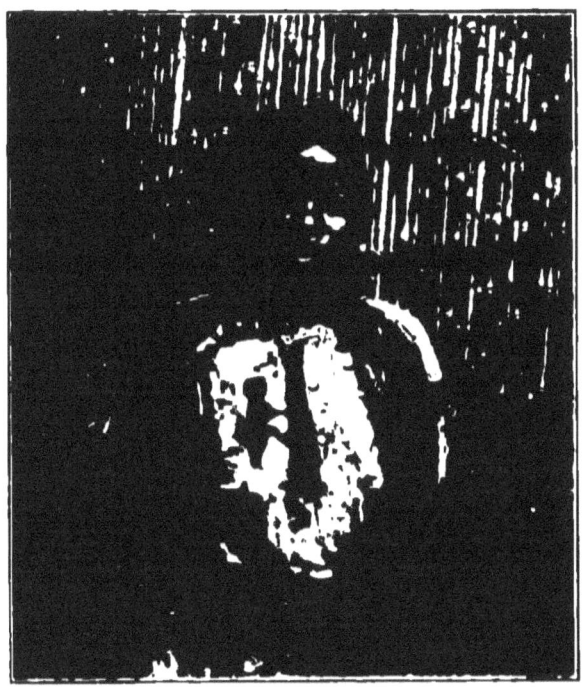

THE REED WALL BEHIND "EDGAR" SHOWS THE UGANDA METHOD OF BUILDING.

dwelling were only women and children ; at any rate, they retired into the house and secured the door. Next day, when light dawned, they went out, and gathering some neighbours they ventured into the tall reeds, where they found the partially devoured dead body of their late companion. The report had only come to Jonathan that morning. The next day, however, Jonathan appeared full of happiness and joy. He said, " I have just met my brother. It was not he whom the leopard ate, but another man." Such incidents as the above helped one to realise a fact which is difficult of belief, and which is yet absolutely true, that as soon as darkness comes on these prowling monsters, so seldom seen, are yet lurking close at hand, and under cover of night are stalking through our courtyards and sniffing round our houses.

But as clearing and cultivation and building advanced in the neighbourhood of Mengo the visits of leopards became less common, and the capital began to assume a well-kept and prosperous appearance, which it had never displayed since the palmy days of Mutesa. But if there was a distinct improvement in the temporal surroundings of the people, what was really of far deeper import for Uganda and all the countries in that region, was the steady advance made in missionary work. There were, amid all the jarring of rival political interests, a number of humble-minded men and women who were seeking a city with foundations, and a kingdom that would not pass away. There were among these " cantankerous and rabid Protestants," these " scheming and plotting Papists," men whose first idea was the advancement of the kingdom of heaven. Mugwanya, the " French " Kimbugwe, had held his high office, I think I may venture to say, with the one idea of advancing the cause of true religion, while among the "English" were such men as Samwili,* Natanieli, Bartolomayo, and others who resigned important and lucrative chieftainships, in order to devote themselves entirely to the work of teaching. The earnest desire which the Ba-ganda people displayed to obtain books presented a really remarkable phenomenon. The anxiety on the part of the people to buy, and the great crowds that came in the earlier days to purchase portions of Scripture, could hardly be exaggerated. People brought to my house more than ten thousand cowrie shells, in order that I might write their names down as purchasers of books not expected to arrive for five or six

* The following touching letter from Samwili to Bishop Tucker has been widely circulated by the Church Missionary Society.

(COPY OF TRANSLATION OF LETTER FROM SAMWILI NAGANAFA.)

" NAMILEMBE,

"*January* 18*th*, 1894.

" MY DEAR BISHOP TUCKER,—

" How do you do, my friend? I write to greet you, and to thank Jehovah our God for bringing you safely, and for protecting you from all danger on the road and on the sea, which I hear is very great. And as He has kept you now, so we pray He will keep you, and bring you back again, as all of us, who are here, hope.

" I rejoiced very much to hear to-day that you had reached England, and all my friends who love you will not fail to rejoice; but again we pray God to give the Englishmen who are there (in England) a pitying remembrance of us, that they may be willing to leave their country, which has great honour, and to come to teach us, as the Son of God got up and left His first position, which exceeded in glory all estates of the archangels, which have honour in the presence of God, and strengthened Himself to come and die for us. Good-bye. May the Grace of our Lord, which exceeds all things, be with you always, for ever.

" I am your friend who loves you very much,

" SAMWILI MULAGO."

months. To several I had said, "You had better keep the shells till the books come"; but the invariable answer was, "We fear to keep them, lest we be tempted to spend them on something else." *

As Easter-tide drew on there was a large number of candidates for baptism, and all the missionaries were kept busy preparing for the solemn event which was to take place on Easter day, when sixty people were baptised.

On June 10th Captains Macdonald and Pringle, R.E., of the Railway Survey, arrived at Mengo. Their report has since proved to be highly satisfactory, and has shown the practicability of making a railway to Uganda. While these officers were at Mengo they set themselves to make inquiries regarding various native products, especially grain and other food stuffs. The question of whether a railway would pay must depend on what commodities the countries connected with the coast by a railway can offer. It is evident that for some time a railway could hardly be expected to pay any dividend on the outlay ; but as a means of opening up the Nile basin, checking the slave trade, and lessening the cost of men-of-war on the coast, the construction of the line cannot but commend itself to the common sense even of those who are most strongly opposed in the abstract to Imperial extension. But the strongest argument of all for it is that Uganda, having now become an English protectorate, some better and quicker and less costly means of transport must be

* Possibly a bank, on the model of our penny banks in England, might prove a valuable aid to economy in the country.

HE LEFT WITH ME TIMOTEO.

inaugurated, than, at its best, the inhuman method of employing native carriers. And there is no means so economical as a railroad. It must be remembered that for many years past there has been a steady payment of some thousands per annum in the transport of goods. This traffic would pass at once into the hands of a railway company. Carriage now costs half-a-crown per pound, or £280 per ton. Some estimate it as high as three shillings per pound, or £336 per ton. If the directors of the railway were wise and charged low tariffs they would secure, I believe, large custom, both European and native.

One of the chiefs had sent Walker and me a "*Musu*," a large kind of rodent resembling a huge rat. It is a very favourite dish in Uganda. The creature lives on the tall reed-like grass, it has coarse, bristle-like hair, and when dressed for the table is plucked and singed, not skinned. We invited the officers of the Survey to dine, and treated them to this dish. I think they approved of it. Our way of living was somewhat primitive, as we had lost most of our belongings in Budu. The officers of the Railway Survey only remained a few days, and when they left Lugard decided to leave Uganda with them, which he did.

In spite of sometimes grave differences all were sorry to part with him, both white men and natives, since he had displayed qualities which commended him to all ; and possibly also the feeling which he has himself drawn attention to existed in the minds of those whom he was leaving behind,* that his successor,

* "Rise of our East African Empire," vol. ii., p. 514.

Captain Williams, was even less fitted to deal with the grave difficulties of Uganda than he himself had proved —a feeling, however, that there is no reason to say that subsequent events justified.

Captain Lugard and the staff of the Railway Commission left Uganda *en route* for England on June 11th. He reached home the following October ; and there is little doubt that his able and energetic action contributed largely to moving public opinion on the question of Uganda, and in bringing about the English Protectorate. So that whatever judgment may be finally pronounced on Lugard's conduct of affairs in Uganda under the most trying conditions, there is no doubt that he has been largely the instrument, though sometimes a little unwillingly, in securing for the Nyanza region the blessings of British rule.

A day or two later Walker (now Archdeacon) left, to visit England, after a sojourn of five years full of difficulties, dangers, and trials, some account of which it is to be earnestly hoped may hereafter be given by himself. I accompanied my friend and companion for two short days' journey on the way. Walker took with him Mika Sematimba, who was now an important chief (Makamba). He left with me the boys, Timoteo and Kangiri, formerly my old pupils, and subsequently his little followers. Walker and I had been together a little more than five months, and it was with many regrets that I bade farewell to one of the most loyal of friends and the truest of men.

CHAPTER VI

A JOURNEY TO KAVIRONDO

Enthusiastic Greeting of Mwanga—A Split in the English Faction—Appealing to Mwanga—Mwanga gives Way—A Fatal Tropical Disease—Wakoli requests Smith to meet him—Lynching of the Man who fired the Salute—Smith finds himself in a Cul-de-Sac—Smith's Hiding-place discovered—The Horrible Suspense ended—Death of Wakoli—Dr. Wright ordered Home—Good Effects of Change of Scene—Arrival at Luba's—I go on to Kavirondo—A Challenge thrown Away—El Gon Mountain—An Amputation under Difficulties—Herr Wolf's Kindness—The Ripon Falls (Jinja)—A warm Welcome—Men of Holy and Humble Hearts.

CHAPTER VI

A JOURNEY TO KAVIRONDO

AN event of great importance which now took place was the opening of the grand new church (July 31st) on Namirembe Hill. The roof of the church is a framework of the reed-like grass called muli, supported by some three hundred pillars, each pillar being the trunk of a tree. It is thatched with strong grass, and projects in the form of a verandah over the walls, which are (in the style of ordinary Uganda houses) of fine white stems of the reed-like grass laced vertically side by side, and fastened longitudinally to bands of reeds. The walls are double, the hollow space between being filled up with grass. The pillars inside run in rows about six feet apart. The building is some one hundred and forty feet in length by seventy broad, and about forty feet high along the ridge, sloping down to some six or seven feet. The church is capable of holding about three thousand people.

Mwanga, who was now an enthusiastic supporter of the English faction, expressed his intention of becoming a Protestant, and attending church in state. A low platform, about six or seven inches high, was made for him at the south side of the church, while a space was preserved on the opposite side of the church for the Company's representative, and the Company's flag was hung above the Resident's seat.

Mwanga and his suite waited in the vestry at the south side, until the beating of the church drum* announced the time for the beginning of the service. They then went to the place arranged for the king. On his entrance all the people spontaneously arose, and with sudden enthusiasm uttered a long and loud cheer as soon as they recognised the king. When the tumult was hushed the king took his seat, and the service began. The preacher was Henry Kitakule,† Bishop Hannington's favourite boy, who had accompanied the bishop to the Nyanza on his first journey.

Next day, in the old disused church, a grand feast was held in honour of the occasion, to which large numbers of guests were invited. The proceedings, however, nearly ended in a disastrous manner. One of the guests secured a piece of beef, and being in great haste to dispose of it, he endeavoured, unsuccessfully, to swallow it whole, with the result that it choked him, and soon he was *in extremis*, and lay dying amid the laughter of the bystanders (slaves and dependents of the chiefs), who seemed to think it a capital jest. Some of the missionaries heard of the

* The tattoo for the prayer drum in U'ganda is the ordinary Unyamwezi caravan drum-beat, probably introduced from Usambiro, the Church Missionary Society station in Unyamwezi.

† Henry Wright Duta Kitakule, now the Rev. H. W., etc.

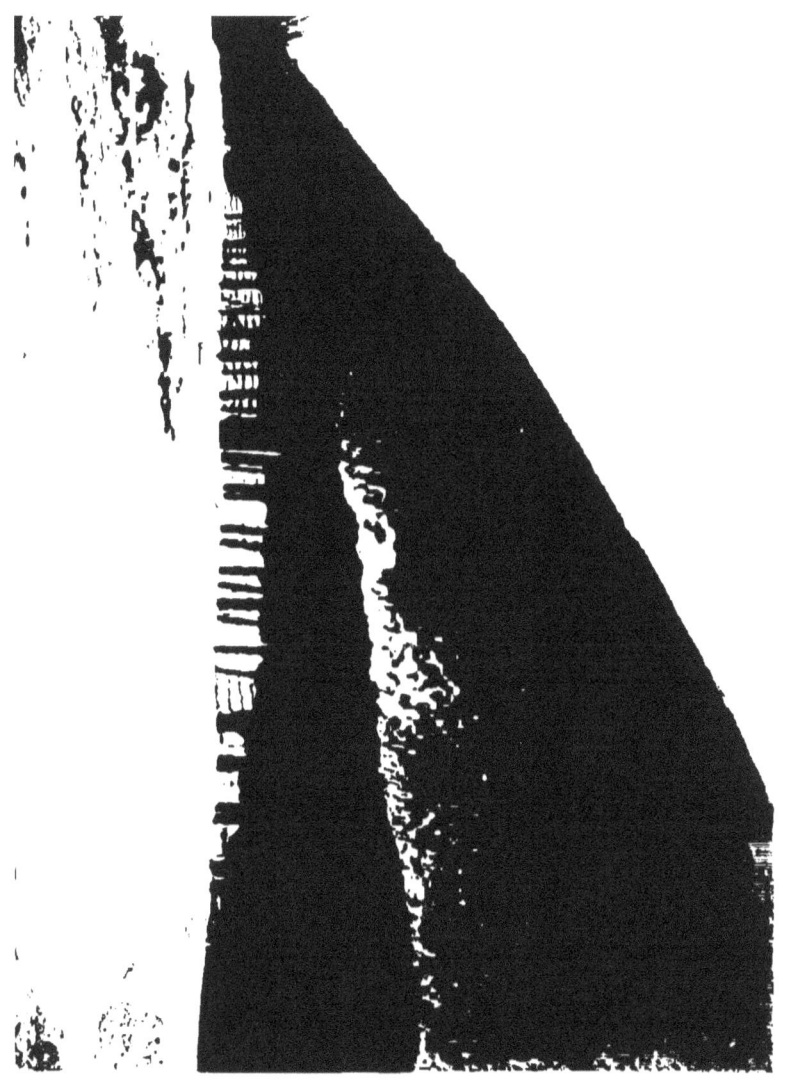

mishap in time, and with Henry's help carried the dying man to the doctor's house close by. Dr. Wright succeeded in withdrawing the huge piece of meat with a pair of forceps, and the man was snatched out of the very jaws of death. For a time he was delirious, but soon came round, and went away very much ashamed of himself, and I never heard more of him.

But though the new church was opened, and things seemed to be settling down at Mengo, and Christian work was progressing, the political element continually crept in to mar and disfigure the spiritual results.

A circumstance now happened which went far to strengthen me in my belief that the late war had not been a mere *fracas* of contending religious bigots ; for no sooner was the English party consolidated than unmistakable signs of a split began to appear, the two camps being divided into the Katikiro's and the Sekibobo's, Apolo and Nikodemo. Nikodemo was, and is, one of the kindest of men, but he was not always the wisest, and in his zeal for the English Company he now sent into Chagwe to obtain some ivory for them without having received the sanction of the king, which, according to Uganda custom, he ought to have done. The officers he sent, in their endeavour to procure the ivory demanded, had roughly used the Katikiro's uncle. This was a grand chance for Sekibobo's young rival, who was most anxious to seize old Nikodemo and lead him in chains from the presence of the king. Hearing of the trouble I visited Apolo, and reminded him that, but for Nikodemo, there would have been no English party at all; and I urged that if Sekibobo had done wrong they should make him pay as heavy a fine as they wished, but they should not humiliate him before the whole country by rigorously carrying out one particular custom, when so many, practically all, the old customs had been abrogated.

Apolo gave way to my reasoning, and promised that he would not press the case. I thought the incident was over. But Mwanga was only too delighted to assert his own privileges, and to humiliate one of his foremost chiefs; and so the whole matter was reopened by the king and some others, notoriously Lutaya, a Muhammedan favourite; and old Sekibobo came to me in great trouble, to say he was to be publicly seized and tied up. I was greatly concerned, because I knew if once this sort of thing were set on foot there was no saying where it might end.

A day or two more it might be Apolo who was to be seized. So I asked my fellow-missionaries to come with me in order that we might plead for our old friend, and ask that, if he had done wrong, he should be fined and not imprisoned.

So, when the king held his next court, we made a point of attending, and Sekibobo was duly tried and condemned; and then came the question of tying him up. His enemies were triumphant. Apolo had forgotten his promise to me. So I got down from my chair, and kneeling before the king, who was seated on his mat, I said in a low voice: "Sir, I pray you not to tie up Nikodemo, who has been the chief man of the Protestants and our father."

INTERIOR OF ST. PAUL'S CHURCH, SHOWING THE COMMUNION TABLE AND RAILS.

Apolo now lost his temper, and said, " Do you plead in secret ? "

I answered : " I did not wish to say in public that you had deceived me ; you promised not to press the case."

FONT. DRUM USED INSTEAD OF A BELL. COMMUNION TABLE.

CHURCH FURNITURE, ST. PAUL'S, UGANDA.

Apolo was silent, and Mwanga felt that it would be wiser to give way.

Times had changed since Mackay and I, in fear of our lives, had come before this man to ask news of Hannington, whom he was about to murder.

Mwanga then said, " Very well ; we will fine him."

Whereupon all on Nikomedo's side tweanziged, which is done by waving the clasped hands up and down, uttering the words, "Tweanze, tweanzege" ("We thank you, we thank you").

The king then said to me, "You may decide what he is to pay," as much as to say, "You had better take my place!"

I said, "We only prayed that the Sekebobo should not be seized. We do not want to interfere with the judgment."

A fine of ivory was then imposed by the king, and Nikodemo was discharged.

The last time we had ventured to plead had been for the inhabitants of Sesse, whom the king was mercilessly bleeding of cattle. The unjust tax was accordingly almost entirely remitted.

After Lugard's departure for England a new enemy appeared in Uganda in the shape of fever, which attacked the Europeans both at Kampala Fort and the English mission. Captain Williams had a most severe attack of hæmaturic fever, brought on by becoming wet through on a cold and rainy evening. He came very near to death's door, but recovered sufficiently to resume his duties at Kampala, to which he stuck with characteristic courage. Dr. Wright also, who had come up with me, and had never seemed to rally thoroughly from the weakening effects of the dysentery from which he had formerly suffered, was also struck down with the same fell disease (hæmaturic fever), so fatal to Europeans in tropical Africa.

Meanwhile a terrible tragedy had been enacted in

Usoga, where another missionary was nearly losing his life in the person of Mr. J. C. Smith, who had gone to take up work at Wakoli's, the paramount chief of Usoga, who was the staunch ally of the English Company.

Smith, who with Gordon had visited Wakoli in 1891, returned there in 1892, and was recommended to Wakoli's care and protection by Captain Lugard, when the latter, in company with the officers of the Railway Commission, passed through on his journey to the coast.

Two days after the survey expedition left, Wakoli was summoned to their camp to undertake the recovery of three valuable loads which had been stolen. Wakoli was absent on this business for about a fortnight. In the meanwhile Smith had busied himself in building a house and making friends with the people. At sunset of a hard day, during which he had been working navvy fashion, he heard a sound of distant horns announcing the return of the chief. At the same time a hot and panting messenger arrived with compliments from Wakoli, and a request that Smith would go and meet him. Smith at first demurred. He was dirty, tired, and hungry, and felt in no condition to present himself before the chief. However, being urged by the messenger, he consented, and went with the man. One or two of the Company's porters who were stationed at the fort hard by followed him, one carrying a Snider rifle.

As soon as Smith reached the procession of the returning chief, Wakoli came forward and welcomed him, and fired a gun as a salute, holding the barrel downwards that the charge might bury itself in the ground. The man who had followed Smith then fired his rifle past Smith holding it horizontally, and was sharply rebuked for his folly in so doing.

The chief then entered his enclosure, and in the first courtyard turned round to shake hands with his white guest. He then embraced Smith in Uganda fashion, and no sooner was the salutation over than the same officious porter, having inserted a cartridge into his rifle, fired a second salute, the charge this time entering Wakoli's side. For one instant, before the shot was fired, Smith had a nightmare vision of what must happen, but had no time to dash the gun aside before the bullet sped. Wakoli did not at once fall, and kept perfectly cool. Not so his warriors, who with wild yells pursued the wretched man who had so rashly fired the fatal salute, and who, terrified by what he had done, now endeavoured to effect his escape. In an instant he was in the grasp of the infuriated warriors, and Smith caught a momentary glimpse of him, deprecating their anger, and endeavouring to plead for mercy. Next moment he saw a ghastly gash where the man's skull was laid open, and the next, the unhappy fellow's head was dashed into a pulp at Smith's feet. Wakoli was able to give some orders about gunpowder —possibly he feared this was a preconcerted attack— then he bade Smith save himself. Smith urged him to lie down and allow himself to be carried into his house. At first Wakoli refused, but then allowed himself to be borne into the inner court. The position of Smith was now almost desperate. The only man with a head on his shoulders was desperately wounded, and his uncontrollable young warriors were thirsting for the blood of another victim; they had only whetted the appetite by the speedy lynching of the unhappy porter. Smith has graphically described how a brutish man, with horrid yells for bullets, came to lead him away. At first all believed that Wakoli had been shot by Smith's orders. The man came and shook Smith by the shoulder, and Smith warned him off, and, in spite of angry resistance, struggled after the bearers who were carrying Wakoli. He felt that his only chance for life was to keep close to the chief.

Wakoli was now placed in the centre of the courtyard, which was soon filled with a surging crowd. One, who appeared to be a chief, gave an order, and immediately seven or eight warriors rushed upon Smith, and violently pushed him out of the inner enclosure. Hurrying and dashing him through three courtyards, they bade him go home. One had snatched his hat from him. Smith saw that they had landed him in a sort of *cul-de-sac*, and he felt that, at all hazards, he must get back to Wakoli's presence. Up to this point he had made but little resistance, but now he threw the warriors from him right and left, and rushed back by the way he had come. There was a block here, and the sliding door was closed; he dashed it down, passed over, and seizing one of his assailants, turned him round between himself and the spears now poised threateningly on all sides. The chief who ordered his expulsion was furious, but Wakoli now intervened and bade them not molest Smith, who had for some time evaded the whirling clubs and flashing axes brandished by many; but up to this point there yet wanted one bold enough to strike.

Wakoli now ordered his people to carry him into a house. Again an agonising struggle with the angry crowd, and Smith found himself inside the house. Wakoli was now lying between him and his would-be murderers. Some one whispered hoarsely to him *to hide* himself. He was able for a time to conceal himself, but could hear the maddening yells of the warriors demanding his blood. These, in their fury, almost trampled their dying king underfoot. Wakoli, seeing how things stood, assured the multitude that the white man had vanished, and that they could not find him here. The mob then rapidly diminished, and were turned out of the courtyard. The attendants then removed Wakoli outside, in order to wash his wound.

Smith was now alone in the house. Presently three men came in, and then a fourth; they said nothing, but began to blow the embers of the fire on the hearth into a blaze. The house had become almost pitch dark by this time, a kindly darkness which served to conceal the white stranger in hiding for his life. The sudden flame now illumined every corner of the building, and Smith, seeing he was discovered, politely saluted the men who had entered. They made no reply, but looked at one another, and then sprang upon Smith. He deprecated their violence, saying if they wished to make him prisoner he would submit quietly.

Accordingly they stripped off his coat and waistcoat, leaving him with trousers and vest. They then tied his hands, but immediately caught up their spears, showing Smith that their tying his hands was only a ruse to make it easy for them to murder him.

With a sudden violent effort he wrenched his hands loose, and was once more free. Again they brandished their spears, and one even aimed a gun at him; but partly from awe of the dreaded white man, partly from fear of what the consequences might be, they did not muster up courage to use either weapon. The horrible suspense was at length ended by the reappearance of Wakoli, whom his attendants again placed in the house; and Smith's assailants then ran off as if for their lives, and, overcome with overstrain and exhaustion, Smith fell into a deep sleep. After some hours he awoke, feeling bitterly cold, his teeth chattering uncontrollably. Wakoli's mother now came and bade him follow her, and she conducted him safely to the Company's camp,* and begged of him to find some medicine. Smith had little medicine of any kind with him, except quinine, which most of the native chiefs know. So he procured some quinine, and followed the chief's mother back again. He had hesitated about relinquishing the shelter of the stockade, such as it was; but feelings of humanity, and a desire to help his sick friend, conquered, and there is little doubt that his so returning saved his life, since his refusal to have done so would have been looked upon as an act of hostility, and a proof that

* The Company's fort at Wakoli's was a stockade made in native fashion.

he felt guilty of the attempt on Wakoli's life. The Company's few porters could never have held the stockade against Wakoli's warriors. On returning, though he was robbed of his boots by some of the warriors, he was allowed to see Wakoli, where a council was going on. The subject appeared to be as to whether or not he should be killed. The women, however, entreated that he might be spared. There was then a whispered consultation between Wakoli and others. The dying chief then called his sister,* and bade her accompany Smith safely back to the Company's stockade. At sunset of that day Wakoli died. Smith remained in the stockade for three weeks, until the arrival of Captain Williams, who had hastened from Mengo as soon as he heard of Smith's great danger, and of the critical position of affairs in Usoga occasioned by Wakoli's death.†

* An African chief's sister is usually a person of great consideration.

† I am indebted to Mr. Smith for very full notes of the above account, enclosed with which was the following letter:—

"CHILWORTH VICARAGE, ROMSEY, HANTS,
"*August 11th*, 1894.

"MY DEAR ASHE,--

"Very rarely do I care to renew the memory of one of the most wonderful experiences a man can claim to have had. It is too wonderful for many to believe, and that is one cause of my reticence about it; another cause is its horrible reality for me, and the vision of the man's head dashed to atoms. There was a Divine power helping me. You knew Wakoli, for whom I want you to express my deepest admiration, and I also must supplement his name by that of Major Williams, as calling for my unfading gratitude.

"Believe me,

" Yours ever affectionately,

" F. C. SMITH."

Such in brief is the story of the tragedy of Wakoli's death, and of the frightful adventure that the devoted missionary was called upon to undergo in the same country, not many leagues distant from the ground which had been stained with the blood of James Hannington.

But to return to our sick doctor at Mengo. Dr.

W. WILSON
OF I.B.E.A. CO.

F. C. SMITH
OF C.M.S.

Macpherson gave so grave a verdict upon Dr. Wright's case, and so strongly urged his return to England, that we felt it right to ask him to leave Uganda for a change that was so necessary ; at the same time we asked Mr. Smith, who had just undergone the terrible experience narrated, and who we also felt required a change, to accompany the doctor, and to look after him on the long and trying journey to the coast. Captain Williams very kindly put the Company's boat at the disposal of the mission, and sent one of his own officers (Mr. Wilson) in charge. Very shortly after Dr. Wright's departure Dr. Macpherson, who had shown much kindness in attending him, was prostrated by a very severe attack of fever. I had gone up to Kampala to help Mr. Bagge a little, upon whom now devolved the trying work of looking after both the patients—the doctor in a very serious condition, while Captain Williams was only recovering from a severe illness.

There is not infrequently accompanying African fever, especially in its acute stages, a despondency which it is difficult to describe, and which is always a very dangerous symptom; and this acute stage Macpherson had now reached. I felt sure that the best thing for him would be to move him out of Kampala, where new scenes would tend to rouse him up. I had known the almost miraculous effect it had produced upon the late Bishop Hannington, when he lay at death's door years ago at Uyui, when we simply took him up and carried him off in a hammock, with the result that he completely shook the fever off—at any rate, for a time. Mackay, too, in his last illness, over and over again had desired to be carried out of Usambiro, but the request, made as it was amid the wanderings of fever, was put down to mere delirium, and disregarded.

Dr. Macpherson had overstayed the time for which he had taken service under the Imperial Company, and everything was ready for his journey to the coast.

But he was too ill to start alone. Bagge could not leave Captain Williams, Grant was in Ugogo, and Wilson, the only other official of the Company, had gone in charge of the boat with our missionaries, Smith and Wright. Under these circumstances, having duly obtained the sanction of the Mission Finance Committee, I gladly volunteered to accompany my sick friend a little distance on the journey. I was not at all sorry that the path of duty was leading me for a time out of a country which may not unjustly be termed the "Ireland of Africa." Macpherson was returning to the coast by the English, and not the German route, with which latter I was familiar. Captain Williams had decided to send down to the coast with the doctor a few Sudanese soldiers, and one or two of the Egyptian officials who had formerly belonged to Emin Pasha's administration. Our way led us to the Nile, where it flows out from the Lake near Lubas, where Bishop Hannington met his death. Roscoe, whom I mentioned as having gone to Lubas to open a mission station, had only stayed there a very short time, and had returned to Mengo with Smith. A faithful Muganda, Yoana Muira (now Rev. Yoana Muira) had come to take his place, and he kindly received us in the house which Luba had built for Roscoe. Next day a short march brought us to Luba's own village. We were travelling very slowly on account of the sick man.

I was, as may be imagined, deeply interested at everything here. The fine-looking old chief, Luba, received me most courteously—the same who with his wives had come to look on Hannington while a prisoner here in "cruel adversity." At some little distance was the hill, from the summit of which the bishop had seen his first view of the Nile. How strange it seemed that the road he had given his life to buy was now open, and an English missionary passing along it in peace! Slowly we journeyed to Wakoli's, the scene of Smith's late adventure. Wakoli had been succeeded by his son Mutanda, a drunken and dissolute sot. I found that very many of the people of Usoga could speak the language of Uganda, which made me feel more or less at home among them. At Wakoli's we found Grant, one of the Company's energetic officers already mentioned. The doctor, though better, was still hardly out of danger, and I did not like to leave him at this point, so I thought I would go on into Kavirondo. Here we forsook the net hammock in which the patient had been hitherto carried, and slung his light wooden camp bed on a bamboo pole. I commend this plan to every African traveller, in case he should need to be carried, as being infinitely more comfortable and safe than the hammock; for in case the carriers let the camp bed fall, the occupant is not brought heavily to the ground, as he would be in a net hammock, for the legs of the bed break the fall.

The country through which we were passing looked almost like a magnificent forest, so thickly was it wooded with splendid trees; while each day we wandered on through endless banana groves.

An amusing incident happened at one of our camping grounds. I had a large Masai donkey with me, and when the cattle came home a great bull saw the donkey, and immediately challenged it to mortal combat. First of all the bull slowly advanced, bellowing savagely, then it stopped for a while, and pretended to graze, then it tossed up the earth, and advanced further. The donkey the while stood perfectly quiet, hardly even pricking its ears. When the bull came quite close the donkey simply looked at it with all the contempt a donkey can express, as much as to say, " What does this great bellowing 'ass' want ? " Not one foot did the donkey budge; and the bull, as if realising that his challenge was somewhat thrown away, sneaked back again, trying to appear as if he had had no hostile intentions with regard to the donkey. He found, however, on his return, a combatant ready for him in the shape of a big black bull which we had brought with us, and then there was a grand battle between these two champions of the herd. It is a curious fact that it is fairly safe to leave donkeys to take care of themselves against all comers ; for when free to use their heels leopards and even lions are very chary of attacking them. It is generally when tied up or enclosed that they are killed by these mighty carnivora.

Passing out of the banana groves of Busoga we entered the wilder and more naked country of Kavirondo, or Bakedi, as the people of Uganda call it. Like country, like people, for the Bakedi were without exception more absolutely devoid of clothing than any people I have ever come across. Naked men I was accustomed to in Unyamwezi and Ugogo, but the women always wore some slight apology for a covering. Here some of the women indeed had a little fringe both before and behind attached to a string tied round the waist, but it seemed quite immaterial whether it was worn or not.* Yet from this country to Busoga is but half-an-hour's walk, and the Busoga are clothed from head to foot.

We had a fine view as we neared the Nzoia River of the great El-Gon mountain, or Masaba, as the Baganda call it. While encamped in this region an unhappy incident occurred which I will relate.

Dr. Macpherson was decidedly better, and had been able to ride the donkey a little, and we were making steady progress to the river. We had several cattle, among which were a cow and her calf, in charge of a Wahuma herdsman and his boy, whom I had brought with me. Grant (who was now with us, and his detachment of Sudanese soldiers) also had some cattle. It appeared there was some little disagreement between my cowman and the Sudanese who looked after Grant's cattle. Whether what occurred had any connection with it or not I must leave the reader to judge. Late on the night in question, a leopard seems to have succeeded in getting into the cattle enclosure, and in either carrying off or frightening away a calf. The Wahuma, it may be observed, look on their cattle much as they

* I was anxious to purchase one of these fringes, but found some difficulty in procuring a spare one. One of the bystanders immediately divested herself of the one she was wearing and brought it to me. I bought it. There was not the slightest immodesty. She had only made herself like many of her sisters standing by.

do on their children, and my man was immediately on the alert. My man Kakonge followed the cries of the calf, and called loudly to another man, a Muganda sleeping near him, to bring a wisp of lighted straw in order to search for the young creature. The Sudanese sentry heard them shouting. Kakonge said in Luganda, "A wild beast is after the calf." The sentry went and told the corporal or sergeant, who came out with his rifle, and without challenging fired point-blank at Kakonge. I heard the shot. Presently Timoteo came in and said, "They have shot Kakonge." I lighted a candle and went out, and there stood poor Kakonge, with his hand smashed to pieces, hanging by the skin and sinews. Happily the doctor, though still very weak, was able to deal with the case. On looking at it he said, "It's a bad business. The arm must come off." He happened to have a case of surgical knives with him, so there and then, by the light of a couple of candles, the operation was performed. He had no chloroform, but Kakonge bore it well, and the doctor, though so weak and ill, did his work splendidly. A little later all was quiet again, and old Kakonge lay in my tent smoking a pipe.

Next day we reached the Nzoia River, and crossed in the Company's Berthon boat, and camped in the large village of Mumias. But as we were crossing news reached us of the near approach of a large European caravan, and the same day there came into Mumias Major Eric Smith, with Martin, the Company's caravan agent, also Herr Wolf, the German newspaper correspondent, who was coming to Uganda to find wherewith to fortify the *ex-parte* statements he had written home from the mouths of the French priests in Zanzibar. Major Smith brought news of the intention of the Government to subsidise the Company for three months, in order to give them time to evacuate Uganda.

At Mumias I bid farewell, with many regrets, to Dr. Macpherson, whose experiences during his service with the Company would fill an interesting volume. He had accompanied Lugard to Kavali's, had seen the glorious Ruenzori, and many other African wonders. I am happy to say he made a prosperous journey to England, where his native air soon set him on his feet again. Major Smith rested two or three days at Mumias, and I accompanied him back to Uganda. He brought with him a Maxim gun, and a considerable quantity of ammunition, the surest sign of all to me that no evacuation of Uganda was intended.

Poor old Kakonge, the cowman, was a heavy burden on my hands; but Grant most kindly detailed men to carry him, for indeed he was too weak to walk. To add to his discomfort, not long after the loss of his arm he was attacked by dysentery, from which I suffered also; but three days' rest at Mumias made me well enough to mount the donkey. Herr Wolf, however unkind his judgments against Englishmen and English missionaries may have been, was kindness itself to my poor cowman, earning thereby my eternal gratitude. He constantly attended him and dressed his arm. And largely owing to his attention Kakonge recovered, and reached Mengo with me in safety. We recrossed the Nile at Jinja (the stone), the name given to the Ripon Falls, which are grandly beautiful, though not awe-inspiring in the sense that Niagara must be. The highest fall at any one point is not more than a dozen feet, yet for a long distance there is a succession of cataracts. The water at the

SOME OF MY HOUSEHOLD.

highest point flows over in two main streams, with a little island separating them. I sat for a time listening to the ceaseless roar of the falls, whose mighty tones ever and anon seemed to deepen as a greater gush of water was precipitated to the gulf beneath. Strange to gaze on that tumult of sparkling waters, and to hear its countless voices, which seemed to be uttering in musical ravings thoughts which the poorest of mortals may feel, but which the greatest can hardly put into words.

A few more days brought us back to Mengo, where I received a warm welcome from my household, my cooks, Mabruki and his wife, and a small colony of Wahuma, who lived in my enclosure and battened on my cows. I had, by the kindness of Zakaria in the Budu flight, saved a few bales of cloth, and I spent most of these in redeeming some of the cattle which were destined for the meat market, and which were frequently driven past my house for slaughter.

I was very glad to get home to Mengo once more, as during a good part of the journey I had been far from well. Timoteo Kaima had proved a most faithful little attendant, and had, with several other boys, accompanied me to Kavirondo. They and I were soon to undertake what was for them a far more important journey, as they were destined to behold the wonders of " Pwani " (the coast) and Zanzibar.

During my absence in Kavirondo I learned some particulars of a quarrel between the chiefs of the English faction which narrowly missed causing a division of the party.

I used sometimes to say to them sadly, "I would give you three months of power, after which I should expect to see you split up into two factions so hostile that you would stand face to face with loaded rifles ready for battle."

The reader will understand how terrible a hindrance

to the work of the mission these eternal squabbles and quarrels were ; but in justice he will remember also that there is a Parliament in England where blows are sometimes exchanged ; duels are fought in France ; while in America revolvers are flourished and fired on manifold occasions. And these also are Christian states!

The sneers and sarcasms hurled at missionaries and their converts, though perhaps fully deserved, are not just from the lips of that class of English people who themselves are notoriously deficient in the virtues which they expect inferior races just emerging from heathenism to exhibit. Virtues and goodness, however, are found among these races, and there are among them men of holy and humble hearts, who are a living witness to the transforming power of the Holy Spirit in those who believe the Gospel of our Lord Jesus Christ.

CHAPTER VII

QUESTION OF UNYORO AND UVUMA

The King sends for Roscoe and Me—An awkward and intricate Question—Arrival of New Missionaries—I send in my Resignation—The Remains of the murdered Bishop brought to Uganda—The Funeral Service—Reason for arresting a Chief—Armed Burglary—A very lengthy Memorandum—Favourable Impression of Kabarega—Advantages of peaceful Policy—An unreasonable Demand—Islanders of Uvuma—The Bavuma beat the Ba-ganda—Frightful Treachery of Mutesa—Efforts to prevent the Attack—Last Act of the Imperial British East Africa Company in Uganda.

CHAPTER VII

QUESTION OF UNYORO AND UVUMA

THE end of this year was marked by the return of Captain Macdonald of the Railway Survey, who, when on his way to the coast, had received instructions ordering him to re-enter Uganda, and conduct an inquiry as to the cause of the outbreak of the fighting in which the Imperial British East Africa Company and the two Christian factions had taken part.

Just as he arrived Mwanga had evolved a scheme of sending an envoy to England, and for this duty had selected Zakaria, than whom no one could have been better for the purpose;* but the acting Resident did not wish any one to be sent at this particular juncture. He therefore visited the king, and suggested that Mwanga should wait awhile, and then send three envoys, one to represent each party. This immediately touched the sore place in Mwanga. It was true that there were three Bakabaka (kings) in Uganda—himself for the English faction, monseigneur for the French, and Embogo for the Muhammedan.

* See p. 180, for the late Sir Gerald Portal's description of Zakaria.

"No," said Mwanga with some spirit, "I am not going to send three envoys to woza musango" (plead a case), "but one ambassador to represent me."

The Resident, in trying to persuade the king to delay sending his envoy, unfortunately referred to Mwanga's having murdered Bishop Hannington, urging this as a ground why his envoy would not be favourably received. Immediately all the king's terrors and haunting fears came back upon him like a flood, and in great agitation he sent for Mr. Roscoe and myself. Mwanga seemed in some way to connect Captain Macdonald's return to Uganda with a possible scheme of long premeditated revenge which was being hatched against himself, and with undisguised fear he asked us what it meant.

It must be remembered the French party never wearied urging the king to oppose the Company on the ground that they intended, when strong enough, to take revenge upon him for Hannington's death.

Roscoe and I assured him that the matter had been condoned; but as it seemed to agitate his mind, at the king's earnest request I said I would myself go and ask Captain Macdonald to explain the object of his coming, and to assure the king that he had nothing to fear upon this score. I accordingly called at Kampala, and told Captain Macdonald what had occurred, and he agreed to go and see the king, and explain matters to him. He asked the Company's Resident (Captain Williams), Herr Eugene Wolf, the Father Superior of the French mission, and myself, as representing the English mission, to accompany him.

It fell to my lot during part of the interview to interpret between Captain Macdonald and Mwanga. Captain Macdonald's object was to make clear to the king the reason of his coming, and to disabuse his mind of the terror which possessed it, and, in fact, generally to smooth matters and to explain anything which puzzled or alarmed the king.

After Captain Macdonald had explained his own position, and given Mwanga to understand that the death of Hannington had been condoned, the king asked him, through me, whether the Company had been sent by the British Government, meaning practically, were they really authorised Government agents. Any one who knows the history of the political relations between Uganda and Zanzibar from Mutesa's days will understand the full significance of Mwanga's question. I refer to the misunderstanding produced in former days by the missionaries having carried letters to King Mutesa signed by Lord Salisbury, and the consequent cross purposes with the Zanzibar Consulate.

The question was an exceedingly awkward, intricate, and difficult one to answer. If Captain Macdonald had said the Company were not authorised, and had no power to make treaties, then what of the Royal Charter? If, on the other hand, they were authorised, and had power to make treaties, then Captain Macdonald's affirmation of this would make the responsibility of the Government all the more complete.

After considering Mwanga's question, Captain Macdonald said the only thing that he possibly could say which would not utterly stultify the Royal Charter of the Company in the eyes of the King : " Tell the king that the Company have been sent by the Government—that is, they are authorised by the Government." I did so most explicitly and clearly, so that the impression conveyed by the Company's officials was made absolute by me, interpreting for Captain Macdonald that what the Chartered Company did had the sanction and authority of the British Government.

The king's mind was greatly relieved on hearing form Captain Macdonald's own lips that his fears regarding the killing of Bishop Hannington were groundless, and from that day was far more in the hands of the Company than he had ever been before.

At Christmas time Bishop Tucker and a new party of English missionaries arrived in Uganda, and shortly afterwards the *Times* special correspondent, who, like Herr Eugene Wolf, had certain theories of his own to maintain. He was not and could not have been quite an unbiassed inquirer after truth, since he himself had tried his 'prentice hand in Uganda affairs as an agent of the Imperial British East Africa Company before Captain Lugard's arrival in Uganda ; and in a state of affairs already far from settled had proved rather a disturbing element than otherwise.

His position of *Times* correspondent, coupled with a graphic and interesting style of writing, have perhaps given his opinions a weight which they cannot claim on their own merits.*

* Bishop Tucker and others have answered at some length the strictures of the *Times* correspondent on the English mission, and have drawn attention to his inaccuracies and omissions.

The arrival of Bishop Tucker and his goodly reinforcement of missionaries was a great relief to my mind ; for it had become evident to me that, for some reason or other, the view of the Company's representatives, rather than that of our own missionaries, was accepted by the Committee of the Church Missionary Society at home. I knew that my own Committee was on very close terms with the Directors of the Company, and, owing to letters received by me, I felt it necessary to send in my resignation, which I did, to Bishop Tucker. I felt it, moreover, expedient to return home, as I desired to ask for an explanation of the letters addressed to me from the secretary of the mission— letters which I felt sure must have been despatched owing to some misunderstanding on the part of the Committee.* I waited, however, until the month of

The Church Missionary Society may certainly be congratulated that so hostile a critic of its work in Uganda was even reduced to the necessity of finding fault with the arrangement of the interior of the church. He launched the terrible indictment against the Mission that there was "*no fixed communion table in the church.*" *Ex pede Herculem*, and from "no fixed communion table" the *Times* correspondent!

* Captain Lugard writes : "Though they" (Committee of the Church Missionary Society) "never dissociated themselves distinctly from the action of their missionaries—an omission I regret—I think I am within the mark in saying that by their conduct and words on my return to England they wished me to understand that they approved my course."—" Rise of our East African Empire," vol. ii., p. 454.

Captain Lugard had the advantage of laying his own views before the secretary, and of apparently commenting in such a manner on one of my letters as to lead to its entire misapprehension. Captain Lugard is probably right in saying that he led those he spoke to in my absence to approve his action, also that

March, when an opportunity presented itself of crossing the Lake in canoes with Mr. Nickisson, who had come up with Bishop Tucker, and who was about to proceed to Nassa, on Speke Gulf, to take up missionary work with my friend Hubbard at that station.

Shortly after Bishop Tucker's arrival a somewhat dramatic incident occurred which is worth relating. Mr. Martin had buried the bones of the murdered Bishop Hannington at Mumia's village in Kavirondo; and Bishop Tucker, on arrival at that place, determined to exhume them, and carry them to Uganda for interment there, and this he had done.

On a day appointed the funeral service was held in the church on Namirembe Hill. The Resident attended, as did also the king and great chiefs. It had been our first intention to inter the remains within the building, but the chief men in the church objected that the people would say we repaired to the church to worship the spirit of the departed bishop, as the heathen went

the Committee's conduct to me bore this out cannot be denied; for on the strength of the letter of mine referred to above a letter was at once addressed to me in terms such as could leave me no other alternative but to resign my connection with the Church Missionary Society. As soon as I had the opportunity of asking for an explanation of the Secretary's letter to me, relating to matters between the Company's reputation and myself, I was referred to my own offending document. It was produced, and a few words of explanation showed that the strictures which the Committee felt it was out of place for me, in my capacity of secretary to the mission, to address to Captain Lugard as official head of the English administration, had not been so addressed by me at all. The letter containing them, and of which Lugard had a *résumé*, was written not to Captain Lugard, but to the secretary of my own Committee.

to their tomb houses to worship their deceased chiefs. We therefore had the grave made outside, close by that of young de Winton. Bishop Tucker preached a very effective funeral discourse, the point of which was that all enmity and every feeling of revenge or fear were now to be buried in that open grave. This, at any rate, was the most important part as concerned Mwanga.

We then began the beautiful service for the burial of the dead, Baskerville reading the first parts while I read the prayers at the grave. How many conflicting emotions were there in our hearts at such a scene! Time had passed with soothing hand to soften down every element of horror. I could not but recall how often, in earlier days, I had been with Hannington in sickness and the sore straits of travel. I, too, had seemed to have tasted in Uganda that bitterness of the death cup which he had drained to the dregs in Usoga. And now in the providence of God it had fallen to me, in Christian Uganda, to breathe over his grave the words of sure and certain hope of the resurrection to eternal life through our Lord Jesus Christ.

As the weeks rolled on the relations between the fort and the missions did not seem altogether to improve. The missionaries complained that the Company's soldiers and servants treated the chiefs and people, and even themselves, with only half-disguised insolence.

These Kampala soldiers and porters would come stalking into the church and interrupt the service, in order to call one or more of the chiefs to a consultation with the Company's representative, or they would come marching into our private houses to deliver a letter without a word of permission on our part.

Bishop Tucker, on his arrival, had to suffer from the same kind of indignity. It must be remembered that these are examples of the general treatment accorded by these dependents of the Company. They treated Uganda as a conquered territory. The Sudanese, moreover, constantly stole the produce of the people's gardens, and not infrequently committed much worse crimes than this.

On one occasion an important Uganda sub-chief arrested one of the Company's porters who had stolen some of the reeds (muli) used for building; but on the man's stating, though falsely, that he had bought them, the sub-chief at once released him. The porter complained to the Company's officers of his arrest, and the Resident sent soldiers, seized the chief, and put him in the guard-room for the night, for daring to stop an Imperial Company's thief!

The Company argued that this sub-chief in question should have followed the thief to Kampala and have complained of him there; but the injustice of this will appear more clear, owing to the circumstance that the Sudanese guards had received orders to admit no person to Kampala Fort except the great chiefs, unless he brought with him a letter; and it is evident that the guards stationed at Kampala would take great care that no one should enter on the errand of lodging complaints against themselves or their companions.

The result of such regulations as these was that the ill-disciplined soldiers and porters of Kampala felt that they had *carte blanche* to rob and ill-treat the natives, and pilfer from them with impunity.

But if small depredations were committed by the Sudanese during the day, the repatriated Muhammedans signalised their arrival by a series of armed midnight burglaries. Nearly every morning some outrage was reported. There is little doubt, moreover, that many of the worst class of thieves, seeing that suspicion would naturally fall on the Muhammedans, availed themselves of the opportunity to rob when they might so easily throw the blame upon the hated Muhammedans.

I had two experiences myself of these midnight robbers.

A sub-chief in Chagwe had sent me, with greetings, a small present of bananas, and the messenger was spending the night in my enclosure in a house near the road. Late at night some thieves broke through the gate, and, hearing people forcing the reed door, my guest challenged them. Next moment a gun was fired point blank at him, the bullet making a clean cut in the fleshy part of his arm, but doing no serious damage. On hearing the report of the gun I immediately came out, but as soon as the alarm had been given the thieves ran off.

Another night, Nelly, Mabruki's wife, thought she heard the noise of some one outside, so she got up and went out. Immediately there was a stampede of thieves. Mabruki and she lived in a small house near mine. I heard the commotion, so I went out with a gun. We found, on examination, that the thieves had made an enormous hole at the base of the house, and were in the act of burrowing under the wall in order to gain admittance. It is the common method of robbery in Uganda, and usually successful.

Some persons, in building their houses, place stones under the walls, so that the midnight excavators may come on them, and wake the sleepers inside by clinking the stones as they pull them out of the pit they are digging under the wall.

But whether the Muhammedans were, in every case, the authors of the burglaries, they certainly were a new element of discord and trouble in the country, which in no little time was destined to reach an acute stage.

Whatever Captain Williams may have thought of Lugard's system of dealing with the Muhammedans, he himself had gained a good deal of influence over them. He was genial and pleasant in his bearing towards them, and at the same time absolutely fearless, and while paying little attention to mere rumours, he neglected no means of satisfying himself of the truth of reports which reached him on anything like good authority.

Captain Williams' administration has been severely condemned in certain quarters, and to some extent, I believe, justly ; yet it must be remembered that he was not carrying out methods of his own conception, but rather those of his predecessor, who, even on his departure, left him with a very lengthy memorandum, detailing his plans for the future. Lugard, as he has mentioned, had also explained to Williams some forty or fifty matters of importance ! One of these questions, he tells us, was that of making peace with King

Kabarega of Unyoro, and I should imagine that another was probably that of dealing with the warlike inhabitants of Uvuma, an island which lies in the direct waterway between Mengo and Kavirondo. There was also the great question of the Sudanese in Toro, and of the Muhammedan faction in Uganda.

These matters I propose to touch upon in this and the following chapter.

And first, what had been in the past, and in the future what was to be the relation of Uganda with Kabarega, the king of the important country of Unyoro?

In the year 1891 Kabarega had sent to Mwanga, just before Lugard's expedition against the Muhammedans, to sue for peace. Captain Lugard, without giving the slightest proof, says that Kabarega's proposals were insincere, and that he was entirely opposed to Europeans. Some of the specimens of Europeans whom he had met with he had encountered under such circumstances of prejudice as hardly to give him the best opinion of them.*

The late Emin Pasha, however, has given a most favourable opinion of Kabarega, and contrasts him with Mutesa, the friend of Europeans, entirely to Kabarega's advantage.

Emin wrote : " During my repeated visits Kabarega gave me the impression of being a thoroughly hospitable and intelligent man." He also gives an instance of gentlemanly feeling, forbearance, and self-control on the

* It would be interesting to know Kabarega's reasons for treating Major Casati as he is said to have done.

part of Kabarega which puts that ruler in a most pleasing light.

The evidence of Emin Pasha, who personally visited him and saw much of him, is very important. Kabarega is, by all accounts, an average, if not favourable, specimen of a powerful African chief. He naturally dislikes militant Europeans who carry fire and slaughter into his country in the teeth of his earnest efforts at making peace.

No one can feel more strongly than I do the necessity of bringing African chiefs into a proper subordination to European rule undertaken for the good of the people themselves ; but I advocate the policy of exhausting every peaceful effort, and the spending even a little money to attain this object, especially in such cases as this of Unyoro, which owns the suzerainty of Mwanga ; and this in itself is a very strong reason for adopting a conciliatory and peaceful policy.

On March 25th of the year 1892 Kabarega made another attempt to make peace, and sent a tusk of ivory to Lugard, and a bundle of salt to the Prime Minister. Reverting to these overtures, Lugard again says he knew them to be insincere, but gives no word of proof of his statement, and is even driven to quote Gordon,* Felkin, and others, as agreeing that Kabarega's power must be broken. But why by force ? This is not the method England adopts with other inferior races.

* The English people require some more solid reason for precipitating armed mobs on Unyoro than a statement even of the late General Gordon, or Felkin, who were in those regions under very different conditions from the present.

An Unreasonable Demand

Force surely should be the last, and not the first resort. Lugard concludes by stating most gratuitously that the probability is that the men sent by Kabarega were spies. The same methods, when applied to Captain Lugard himself by high ecclesiastics of the Roman Church, he very properly and rightly resented. Captain Lugard was not likely to accept envoys of peace, since he tells us "my pet scheme was to conquer his (Kabarega's) country."*

And this policy his successors seem to have followed with unquestioning fidelity, for on Lugard's departure the Company's representative sent Mayanja (called Isaya)—an old Uganda patriarch and a former chief under Mutesa—to demand from Kabarega an almost fabulous amount of ivory as the price of peace—an amount so great, as in my opinion to assure, on Kabarega's part, the rejection of the terms.

No doubt the Imperial British East Africa Company has full particulars of this transaction, since, I presume, it was noted in official despatches.

In the year 1893, after Captain Williams' departure, Kabarega sent messengers to Uganda, previous to the expedition against him in that year, with presents to Mwanga, asking what the white men really wanted, and offering a free pass to envoys who might come and inform him. These overtures were, however, not attended to, and in consequence of Kabarega's attack on Toro, from which place the Sudanese garrisons had been raiding Kabarega's country, and inflicting inhuman and unspeakable outrages upon his people, Major Owen

* "Rise of our East African Empire," vol. ii., p. 415.

led an expedition far into Unyoro, inflicting a severe defeat upon Kabarega's army. The king himself, however, escaped. See Appendix C, " War in Unyoro."

To come now to the important matter of the large and independent island of Uvuma. This island was inhabited by a brave and warlike people, who had never yet been subdued by the armies of Uganda. It had been the policy of earlier Uganda kings to keep on good terms with Uvuma ; but when Mutesa came to the throne he determined to make it his boast that he was lord of Uvuma. The Bavuma had always kept on friendly terms with Uganda, and their chiefs had been fast friends with Suna, Mwanga's grandfather, and therefore Mutesa's action was a new departure, and had not, I believe, the approval of his more sensible chiefs. Mutesa's efforts, however, ended in humiliation and disaster for himself. The Bavuma were splendid canoe men, and though they might not build better boats than the Sesse islanders built for Uganda, they were warriors as well as sailors, whereas the sailors of Sesse left all the fighting to the Uganda soldiers.

My readers may remember how Stanley came upon King Mutesa as he was prosecuting a war against Uvuma, and how he manufactured a kind of moving fort, which would resist the stones slung by the Bavuma, who were very skilful with the weapon which the tribe of Benjamin had learnt to use with such precision. Moreover, it was said that the Bavuma were accustomed to dive from their canoes, knife in hand, and to come up under the Uganda canoes and cut the withes which bound the planks together. At any rate, they were a terror to the Uganda soldiers, who would not face them on the Nyanza, however willing they were to meet them in battle on land. Mutesa's expedition against the Bavuma, in spite of Stanley's presence and advice, proved a dead failure; and the baffled king retreated with the loss of some of his important chiefs, and retired to Nabulagala, to comfort himself with the pleasures of his capital after his unsuccessful military undertaking.

After a while, the old friendly relations were renewed by the two peoples, and the Bavuma came as of old to Chagwe to hold, what would be called in Lancashire, their "pot-fair"; for they were celebrated far and wide for the excellence of their pottery. They ventured, also, to send to Mutesa to ask if he would receive a deputation, carrying some small presents. This the Kabaka (king) graciously promised to do, and the deputation duly arrived. Huts were provided for their accommodation, and they were subsequently introduced to the presence of the king. Their presents were received with condescension, and the visitors remained for some time. There was a considerable number of them, nearly one hundred all told. One day, as the Kabaka and his guests were talking together, the conversation turned upon the late war and its various episodes, how this Uganda chief and that Uganda chief had been killed. The subject was a pleasanter one for the guests, whose side had been triumphant, than for the royal host, whose armies had been worsted, and whose leaders had been slain. I myself have seen Mutesa's face fall when he was wroth, and can imagine vividly how his large eyes dilated with anger as he listened grimly to the glib account of his own humiliations, told with guileless glee by the simple islanders.

"And it was thus you killed my chief?" he suddenly asked. "Yes, thus," they eagerly replied, not yet suspecting evil. "And how did you dare so to treat my slaves?" asked the angry tyrant. The guests now saw their mistake, and sought to deprecate Mutesa's rising wrath; but it was no use. "You come," he cried, "to my very presence to tell me of your evil deeds"—his warriors, be it observed, had been killed in open war and in fair fight: but that was no matter. "For these deeds you shall die," continued the angry king. "Take them," he shouted to his executioners; "let not one escape." And in a minute or two a ghastly heap of corpses witnessed to the treacherous cruelty of Mukubya, the causer of tears, for that was Mutesa's name.

On Mutesa's death Mwanga reverted to the more sensible policy of his grandfather, and friendship was once more cemented between the two peoples.

And so when Mwanga was forced into opposition to the Company he sent to his Uvuma allies to come to his assistance. It is said that they made a demonstration against Muwambi's, but were beaten off with heavy loss.

It appeared to be part of the definite policy of the Company "to smash" Uvuma, in order to gain full control of the waterway between Chagwe and Kavirondo.

But however this may have been, in the beginning of 1893, on more or less frivolous pretexts, the

Company's representative determined to attack Uvuma. The grounds stated appeared to me so wholly inadequate, that I ventured to ask Captain Macdonald, who had volunteered to give his assistance, if he had considered how very serious the matter was to which he was about to lend his countenance.

Although Captain Macdonald was a Government Commissioner, he entirely repudiated the idea that he went in his official capacity ; he simply volunteered to help a brother officer. In consequence of what I had said to him, he very kindly arranged an interview between Captain Williams and myself, and the latter received me most courteously, and promised even at the eleventh hour, to send in order to try and bring the people of Uvuma to accept his terms.

It was too late, however, and there was no reaching the island. The whole fighting force of Uganda had been collected, and the people of Uvuma knew perfectly well that they were to be attacked.

Bishop Tucker had also tried to do what he could in the matter, but his knowledge of the case was so small that he was soon silenced.

The French bishop was too busy to intervene, though I begged him, in the interests of humanity, to do so. But though he would not lift a finger or say a word to prevent it, his missionaries wrote home to Europe grossly exaggerated accounts of the affair, throwing the whole blame on the English missionaries !

The attack was made in Stokes' boat and the Company's steel boat and a host of canoes. Two

Maxim guns were employed. The Bavuma, as soon as their enemy appeared, came on splendidly; and had it not been for the frightful effect of the Maxims, which literally mowed them down before they could come within striking distance, it might have gone badly for the Ba-ganda. The islands of this brave people were then occupied and looted. Captain Williams behaved, as was to be expected from an English officer, with humanity and moderation, and was backed up by the Christian chiefs, who returned a vast host of captured women; nevertheless, the Muhammedan Ba-ganda auxiliaries, and no doubt others, carried off numbers of slaves, and openly brought them to the capital. The Muhammedans, who were located some little distance from Mengo, had to pass my house in order to reach their encampments, and numbers of slaves were led past my gate. I immediately wrote to Mr. Grant, who remained in charge of Kampala Fort, to inform him of this circumstance. Mr. Grant acted promptly in the matter, and sent out soldiers to patrol the roads. Fourteen slaves were seized; but as soon as it became known that the highroads were watched the slaves were conveyed secretly by other means. The expedition returned on February 10th, 1893; and this raid was the last act of the Imperial British East Africa Company in Uganda.

CHAPTER VIII

THE MUHAMMEDAN REVOLT

The Fruits of Hostility to England!—Question of Missionary Extension — A Christian Conscience in England — The Muhammedan Question assumes an acute Phase—Muhammedans demur to the King's Orders—Juma appeals to the Sudanese—Difficulty of Selim Bey's Position—Selim Bey's reported Oath—Apolo ordered to collect his Guns—Captain Macdonald summons the Europeans to Kampala—The Sudanese profess themselves Loyal—Captain Macdonald disarms the Sudanese—Protestant Chiefs once more uphold English Rule —Arrest of Selim Bey—Death of Selim Bey—Capture of a Thousand Women — Macdonald demands Unconditional Surrender of Muhammedans—" Every Man goes to the House of his Father."

CHAPTER VIII

THE MUHAMMEDAN REVOLT

I MUST now speak of perhaps the most important question of all in reference to Uganda—that of the Muhammedan native Ba-ganda, and the Sudanese introduced by the agent of the Imperial British East Africa Company. An exhaustive account of the events which led to the mission of Sir Gerald Portal to Uganda, and of the results accomplished by it, would be far beyond the limits of the present volume. I must content myself, therefore, with merely stating that the great interest which had been evoked throughout England by all that had taken place in Uganda resulted in the appointment of Sir Gerald Portal as Government Commissioner. He was instructed to journey to Uganda to report upon the best means of dealing with the country, in view of the withdrawal of the Imperial British East Africa Company on March 31st.*

On March 17th the Commissioner entered Uganda, and was gladly received by all classes in the country, except the Muhammedans. He succeeded, with the

* See instructions to Sir Gerald Portal in Appendix A.

help of the missionaries, in bringing the contending Christian factions to an understanding. The main difficulty, indeed, had disappeared, since there was now the almost moral certainty of continued British occupation. It was to be regretted that the arrangement the Commissioner sanctioned permitted the eviction of numbers of poor Protestant peasants, who had been located in the various chieftainships handed over to the Roman Catholics, and who had built houses, and cultivated land on the estates belonging to them. But no doubt they were eagerly welcomed in other districts, since, in spite of assertions to the contrary, it is population, rather than land, which is scarce in Uganda.

Sir Gerald Portal has given a vivid account of his mission to Uganda and what he saw there. He secured for the "French" party the districts of Kaima and Luekula, and the island chieftainships of Sewaya and Semugala and Jumba, also gardens on the road from Budu to the capital. They were also given a Katikiro (an important office equal to that of Apolo, the Prime Minister), and a chief of soldiers, also a chief of canoes; so that they had little cause to regret their hostility to England, as represented by the Imperial British East Africa Company.

It must be assumed that Sir Gerald Portal's award was based on the inquiries made by Captain Macdonald, who apparently found it impossible to unravel the knots of conflicting evidence. He seems, however, to have thought Captain Lugard wrong in his action of accepting armed help from the Protestants against the hostile French faction ; but, by a kind of poetical justice, he was soon to find himself in much the same kind of situation with regard to the Muhammedans, when he was himself forced to adopt a very similar method to that of Captain Lugard, by accepting armed help from the Protestants against the Muhammedan faction.

But there is one point in the understanding which merits notice. It was the question of confining missionary operations to particular spheres. So important did Sir Gerald Portal conceive this to be, that he addressed a letter of some length to the Earl of Rosebery on the subject.*

The point was really the question of missionary extension to the intelligent Wahuma of Toro. It must be remembered that Bikweamba Yafeti, their Prime Minister, was a Protestant Christian ; and that a very definite attempt had been made by us to open up mission work in Kasagama's kingdom. I had, during 1892, with much trouble translated the Creed, Lord's Prayer, and Ten Commandments, into the language of the Wahuma, and printed one thousand copies, which I sent to my old pupil, Bikweamba. These the Sudanese soldiers managed to get hold of, and tore up. Kasagama, knowing of the efforts already made to reach his people by the Protestant missionaries, sent messengers to his own friends, the Protestants, to ask for teachers. These messengers arrived, and were sent to Sir Gerald Portal by Bishop Tucker. Sir Gerald Portal suspected that this may

* *See* Appendix B. Letter of Sir Gerald Portal to Lord Rosebery.

have been a plan to prejudice the spheres of influence. What I have said, however, I venture to think will show that he was mistaken.* It was, indeed, the natural outcome of missionary effort already made, and which it seems to me should have influenced, and rightly influenced, any attempted arrangement of defining spheres of missionary effort.

As a matter of fact, however, it is most difficult to have any such arrangement as Sir Gerald Portal suggested. It was tried before in the case of Uganda itself. A prominent member of the committee of the Church Missionary Society waited on Cardinal Lavigière, and obtained his consent to a scheme which would have prevented the Algerian missionaries from entering Uganda. It was just such an understanding as Sir Gerald Portal tried to induce Bishop Hirth to consent to. The understanding, however, attempted in former years was not held to on the Cardinal's part. His missionaries did come to Uganda with results both good and evil.† We hear a good deal of the Nonconformist conscience; but it is a solid reality that there is a *Christian* conscience in England, which will not consent to leave the matter of the conversion of the heathen to arrangements and understandings between the Vatican and any other persons.

Sir Gerald Portal left Mengo on May 30th to return

* Sir Gerald Portal's " Journal," p. 215.

† The story is well known, how, when Père Lourdel denounced the Protestant religion before King Mutesa, the king suggested that both sets of teachers should return to Europe to settle which really had the truth, and that then they should come back and instruct him.

to England, in order to make his report upon Uganda, with the result that Her Majesty's Government determined to establish a regular administration, and for that purpose to declare Uganda to be under a British Protectorate.

On his departure Sir Gerald Portal appointed Captain Macdonald as representative of the administration, leaving under his orders some of the officers whom he had brought with him. His own brother, Captain Raymond Portal, sad to say, had died.* The *Times* correspondent also remained in the country for a while, and afterwards rendered valuable service to Captain Macdonald.

Sir Gerald Portal had hardly left Mengo when the Muhammedan question suddenly began to assume an acute phase. The Muhammedan chiefs had agreed, under compulsion, to recognise Mwanga as their king, and to work for him and pay him tribute. At the same time they could not forget that they had never been crushed by the English infidels in battle, and that they had come back to Mengo rather as a compliment to Selim Bey than because they had been conquered by the English. Hence they were bitterly aggrieved that they had received no increase of territory by the Commissioners' award, while the " French " rebels had obtained a slice of country almost double the size of that they had occupied before the arrival

* One cannot help feeling that had these two gallant young Englishmen been better provided with English stores, so essentially necessary for Europeans in Africa, they might have better withstood the hardships they were called upon to undergo. See Sir Gerald Portal's " Journals."

of Sir Gerald Portal. The Muhammedans, however, had no French Government behind them, while in Captain Macdonald they had a man before them who knew his own mind.

The Commissioner had left orders that if the Muhammedan faction continued to refuse to do the king's work, and pay the king's taxes, their leaders should be seized and sent to Kikuyu.

On June 4th the handsome young Muhammedan and king's favourite, Lutaya, came, with several other half-hearted co-religionists, to tell Apolo, the Katikiro, that the Muhammedan faction were bent on fighting.

Apolo at once informed Captain Macdonald of what he had heard. Macdonald affected not to credit the report. Ten days later, however, he bade the king summon both the Roman Catholic and Muhammedan chiefs, and tell them to work for him.* The king did so, and told all the chiefs that they must build for him. The Roman Catholics at once agreed, but the Muhammedans demurred, and begged of the king to appoint them a day on which to lay their grievances before him. They asked also that they might be allowed to refer the matter to their party. Mwanga, however, said, "I give you till this afternoon, when you must return and tell me your intention."

They went therefore to Natete, where their canton-

* The work consists of building and fencing, and a fixed amount of such feudal labour for the king is attached to every chieftainship; for every chief holds direct from the king. The Muhammedans had accepted these feudal chieftainships, but now refused to contribute the quota of work for the king belonging to their offices.

ments were situated, and held a hasty counsel, with the result that they arranged to appear for the present to acquiesce in what the king demanded. At the same time they sent off one of their trusted adherents, Wanimba by name, to gather their fighting men, for in reality they had decided on war. The chiefs then returned to the king, saying, " We agree to work." But Juma, their principal man, repaired to Kampala to try and win over the Sudanese to give assistance to those who, like themselves, were people of Islam. Juma's pleading, it is averred, was not in vain. He said to the Sudanese, " Selim Bey brought us here. We came under his protection, and now the infidels are about to coerce us into working as their slaves. You have the guns of the white unbelievers in your hands. You, if you will, can give us aid." There is little doubt that Selim Bey, who had been instrumental with Dualla in bringing the Muhammedan faction in, had felt himself aggrieved at the treatment accorded to him by Sir Gerald Portal. He was a most important man, and a high official in the Khedive's service. His position with Lugard and Williams had been rather that of a coadjutor than an inferior. He had proved himself loyal to them in this capacity, and his control over his soldiers was truly remarkable. I myself was present at Mengo when this was shown in a striking manner. There happened to be present in Mengo a large number of Zanzibaris, who had come to Uganda in one of the Company's caravans ; and these men were encamped close to the cantonments of the Sudanese soldiers. A quarrel arose between a Zanzibari and one of Selim's soldiers, which had originated—like so many quarrels—over some dusky Helen. Soon the two camps took sides each with its own member, and a battle royal ensued; but very soon the Sudanese rushed to fetch their rifles, and were deaf to all remonstrances of officers, black or white, till Selim appeared. As soon as the Bey had shown himself discipline was instantly restored, and the storm was stilled.

Moreover, Selim's position as a Muhammedan in the heated religious atmosphere of Uganda was one of the deepest difficulty; but whether or not he really meant to resort to armed measures against the English Government it is a little difficult to decide. He was now receiving pay from the British Government, but seems to have considered that his position was rather to help and advise the administration than merely to obey. Lugard writes of him eloquently as the "veteran selected by Gordon for the command of Mruli, whose valour saved Dufileh, against whom no charge of disloyalty had ever yet been proved amidst all the faithlessness of the Sudan troops." The *Times* correspondent, on the other hand, seems to accept the version current in Uganda, and one, it must be said, for which there is strong presumptive evidence. I give the following extract from his letter, dated from Mengo, June 25th :—

" It has transpired recently, and there seems to be no special reason to doubt the report, that the outbreak was fixed for the night of June 18th. The Muhammedans were to attack and fire the king's palace and the French mission on Rubaga. In the meantime, the Sudanese at Kampala were to secure the fort, with all the Europeans, which they could undoubtedly have done with ease. Selim Bey, after disposing of Mr. Reddie and myself, was to join them with his troops from Fort Alice. The whole country would then have been in their hands. Holding a strong position, and possessing two Maxims (with the mechanism of which some of the Sudanese are well acquainted) and a large supply of arms and ammunition, they would have been completely masters of the situation, so far as the Protestants and Catholics were concerned. Embogo was then to be crowned King, and Selim Bey was to hold the position of Acting Resident. It was a bold and ingeniously contrived plot, and all one can say is, ' Thank God it did not succeed ! ' "

But whatever may be said in favour of Selim's loyalty, the utter hostility of the Uganda Muhammedans to their infidel superiors is undeniable. They had no experience of European power, as the Egyptians or Zanzibaris had, and their contempt and rancorous hatred for unbelievers of all kinds is difficult for English people to realise. Their enthusiasm and valour were undoubted, and this enthusiastic religious fervour on their part must have been very difficult for a follower of the prophet, as Selim was, to resist. By all reports, Selim swore on the book that if the Protestants attacked the Muhammedans to enforce the orders of the king he would render them assistance. On June 17th he wrote to Captain Macdonald to this effect. There was nothing secretly treacherous in his action, though, as he was in the English service, it was, to say the least of it, bordering upon open mutiny, since he was well aware that the English Commissioner supported the king.

Captain Macdonald had been obliged to send an ultimatum to the Muhammedan chiefs nearly a fortnight before when they had objected to work, and had threatened, unless they assented within two hours, to attack them. Selim's letter was written from Entebe (Fort Alice), some twenty miles distant from Mengo. The same day that the letter arrived (June 17th), Apolo, the Katikiro, was busy appointing the work in the king's enclosure to the different factions—the Protestants ten parts, the Roman Catholics five parts, and the Muhammedans two parts. While doing so he received an order from Captain Macdonald to collect his guns, for that there were signs of rebellion on the part of the Muhammedans. Captain Macdonald also visited the two missions, asking the Europeans to come quietly to Kampala. He told the missionaries that he had received a letter from the Bey, who claimed the right to be consulted in all disputes with the Muhammedans, who, he asserted, had only returned owing to his promise to protect them.

While one can feel the fullest sympathy with the fine old Bey, it is abundantly plain that the position he took up was absolutely impossible, and Captain Macdonald had no other course open but to settle, once and for all, who were the rulers in Uganda, the English Government or the Muhammedans. His position was most dangerous, and for a weak man who hesitated for a moment the consequences might have been most disastrous. Another element of danger was that the Manyuema Arabs had come into communication with the Uganda Muhammedans, and a powerful coalition seemed to be on the point of coming to a head. But Captain Macdonald was a strong man, and though gentle and courteous to the native chiefs he never allowed his kindness to be mistaken for weakness. He saw clearly the seriousness of the whole position, and acted promptly and energetically. Happily for himself he was in no sense responsible for the mischief with which he was now called upon to deal. He at once sent to recall Sir Gerald Portal, who had only been gone a little more than a fortnight, and who had not yet left Kavirondo. Also he recalled Captain Arthur from Busoga, and sent for the *Times* correspondent and Mr. Reddie (a Government officer), both of whom were at Fort Alice. Captain Macdonald, as we have seen, felt it necessary in this emergency to call to his aid all the Europeans in Mengo ; and, in order to bring them to Kampala without exciting suspicion, they were asked not to come all at the same time. It had been arranged that two of the English missionaries, Millar and Leakey, should go up to the fort for luncheon (this was on Saturday, June 17th). At 2 P.M. came Roscoe and Pilkington, accompanied by Forster * (now in the employment of Government), and later in the afternoon the French missionaries arrived.

* This gentleman had seen military service in South Africa, and had come to Uganda with Bishop Tucker. His work, as mine had been, was largely in the printing office, not that I would venture to compare what we respectively turned out.

Presently Embogo, who had formerly been styled Sultan, came in, with several of the leading Muhammedan chiefs, to ask why the people were getting under arms. This they were doing silently and quietly, without any noise of shouting or drum beating. It was too deadly a crisis for that. Every one knew that the time had come which was to decide the fate of Uganda. Captain Macdonald invited Embogo and the chiefs into his room, and told them he would tell them presently. As soon as they were inside he set a guard on the door, and then went out to deal with his Sudanese soldiers. He had already armed his nine Europeans with rifles, besides some one hundred and fifty Swahili porters from Zanzibar on whom he could depend. The Maxim guns were placed in position to command the spot where the troops were to be paraded. Captain Macdonald then called the Sudanese officers, and briefly told them that Selim Bey had set himself in opposition to the Government, and asked them : " Do you stand by the Bey or the Government ? " They professed themselves loyal. The soldiers were then ordered to fall in, and the same question was put. Those who were loyal were ordered to go to the right, those who recognised Selim were to stand steady. All the soldiers moved off to the right. Captain Macdonald then demanded of Embogo four of the leading Muhammedan chiefs as hostages for the good behaviour of their faction, and went himself to arrest them, with their leader, Juma, who had come into the fort with Embogo. He took six men with him. Juma walked in front, covered by the rifles of two of Macdonald's men, who had orders to shoot him if he should make the least endeavour to escape. When they reached Natete two of the three chiefs were secured, Kamya and Kamyagere ; another was ill, but sent two of his friends as security for his appearance. These, with Juma, made up the number whom Macdonald had determined to secure. They were safely lodged in the fort, and the missionaries returned to their respective missions. Orders were sent to Selim to say that he must remain at Fort Alice, and that he must send no more messages.

However, next day (Sunday, the 18th), in consequence of another message brought by Mr. Reddie from Selim Bey, Captain Macdonald judged it necessary to disarm the Sudanese soldiers. He again sent for the missionaries, whom he armed. He also called out his Zanzibaris, and put the Maxim guns into position. He then made the Sudanese soldiers fall in. He brought out the Muhammedan prisoners to be witnesses of what took place. They, thinking they were to be shot, cried out piteously to Pilkington to save them. Captain Macdonald then addressed the soldiers. He said he did not desire to impugn their loyalty ; but that, as Selim Bey had mutinied, he should be obliged to temporarily disarm them. Only one soldier showed any signs of hesitation, but his courage failed him, and he obeyed the order to ground arms. The rifles were collected, and the soldiers were ordered to their houses. Captain Macdonald then bid the Muhammedans who were collected at Natete to disperse and return to their country places, and he also sent those who were collected round Kampala to Natete, where their main camp was situated. That morning three hundred of their adherents, armed with guns, had arrived to swell the Muhammedan ranks, so that there was a large body of Mussulmans in open rebellion to Mwanga, Selim Bey in open mutiny at Fort Alice, and an unreliable garrison at Kampala. So that a second time, by the irony of fate, it became necessary for an English officer to arm the Protestant chiefs in order to vindicate and uphold English rule. Lugard and the late Sir Gerald Portal and others have represented these Protestants as if they were always on the point of annihilation by some one or other, and yet they were never found wanting when hard fighting had to be done.* The Muhammedans stood their ground for a time, but were defeated with great loss, and driven from the capital. Numbers of the Protestants were wounded.

On June 19th Captain Macdonald determined to go himself to Entebe to deal with Selim Bey, but just as he was about to set out some thirty soldiers appeared on the parade ground. These had been sent by Selim to say that he was loyal, and was guarding Fort Alice, only he begged of Captain Macdonald to stop the Christians from fighting the Muhammedans.

Next day Captain Macdonald went down to Fort Alice, leaving Captain Arthur, who had arrived mean-

* It is absurd to suppose that if the Protestants were as few and as feeble as they were represented to be, they could have secured, as they did, a good half of the country for themselves, before even the arrival in Uganda of the Imperial British East Africa Company.

while from Busoga, in charge of Kampala. He took with him Mr. Reddie and the *Times* correspondent.

Nikodemo, the old Sekibobo, also accompanied Captain Macdonald on his venturesome undertaking of seizing Selim Bey, surrounded as he was by his Sudanese soldiers.

Captain Macdonald went on ahead with six men whom he could depend upon. On arriving, he called out the garrison, and ordered them to ground arms. They replied: " We obey because Selim our leader has ordered us to do so," and asked that they might receive them back at once.

Captain Macdonald then gave the order: " Right— turn! Quick—march!" and the guns were instantly covered by the six loaded rifles held by Macdonald's men. Reddie was near at hand with a Maxim, while Nikodemo had posted his men in the long grass with rifles ready for any emergency.

Selim was soon arrested; he offered no resistance. At first he was sent to an island in the Lake (Nsazi); but subsequently it was decided to send him to the coast, together with Juma (who had been the chief agent in the rebellion) and Embogo, whose presence was a constant menace to the peace of the country. These three important personages Captain Macdonald asked the *Times* correspondent to take charge of as far as Kavirondo, where the late Sir Gerald Portal was awaiting news of the outbreak.

They left Uganda on June 10th, but on July 24th Juma succeeded in making his escape, having, somehow, obtained possession of a file, with which he cut through the chain which secured him. The adventures of this man would prove an interesting story if they could be written. He had been a prominent figure in the desperate fighting which had taken place since the year 1888.

About the third week in August poor old Selim Bey, who was suffering from dropsy, and had been carried all through the march to his last resting-place, died at one of the camps near Lake Naivasha.

And thus practically ended the Muhammedan rebellion and Sudanese mutiny. The Muhammedans were now deprived of two of their provinces, the governorship of Kitunzi and of Kasuju; and on July 13th the former was given to the Protestants, and the latter, and smaller, to the Roman Catholics, who seem to have left all the fighting to the Protestants.

On July 16th, Major Owen, accompanied by Wakirenzi (the same as Captain Williams' fighting chief Mulondo), pursued the Muhammedans, and came up with them not far from the Mpanga River,* and entered into communication with them. They professed their desire for peace. Major Owen then demanded that they should hand over fifty guns, and also a canoe which they had looted. Five of the fifty guns mentioned had just previously been stolen from Major Owen's men. They promised to yield up the guns, and said they would bring them at noon. They, however, determined to effect their escape, and march westward to join the Manyuema Arabs, with whom

* The Mpanga River is given by Lugard as 20° 3' N; 30° 20' E. Map 4, " Rise of our East African Empire," vol. ii.

they had entered into communication ; but Wakirenzi, having received information of their intention, came up with them, and found, as he suspected, that though they had appeared to wish for terms, they were, in reality, making preparations for retreat. A battle ensued by the banks of the Mpanga, the river which separates Unyoro from Toro, and the Muhammedans lost twenty-six killed, while the loss on the other side was only four. Most of the Muhammedan fighting men escaped to the further bank of the river ; but the great bulk of the women remained on the Toro side, and more than one thousand of them were captured. The battle took place on July 18th, and completely upset the plan of the Muhammedans to march towards the Congo.

Major Owen, who was some little distance away, now heard, through one of his Sudanese soldiers, that the defeated Muhammedans wished to return to Uganda. He therefore wrote to them, saying he had no desire to drive them from the country if they would live peaceably. They were glad to hear this, and sent back two of their principal men, Namfumbambi and Kaketo, with the five guns which had been stolen, to discuss the terms. Major Owen also sent two important Uganda chiefs, Stefano Kalibwani and the real Namfumbambi,* to the Muhammedan camp. Stefano, it will be remembered, was the man who, the previous year, had effected the escape of Mwanga from the Roman Catholics. Next day he returned with Kyayambade, the Muhammedan · leader, who said that they surrendered. This was the 20th. On the 23rd, the Baganda

* Each hostile faction usurped the names of chieftainships.

chiefs, who had seized the thousand women spoken of, now held a meeting, and agreed that all the women should be set free (I am giving their own version of the matter); so the captives were brought out to an open space, and they were asked what they wished to do. There is no doubt, whatever, that large numbers of them had been carried away by the Muhammedans against their will. So what follows is at least probable. Three hundred said they wished to return to the Muhammedans, which they were permitted to do there and then. Two hundred said they were Roman Catholics, and would go to their co-religionists; while four hundred elected to remain with the Protestants. The remainder, I suppose, were children.

When all this was over, Major Owen now bethought himself of the captured women, and told the Uganda commander to bring the captives that they might be dealt with. The commander replied that he had set them free. Major Owen was extremely annoyed that this had been done without his knowledge. Kakunguru Wakirenzi apologised most humbly for the omission, and as nothing could well be done no more was said. Peace having now been arranged, the late combatants set out on the return journey to Uganda.

Captain Macdonald, however, when he heard of the return of the Muhammedans, armed and organised, very wisely would not hear of their coming back under such conditions, and demanded that they should give up their arms unconditionally; and these terms they eventually were driven to accept. Captain Macdonald allowed them to settle in any part of Uganda that they preferred.

Some fifty of them, including Kyayambade the leader, elected to go to Budu : many went to Bulemezi and other places ; and, to quote the Katikiro's words, "every man went to the house of his father," and thus, on August 15th, happily ended the long and weary war with the Muhammedan faction. King Mwanga now, by Captain Macdonald's advice, conferred estates and gardens upon the returned prodigals, not in their capacity as members of a powerful religious or political faction, but as subjects of the king of all Uganda. In all this appeared the hand of a man who knew how to be both determined towards the rebellious, and, when such action could not possibly be mistaken for weakness, wisely generous to the defeated.

But long ere the arrival of this happy consummation I had left Mengo in company with Nickisson, *en route* for Nassa and the coast.

BOOK IV

FROM UGANDA TO ZANZIBAR

—

CHAPTER I

PERILS OF WATERS

Sorrowful Farewells—The People of Nassa—Members of my Party —Timoteo stung by a Scorpion—Wholesale Thieving—How is the Nyanza supplied with Water?—Making a Raft—A Stream like a Mill-Race—Making a Rope—The Raft swept from under Me—An unpleasant Predicament—A hospitable Reception—" Down on my Luck"—A severe Illness—True Story of a strange Incident—We owe our Lives to a small Act of Kindness—Oriental Embellishment.

CHAPTER I

PERILS OF WATERS

ON March 5th Nickisson and I left Mengo together. Many friends, both English and native, bade us farewell, and I was not a little touched by the kindness of Père Gaudibert, of the French mission, in coming to bid me good-bye. It was a true satisfaction to me, that in spite of the bitterly hostile attitude the converts of the French fathers and our own had held towards one another, and the serious political and religious difference dividing them, yet these courteous opponents, and especially the kindly Englishman, Père Gaudibert, and the English missionaries, always kept up a pleasant intercourse, and interchanged those small amenities which helped to smooth our necessarily difficult position.

My faithful friend, Samwili, who had been the first of the chiefs to welcome me to Uganda, was the last to bid me farewell; for he as well as the kindly old Nikodemo, the Sekbobo, came down to the Nyanza to see Nickisson and me embark in the canoes which were to take us across the Lake to Nassa on Speke Gulf, where I hoped to make up my small caravan for Zanzibar.

A day or two later we left Entebe (Fort Alice), the last point on the mainland of Uganda we should touch. At Entebe we had the saddest leave-taking of all. When we entered our canoe poor Kakonge, my good old cow-man with his one arm, waded into the water, and lifted up his voice and wept, while the warm-hearted Mabruki, my faithful follower standing knee-deep in the water, joined him with equal fervour. Other friends stood weeping on the bank, and my own eyes filled with tears. The word to start was now given, and soon nothing was heard but the rhythmical beat of the paddles, as twelve lusty canoe men sent the graceful boat flying through the water, and soon the sorrowful figures on the beach became indistinguishable. A little later, and the shore itself had become distant and dim as we pulled out towards the far-off island where we were to make our first camp ; and thus for the second time I bade farewell to Uganda and its kindly inhabitants.

Nickisson and I had a long but pleasant journey to Nassa, passing the German station at Bukoba, where we met Hubbard, my old companion in travel, bringing the new mission boat, the *James Hannington*, to Uganda. My former boy, Songoro,* was now

---

* When I first made Songoro's acquaintance he was a poor, half-starved, runaway slave, who had been raided by the Arabs, and taken refuge with my caravan seven years before. He accompanied me to Zanzibar, where I procured letters of freedom for him.

NASSA MISSION BOYS.

ENKOKO. MUHASSA. HENRY MUKASSA.

captain of the boat; he had become a fine strapping fellow. The poor lad was drowned a few weeks later, while attempting to do something to the anchor of the boat. He had dived into the water, but never came up alive. His body was recovered the next day.

At one of our camps we saw great numbers of hippos, so we went out in a canoe to try and get a shot. Nickisson landed on a rock which stood up some distance out in the Lake, and from that point was able to take a steady aim at a huge cow. On receiving one shot from the Martini she turned over instantaneously. We saw her four feet for an instant in the air, and then she sank. The same afternoon the carcass floated, and the canoe men towed it in. In a couple of hours the huge monster was cut up and carried off to be eaten. We tried some of the meat, but did not find it altogether a success. We had so many ducks that hippo meat was rather at a discount.

We did not finally reach Nassa until the end of March. The people here are very primitive, but kindly disposed, and apt now to be somewhat cringing, owing to their great dread of the Germans, who have a military station at no great distance. Some little progress has been made in teaching them; but those among them who appeared most impressed with Christianity were more or less outsiders, the chief Christian being half a Muhuma, one of the most intelligent tribes of the Bantu people.

I remained at Nassa some fourteen days, kindly entertained by Nickisson, but suffering from an attack of incipient dysentery, which afterwards on the journey nearly proved fatal. It was now the rainy season ; but in a fortnight's time from my arrival at Nassa the rains had sufficiently subsided to make a start possible. My party consisted of the following : Alberto Namenyeka, an Uganda chief, who had accompanied me, the boys, Timoteo Kaiyima, and Kangiri, already mentioned, who were about the same age (fifteen years), and of the same tribe, and one or two other lads. I had with me also a good-humoured Muganda named Musa, who had formerly served as a soldier in the German garrison at Bukoba. On his return to Uganda subsequently he had lived with me. He now acted as one of my guards, and was armed with a Winchester rifle. Alberto had a double-barrelled express rifle, Timoteo a Snider carbine, and Edgar * a faulty Snider rifle. These completed the list of my armed guards. I had besides about a dozen Nassa men carrying my baggage, and a mixed company of Wasukuma natives, who followed me with the intention of going to the coast to hire themselves out as porters in returning caravans. Subsequently I armed some of my porters with bows and arrows and spears, that they might have weapons of some kind to give them confidence. I then bade farewell to Nickisson, to whom I am indebted for many kindnesses, and not the least, his allowing me to make full use of the interesting pictures he had obtained with his camera.

I had bought a donkey from the Germans at Muanza, an animal which, failing a bicycle, is almost an in-

* A Freretown mission boy, who was returning to the coast.

dispensable adjunct to African travelling. The donkey I secured made my long seven hundred mile journey a pleasure rather than the weariness it must otherwise have been.

KAPONGO, THE CHIEF OF NASSA.

I left Nassa in pouring rain, and the first night of my journey (owing to a mishap which befell my boy Timoteo) proved anything but pleasant. One of the scorpions, so common in this country, stung him. They are not more than an inch or one and a half inches long, small and colourless, but they give a most frightful sting—nearly as bad, I was told, as the dreadful-looking black scorpions, some six or seven inches in length, found further south.

Timoteo came to me in great tribulation, and bemoaned himself all night long in my tent. Had I ever been stung? Yes. How long did the pain last? I said in my case it had lasted acutely for about two hours. In five minutes Timoteo stopped moaning to say, "Sir, is the two hours up?" "No;" and so on till dawn broke.* Neither of us had any sleep during the night.

My train of naked Wasukuma grew larger as we advanced, for we gained recruits at many of the villages, and some of these people, taking advantage of the presence of an European, unknown to me, here and there robbed the villages of the district through which I passed.

In one village I happened to sit down to rest, and presently one of the inhabitants came to complain of being robbed. On inquiry I found that one of my tail-men had loaded himself with all that he could carry away. I made him disgorge the stolen goods at once. I thought of tying him up and ordering him a castigation, but as he had a dreadful sore on his leg, and, moreover, was not actually one of my people, I contented myself with making him give compensation

* *Scorpion stings.*—I have been told since coming home that an onion applied to scorpion stings is a specific. I had, as it happened, some onions with me, but I did not know of their medicinal virtues or I might have tried the effect on Timoteo!

in the shape of an old fez cap, which he possessed, which seemed quite to satisfy the man whom he had intended to rob. This dishonest traveller afterwards proved most useful to me, and in spite of his bad leg and character, assisted, for some small consideration, to carry me when I became ill.

Going in a south-westerly direction, I passed through the districts of Usmao and Urima, and crossed various rivers, one or two of which were normally of considerable size ; but all were now swollen by the recent rains to enormous volume. These swift streams seem to be the key of the puzzle of how the Nyanza is supplied with water. The vast volumes of water that pour themselves into the Lake, rushing in wide and deep torrents through these southern regions, are almost inconceivable. Without resorting to more complicated theories, one can easily understand that during the rainy season a supply of water from these mighty feeders sweeps into the Nyanza sufficient to account for the existence of the Lake. .

I had not thus far been able to shake off my threatened dysentery, a sickness not unfrequently fatal to African travellers, but an unpleasant accident which very shortly happened to me made the threat a dire reality.

I had advanced but slowly, for I found the swamps and watercourses much more frequent than I had been prepared to expect. At last I was brought to a halt, and kept waiting for a couple of days, for one of these raging torrents to go down sufficiently for my caravan to cross over. Each day during my involuntary halt

I sent men to bring the news of the stream, and whether it had yet become fordable. The third morning they told me it might possibly be feasible to attempt a crossing ; but they seemed very doubtful. However, I determined to make the attempt. We successfully crossed one great swamp and river, but soon, on surmounting the next rising ground, I saw in front of me what appeared like a small lake ; however, when we approached it, I thought it seemed fairly shallow, and to be flowing somewhat sluggishly. I therefore cast about for some means of crossing. But there was nothing in the way of a boat. I thought of a raft, but there was no wood of any kind within reach. My eye suddenly caught sight of the poles, on each end of which my porters were carrying their loads balanced over their shoulders. The poles were some eight feet in length, and were usually formed of the lightest kind of wood procurable, notably the ambatch, or failing that the stem of the palm branch. I collected from my followers a quantity of these poles together with the cord (twisted out of strong fibre), which they use for tying up their bundles. With this cord I tied the poles side by side to two or three cross-pieces. Among my baggage I had two zinc-lined watertight boxes. These I emptied of their contents and lashed on to the raft, and then over these a few more carrying poles to form a kind of platform. The boxes were about one foot in depth, so that they gave the raft great buoyancy.

I then launched my novel craft. It floated splendidly, and I took my seat upon it, while the men, wading by my side, propelled the raft through the shallow waters. I was delighted with the success of my invention, and received with complacency the praises bestowed on the masala (cleverness) of the Muzungu (Englishman). Presently we reached a little island, where I disem-

"EDGAR," SHOWING ALSO UGANDA ENTRANCE AND DOOR BEHIND.

barked, and saw, to my dismay, that though we were only some fifteen or sixteen yards from the opposite bank, between the island and the other side there rushed a swift stream like a mighty mill-race, fully seven or eight feet deep. The shallow and sluggish stream already passed was merely the overflow of this watercourse. Edgar, already mentioned, a lad aged about seventeen, was a strong swimmer, so he jumped in, and was soon swept to the other side, reaching the bank forty or fifty yards lower down. I thought if I could get a rope across I might be able to work the raft across by hauling it backwards and forwards. So I went back to my porters and collected all the rope, cord, and string in the caravan. There was a considerable quantity of cocoa-nut rope from Zanzibar, with which most of the baggage was tied, also some Uganda executioner's cord, and an Usoga rope, which I was taking home as a curiosity. Everything in the shape of cord that I could lay my hands on was requisitioned, and we twisted it into a strong rope. Then I returned to my island. Edgar took one end of the rope, and, after two or three unsuccessful efforts, carried the end to the opposite bank, where he secured it. What with the long morning march and the raft making and rope twisting, the day was nearly spent. We had all been too busy to think of cooking. I was anxious to make the experiment of crossing before the light failed. I had established a communication between the island and the opposite bank ; but the weak point in the affair was that I had not sufficient rope to attach to each end of my raft, and so haul it backwards and forwards. Meanwhile a little party of villagers from the other side—people of Urima—having taken the precaution of driving off their cattle, now came down, and for some time watched my proceedings with great interest. They quite saw what I was trying to do, and kindly volunteered to hold the end of the rope at their own side. I thought I might be able to cross on the principle of a chain ferry, and work my light raft across holding on to the rope, which was now stretched across the stream. I therefore embarked, and pushed myself off. At first all went well, and my hopes rose; but as I advanced nearly to the middle of the flood I saw that I had wofully miscalculated the force of the torrent. The strain on the rope became very great, and the result was that one end of the raft went under water, and I found I must either let go the rope and be swept down the stream on my fragile vessel without any pole or oar, or else cling to the rope myself and let my raft go. I decided on clinging to what was a pretty fair certainty rather than risk a lonely voyage in unknown waters. I therefore held on to the rope. In another moment the raft was swept from under me, and went dancing down the stream. I was now in the water, the torrent gurgling in my ears and sweeping along with such force that it was all I could do to retain my hold on the rope. If one of the groups on land had let go the other could easily have hauled me safely ashore; but I dare not shout to them to let go; for then both parties would probably have let go simultaneously, and, weighted with boots and clothing as I was, and weak with sickness, I should most probably have been drowned. So I determined again to hold on, and work hand over hand to the opposite bank. My wisest plan would of course have been to return to the island where my friends and all my belongings were; but I had only room in my head at the moment for the thought that the other side was the place I was bound for, and so to the other side I would go. So I struggled on, and reached the opposite bank very much fatigued. The whole thing, had I been strong and well, would have been merely an amusing accident; but under the circumstances of my being so unwell it was a serious mishap. The sun had now sunk, a cold wind was blowing, and I was wet through and through. I had landed among semi-hostile savages, who entertained a strong grudge against all white men, owing to their hatred of the Germans. I was weak and ill, and an unfordable torrent ran between me and my friends and supplies. I had no inclination to cross the water again; and I thought it would be better to sleep in the village, where I could at least dry myself by a fire, than to run the risk of being drowned. I was, moreover, too weak to make the attempt. A day or two before I had, as it happened, read in a newspaper, which I had with me, of an unhappy man who lost his life in the Mersey. There had been a collision in the river, and he had managed to grasp with his hands the bowsprit of the vessel which had run into his own ship. He was able to support himself for a while, but gradually his hold relaxed, and he was heard to cry out, "I'm done for, I'm going," and when he had said this the poor fellow fell off into the water and was drowned. This narrative had kept occurring most strongly to my mind as I struggled across clinging to my rope, and feeling the while very near being done for and going. I had imagined myself being whirled down the torrent in the manner my ill-starred raft had disappeared.

As soon as they dragged me ashore I said to one of the natives who had held the rope, "Tujage Kaya" ("Let us go home"). I knew a few words of their dialect. And so these kind folk took my two arms and helped me up the opposite hill. We went on for a mile and a half till we reached the village. I was by this time shivering with cold. My hosts now entered a small circular house, where to my delight I saw there was a fire. There was a wild stampede as a terrified little boy tried to climb a high partition in order to effect his escape. However, my guide reassured him sufficiently to prevail upon him to make his exit by the ordinary method, through the door. The women folk also took their departure, and I was left alone with my guides. Very soon several of the villagers came in to hear the news of my disastrous shipwreck and to see the strange white guest. I took the liberty of divesting myself of all my clothes in order to dry them, an operation watched by the spectators with the keenest interest. My host kindly lent me his best suit—a small goat skin—in which I arrayed myself while my clothes were drying. I sat on the foot of the bed—an inclined frame, on which were stretched a couple of hard cow-skins. A small beam at the foot of the bed formed a ledge to keep the sleeper from sliding off. I sat on this ledge till it was time to go to bed.

I had half a ship's biscuit in my pocket, which had been soaked in the water, a small clock, and a note-book. I sadly ate my biscuit, and the kindly host brought me some sour milk, which I drank with great relish. He gave me some Indian corn, but I was afraid to eat it owing to my weak condition. After a while Edgar appeared ; he had kindly come to keep me company. No one else was able to cross the river. I then tried to settle down for the night, but presently the mosquitos came in myriads, and I fell an easy prey to these cruel adversaries. I made Edgar crouch near me on the bed to keep me warm, and covered myself, as far as I was able, with my damp garments, and then towards morning fell into unrestful dreams.

Next day I sent Edgar to go and see if the water had at all abated. When he was gone I went after him and called him back, and told him if he could to swim the river to fetch me some things wrapped in my mackintosh sheet, and to tell Timoteo to pack them. He started on his mission, and I went sadly back to the village, feeling more melancholy and lonely, more "down on my luck" than I had felt for many a long day. My low spirits were no doubt the result of my weakness and want of food. I went into the hut, and sank down on my cow-skin bed to find strength in the tender love of an Almighty Comforter. Before this the stream which I had crossed-had seemed to my agitated imagination like a nightmare torrent rolling between hope and myself. If I had only had Timoteo with me to sympathise a little it wouldn't have seemed so bad. I don't know how long I was thus meditating, when suddenly Edgar appeared with my head man, and chief of the Nassa party, who had managed to cross the river. Edgar brought a parcel containing biscuits, condensed milk, tea, and bovril, wrapped up in a sheet. He brought besides a small copper kettle. He also gave me the pleasing intelligence that my raft had been recovered, and that the river was much abated. Soon the kettle was boiling and the tea made, and the horizon became bright and smiling, and loathed melancholy took her flight. A cup of tea under such circumstances is a fit theme for a Cowper. In the afternoon Timoteo and Kangiri arrived; the latter had been half drowned in crossing. They had been helped across by some stalwart natives accustomed to these torrents, but Kangiri had been carried down the stream, and was only recovered with the greatest difficulty. The poor little fellow suffered nearly as much from his immersion as I did, for in a day or two he developed pleurisy, and became too weak to walk. The result of my wetting was a severe attack of dysentery. I therefore pitched my camp, and awaited with some anxiety the turn affairs would take. I knew it must soon end one way or another, and, humanly speaking, I owe my life to the nursing of Timoteo, who never left me night or day, and also to a good supply of drugs and the cornflour which I had with me. The third morning the symptoms abated, and I made a start on the donkey; but I soon found that I was far too weak to sit up, and so I hired a few of the supernumeraries who were following to carry me. And in this way I travelled for three or four days.

I have given rather minute details of a perhaps

trifling incident, but I have done so as an illustration of the kind of accidents which may befall even a well-equipped traveller in a country like Africa.

Leaving Usukuma, I came southwards to Usongo, Stokes' village, where the great trader was awaiting one of his ivory caravans preparatory to his journey with his hosts of porters to the coast. He treated me with kindness, and gave me a present of goats. While here I met Mr. Muxworthy, who related to me the true story of an incident that occurred the last time I was on my way to Zanzibar from the Nyanza in the year 1888.

Two hundred miles of the road from Mpwapwa to Zanzibar lay through the districts disturbed owing to the armed resistance to the aggression of Germany by the Arabs and their native allies. At Mpwapwa I had joined Dr. Pruen, who had just been recalled to the coast, and who was about to undertake the journey with his brave wife and a six-weeks-old baby, little Stella. As we advanced further and further towards Zanzibar we found that we were in a thoroughly hostile country, and that it would be dangerous in the highest degree to go on. It was with the utmost difficulty that we were able to communicate with the English Consul-General at Zanzibar, and to inform him of the very dangerous position in which we were placed.

Our Consul at once begged of the then Sultan, Seyyid Khalifa, to use his influence for our protection, and this he promised to do, but, as Sir Charles Euan Smith subsequently learned, with no intention of keeping his word.

The Sultan at that time was really bitterly opposed to the Germans, and indeed to all Europeans in the interior, though he was nominally supporting them with his soldiers; but as these soldiers, as I have heard, were supplied with blank cartridges for use against their co-religionists, their presence cannot have been very valuable to their German allies. The Sultan, at any rate, would not lift a finger for our help any more than he did in the case of another missionary, Mr. Brooks, who was afterwards murdered in the same district, governed by the Arab chief, Bwana Heri.

We, however, owed our lives to a small act of kindness which had been performed for the chief in question by Mr. Muxworthy, who was then acting as our business agent in Zanzibar. Mr. Muxworthy's version of the story was as follows: " He had sent one of his own men to accompany the Consul-General's messengers to Bwana Heri, who lived at Sadaani, the small coast town to which we were making our way. The chief and the Arab elders met in the open square of the town to discuss what should be done. All voices were eager that the hated Europeans should be killed, and the question was warmly argued until sunset. At last Bwana Heri addressed the assemblage in the following terms: 'Listen to me,' he said, ' that I may speak. You know how the English not many days since seized my jahazi (dhow), and were about to condemn her as a slaver and to break her up, when my friend Bwana Muxworthy went himself to the Baloza (British Agent), and falling on his knees before him implored him to spare the vessel of me his friend Bwana Heri. The Baloza heard his prayer, and my jahazi was restored to me through the intercession of my friend. Now he has sent to pray me to protect his friends, and shall I not do so? By Allah! but I will. 'Bass' (enough, the matter is ended)."

All applauded Bwana Heri's decision, and our safety was secured. Next day the old man sent his own son Abdallah, with some dozen soldiers, to escort us to the coast. The mission steamer, the *Henry Wright*, had endeavoured to land a boat at Sadaani in hopes of taking us off, but she was fired upon by the Arabs, and had to withdraw. We were eventually, however, safely embarked in Bwana Heri's dhow—the very jahazi, I suppose, that Mr. Muxworthy had been the means of restoring to its owner—and in it we finally made our escape.

Bwana Heri's story was somewhat embellished with Oriental figures. Mr. Muxworthy had not found it necessary to fall on his knees before the British Consul, but in the court he had been able to give satisfactory proof that the suspected dhow was not a slaver, when she was at once restored to her owner. This little incident serves to show on what slender threads our lives often hang.

CHAPTER II

PERILS IN THE WILDERNESS

Our Hosts hold their Noses—Ikungu must be won on Pain of Death—Another Object of Charity—Will he win Ikungu?—My first Patient dies—Price's Bicycle—No One to teach the Glad Tidings—Carried off by a Lion—Disputing its Prey with a Lion—Waiting for the Tide—Generous Kindness of Sir Lloyd Mathews—Interview with H.H. Sayyid Hamid bin Thwain.

CHAPTER II

PERILS IN THE WILDERNESS

A DAY or two after leaving Usongo we entered an uninhabited wilderness, and one morning we reached a river, now merely a sandy bed with here and there a pool. The margin of the river was lined with palm trees, on which were perched numbers of cranes, which had collected to feed upon the fish that now swarmed in the infrequent pools. All discipline immediately vanished from my caravan, my loads were flung down in the river bed, and the men went off pell-mell to secure the fish. They came back loaded, but looking sheepish; for they knew they had done wrong. As each one came up I made him throw his fish on the ground; and when all had come up I said, "Now what have you gained by leaving my loads, perhaps for robbers to seize? How much fish do you possess now?" "We have gained nothing," they replied, "and we have done wrong." Though I had made them relinquish their fishy spoils, I had no intention of allowing them to lose so valuable a provision for the journey. So I now said, as they had acknowledged their fault, I would overlook it, and, what was more, I would forfeit a day's journey, and make my camp here in order that they might collect a goodly supply of fish and partially cure it. The men were delighted, while the theory of discipline had been vindicated. We then made our camp among the palm trees, and soon many hundredweights of fish were brought in. Frames were made on which to place the fish, when cleaned, in order to smoke it. This process went on during the rest of the day and all night through. Many of the fish were enormous, some of them weighing fully twenty pounds, if not more. When we started next morning we were simply staggering under our load of fish, which lasted the Nassa men more than a month—until, in fact, we reached Zanzibar.

A little later, when we entered one of the enormous villages of Ikungu with our stinking provision, we were received with the most ludicrously absurd gestures by the inhabitants,* who, anxious to see us and hear the news, came up holding their noses lest their sense of smell should be outraged by our "fishy fume." This village was visited at night by huge hyænas, which prowled round the tent. Edgar fixed up his rifle with a piece of fish on the muzzle connected by a string with the trigger. When all was quiet a hyæna came and snatched the fish, and in so doing discharged the

---

* It is a curious circumstance that the southern Wanyamwezi, or Badakama, who do not live near the Nyanza, will not touch fish, while that branch of the tribe which lives on the shores of the Lake are skilful fishermen, and largely live on the produce of this industry.

rifle, the bullet passing through his own head. He fell dead a few yards off, and was discovered in the morning lying huge and stark. These great brutes, it is said, can smash the leg bone of a zebra with their mighty jaws.

Ikungu is on the edge of the grim wilderness separating Unyamwezi from Ugogo, a desert of six days' journey. Woe to the weak and feeble of a heavily loaded caravan when once they have entered the terrible Muganda—for that is the name of the wilderness—there is no turning back. Ikungu must be won on pain of death. How many a tale of horror could this mighty waste unfold! We had not gone more than two days' journey in the wilderness when a huge native caravan—fully a thousand people—passed us, all carrying up to what seemed their utmost capacity. The goods consisted of bales of cotton cloth, long muzzle-loading guns, gunpowder in 10 lb. kegs, brass and copper wire, and not unlikely a number of breech-loading rifles and ammunition concealed in the bales.

The next day I was destined to see for myself some of the gleanings of the wilderness. As we passed through a scrubby piece of forest Timoteo, who usually kept in front, suddenly appeared at the side of the path waiting for me to come up. He had halted to draw my attention to a poor creature, who, unable to stagger on, had fallen down to die. Timoteo had feared that I might not notice him, as he lay a yard or two from the pathway. Most of my other followers would have passed by with the utmost indifference.

Timoteo had therefore remained to point out this poor
fellow-creature in distress. It was a piteous sight—a
skeleton with dusky skin stretched over it; a ghastly
sore on the shoulder filled with flies; a filthy scrap
of rag as a covering—yet a brother with life still
lingering in his body. What was to be done? It
was an almost hopeless case. I gave him a little
brandy and some Valentine's beef juice. This roused
him up. I dressed his sore. I cooked cornflour for
him, and forced him to eat it till he wept at my
cruelty in not leaving him to sleep his death sleep
in peace. I improvised a hammock of my tent floor-
cloth, and hired two strapping fellows, who had followed
me from Ikungu, to carry the poor dying creature.
We then started again on our journey, and kept on till
the sun was sinking, when, just as we entered the palm
trees which marked water and our camp, I saw that
Timoteo had again halted, and had another object of
charity by his side—an elderly man with a long staff
in his hand, and carrying on his head a potsheard
containing a half-handful of dried beans, his whole
provision for what would be for him a two or three
days' journey. The poor fellow was now light-headed,
and had been walking almost mechanically, not knowing
whither he was wandering in this night now coming
down on him with its horror of darkness. I gave
him the remains of the Valentine's beef juice and the
brandy which I had mixed for the patient of the
morning, and his eyes were enlightened. As soon as
I reached camp and had a fire lighted, I made the
boys cook a dish of ugali (porridge) and a fowl,

and after a good supper he fell asleep. Next morning I had to move on, and the question arose, What were we to do with Number Two? He said his legs had given out two days since, and he had fallen behind with two others, whose corpses we should pass. They had fallen, while he had staggered on till he chanced to meet us. I told him he had better make up his mind what to do, either to follow us or go forward. It was a good forty miles whichever way he went; but his home lay in the direction of Ikungu—that is, the opposite way to which we were going. He said he would attempt the journey. We therefore cooked a mass of ugali, and tied it up in a cloth for him, and gave him the fat tail of a sheep, and, what he particularly begged for, a box of matches. And, thus provided, he set out on that forty miles' journey leaning on his staff. There was happily plenty of water on the way; and at every stage were deserted camps with plenty of huts surrounded by thorn bushes, left by the caravan that had passed, and also plenty of fuel to his hand, collected for fires by the people who had slept in that camp; he had, moreover, his precious box of matches. But there were, on the other hand, hyænas and hungry lions prowling in the wilderness; there was his weakness and weariness; and I could not but have many misgivings as I watched him take his solitary westward path, and I have often since wondered whether he succeeded in traversing the long forty miles, and in winning Ikungu; but I never heard.

We had not left our camp very long when we came

upon the ghastly sight of the corpse of one of the two men which our friend had told us we should see. It was partially devoured by a hyæna, and was a truly horrible sight. The other dead body had been dragged out of sight.

Such is the result of the present system of caravan travelling, and the moral of these incidents is—let a railway be made. The next night my poor patient, whom I had by this time transported fully forty miles, at last succumbed. My men thought me a fool for bothering a dying man by moving him; but what could I do? I left him lying by our camp fire just as he had died. There was no time to make a grave, for one and all were anxious to be out of the Muganda Mukali—the terrible wilderness.

We had thus passed safely through the great wilderness, and happily without other adventures than those already related. We journeyed on through Ugogo to Kisokwe, the mission station near Mpwapwa, where I found my kind friends the Coles both ill in bed. I was, however, hospitably received by Mr. Briggs, also stationed at Kisokwe. The next camp was Mpwapwa, where another old friend and faithful missionary, the Rev. J. C. Price, was carrying on his work. He had just had some interesting baptisms in the river which runs through the valley at some distance from his house. The heathen stood on one bank with the candidates among them, while those who had already received baptism stood on the other. The candidates then descended into the water, and were duly baptised, after which they came up out of the water, and were received by the little Christian congregation on the other bank.

REV. T. C. PRICE'S MISSION CHILDREN. THE GIRL HOLDING THE
BOOK IS DAUGHTER OF THE UGOGO CHIEF OF MPWAPWA.

Price had a bicycle, but he had injured it in learning to ride ; besides, it was rather too light for rough African work. Still for the level plains of Ugogo, of which country Price may be called the apostle, a good bicycle, I should imagine, would be indispensable. I give an illustration of three young girls who were Price's "children." While I was at Mpwapwa the boys brought in three baby leopards. I thought of trying to carry one to the coast, but it was too young for the attempt, as I could procure no milk with which to feed it.

Bidding farewell to Price I journeyed to Mamboya, my ideal of beautiful scenery, where I was most kindly welcomed by the Missionary Deekes and his wife. She had a fine baby, which was a credit to its mountain home. With them I remained a day or two, and then once more turned my face coastwards. I need not dwell on the incidents of the journey to the sea, which was accomplished without any mishap. I made a point of visiting my friends at Mazengos, whom I have mentioned before. And there, sure enough, was little Kilimo and the others just the same as ever, except that they had grown during my absence.

As I talked to these intelligent people it struck me as very grievous that no one had ever attempted to teach them the glad tidings of the kingdom of God. The French—those intrepid missionaries—had indeed a mission station not very far away, but they never had attempted to teach in the villages of this district.

While here I became acquainted with the story of as curious a lion adventure as I have ever heard.

I happened to be sitting in my tent door, when I saw a number of Wanyamwezi approaching me leading a boy. They came up and saluted me, and asked me for medicine for the lad. I noticed that his head was covered with a piece of calico. On removing the covering I saw that there were two deep furrows, one on each side of the scalp, reaching from the back to the forehead. The skull had been laid bare; the poor boy looked much emaciated from loss of blood. I asked how this had happened, and with many gesticulations a big man, who seemed to be the leader, told me the following story :—

They formed a small party which was making its way to the coast. A few evenings before they had reached a camping ground where there was water, and prepared as usual to turn in for the night. They made a boma (enclosure) of thorn bushes to keep off wild animals, and inside this they put up a few grass huts in which to sleep. One of their number, a lad, went off a little distance with his axe to cut some firewood, while others drew water and prepared to cook their evening meal, consisting of thick porridge (ugali), and made of the meal which they carried with them. The lad who had gone to cut the fuel, however, did not return, and his companions, wondering what had become of him, went in a body to search for him. They found the axe, but the boy was gone—*a lion had carried him off*. With heavy hearts they returned to their little camp, lighted the fire, and cooked their food, and one can imagine, as they sat there with the shadow of their loss upon them, how they related grim stories of similar misadventures, with which African native travel is so abundantly and so fearfully supplied.

They then made up the fires, and lay down to sleep. The fires burned lower and lower, and the sleepers must have been weary with their journey, for none of them arose from time to time, as travellers usually do, to heap fuel on the dying fires.

Suddenly they were awakened by the horrible deep growling of a lion which had leapt their little boma, and had seized one of their number, whose agonising shrieks told my informant that it was his own boy who was the lion's victim. The others, terrified out of their wits, sprang from the enclosure, and ran they knew not whither. But the boy's father, my informant, a great strong fellow, had no notion of so running. He had no time to snatch up even a spear, but went straight for the lion, which had fixed his claws in the lad's skull. He struck the monster over and over again full in its face with his clenched fist, uttering the while fierce cries of anger. And though unarmed, so dauntlessly did he dispute its prey with the savage beast, that the lion was actually cowed, and relinquished the boy from whose wounds the blood was pouring, and leaping back into the darkness from which it had sprung, left the father triumphant, and the boy, though wounded, safe. Their trembling companions now came back, the fires were replenished with fuel, and they bound up the lad's wounds as best they could. There was little more sleep for them that night, and the fires were kept bright, as the little party waited for the rising of the sun to continue their journey.

Such was the story of these simple folks. I

TIMOTEO MUDEMUGGA. BADUBAZE. KAGWA. KANGIRI JIMMY.
R. P. ASHE. ALBERT NAMENYEKA, A CHIEF.

thoroughly washed the poor boy's wounds with carbolic acid and water, and bound them up. Two days later, when I left Mazengos, the little band to which the lad belonged attached themselves to me, that their boy might have the benefit of my treatment, and every day I used to dress his wounds. The injured boy walked behind me all the way to Sadaani, more than one hundred miles, and the wounds were doing well when I left him in order to cross to Zanzibar.

We crossed over on Saturday night, and reached Zanzibar on Sunday morning, to the no small disgust of the agents. It was not my fault, however, that I arrived on a Sunday, for I had embarked in the dhow on Friday night; we had to go on board before the tide came up. The dhow lay over on her side, and we sat miserably waiting for the water to come up and float us. The tide came up indeed, but only dallied near us for a time, and then receded, leaving us where we were; it had not come quite far enough to float us. This was annoying, but no one in particular was to blame, and I had to remain another day to await a more favourable tide. The German officers at Sadaani treated me with much kindness and hospitality. At last the dhow floated, and we made our voyage to Zanzibar, which we safely reached. I was accompanied by Albert, an Uganda chief, and my boys. I had to wait for a full week before the arrival of the European mail, and I employed the interval in showing my Uganda companions the wonders of European and Asiatic civilisation, as represented at Zanzibar. We paid a visit to the Universities Mission, where we were courteously received by the late Bishop Smithies. But the person of all others who loaded us with kindnesses was the Sultan's chief minister, Sir Lloyd Mathews, whose name is so well known in connection with Zanzibar. I think I learnt during my visit to Zanzibar the secret of Sir Lloyd's marvellous influence with the people of Africa and with the Arabs.

His generous kindness to myself (an entire stranger), to the young Uganda chief whom I had with me, and even to my boys Timoteo and Kangiri, I can never forget.

We must come and dine with him, the whole party of us, chief and boys together. Had we all been English noblemen we could not have been treated with greater courtesy, consideration, or kindness. It struck me as strange indeed that a truth which had dimly dawned upon me as containing the secret of missionary success in dealing with natives, as being the basis of Christianity itself—namely, the simple power, without any appearance of condescension, of treating human beings as brothers, without reference to their quality at all. This power was here exhibited as a definite system by the chief minister of Zanzibar. That his rare abilities have been recognised by our own Government appears in the fact of the distinction of a well-earned knighthood which has been conferred upon him.

Before leaving Zanzibar, my friend Albert, the chief, and myself, had the honour of a private interview with the Sultan, His Highness Sayyid Hamid bin Thwain.

He received us most courteously, and spoke sensibly about the opening up of Africa, the price of ivory in the interior, and other topics. We had an interpreter, but both Albert and I understood enough Swahili to carry on a conversation with the Sultan in that language. The Sultan made Albert a rich present, and gave Jimmy, who had followed us, a handsome waistcoat.

Before I left for England I took my Uganda band to be photographed, that I might preserve a memento of my kindly companions.

On July 4th I bade these faithful friends a sorrowful farewell, leaving them in the kind care of Sir Lloyd Mathews, until my friend Walker should arrive at the end of the month to relieve him of the charge he so generously undertook.

I must now also bid my reader farewell, with the hope that I have been able in some measure to interest him in these " Chronicles of Uganda."

APPENDICES

A. *Instructions to the late Sir Gerald Portal.*
B. *Letter of the late Sir Gerald Portal on Mission Extension.*
C. *The War against Unyoro.*
D. *Correspondence relating to Toro and Uvuma.*

APPENDIX A

INSTRUCTIONS TO THE LATE SIR GERALD PORTAL

(SEE PAGE 393.)

(i) The following were the instructions delivered to Sir Gerald Portal :—

"FOREIGN OFFICE, *December 10th*, 1892.

"SIR,

"The Imperial British East Africa Company has decided to complete the evacuation of Uganda by March 31st. With that evacuation Her Majesty's Government have determined not further to interfere.

"2. They have, however, resolved to despatch you, in your capacity as Commissioner for the British sphere of influence in East Africa, to Uganda, there, after investigation on the spot, to frame a report, as expeditiously as may be, on the best means of dealing with the country, whether through Zanzibar or otherwise.

"3. The Company have offered to make over to Her Majesty's Government their establishments and stores in Uganda. It will be for you to judge how far it may be necessary or expedient to avail yourself of this proposal.

"4. It will, of course, be your first duty to establish friendly relations with King Mwanga. It may be necessary for this purpose to give him presents, and even, for the moment, to subsidise him, but you will make no definite or permanent arrangement for subsidy without reference to me.

"5. You will impress upon the king that in following the advice which you may give him he will best be proving the sincerity of the assurances given by him and his chiefs in their letter to the Queen of June 17th, and that your mission cannot fail to satisfy him of the interest which is taken by the British Government in the country.

"6. The other points on which you should dwell in your communications with the king and chiefs are the prevention of broils stirred up under the name of religion, the promotion of peace, the encouragement of commerce, the security of missionary enterprise, and the suppression of the slave-trade.

"7. One considerable difficulty is inherent in the situation. The Company has of late concluded a great number of treaties with native chiefs, including one of perpetual friendship with Mwanga, which last, however, has not been ratified by the Secretary of State. There are many others (eighty-three in all) which have been so approved. Whether an approval of this kind can be held in any way, directly or indirectly, to bind Her Majesty's Government is a moot point. There is no doubt of the liability of the Company, and of the fact that the Company, having concluded these treaties, finds itself compelled to evacuate the country, without making any endeavour to implement them. It is to be feared that this proceeding may have a prejudicial effect on the British good name in these regions, and I shall be anxious to have your report on this point with as little delay as possible, as well as on the course to adopt with reference to these engagements.

"8. A mission to Central Africa cannot of course be conducted according to ordinary precedent; the infrequency and difficulty of communication may require a latitude beyond what is usual, and in entrusting to you these important duties Her Majesty's Government reckon with full confidence on your meeting with firmness and caution every occasion that may arise.

"9. Her Majesty's Government desire that your expedition shall be fully officered and equipped. There will therefore be attached to you Mr. Ernest James Lennox Berkeley, Colonel Rhodes, Major Owen, Captain Portal, and Lieutenant Arthur. You will also take the interpreters and guides that you may deem necessary, and an adequate force of armed natives.

"10. It will be your duty to sign a commission appointing one of the above officials to act on your behalf in case of your being incapacitated. You will use your own discretion as to which it shall be.

"11. During your absence on this mission it will be necessary to supply your place as Consul-General at Zanzibar. Her Majesty's Government will lose no time in sending there a suitable official to act in this capacity. Should, however, any interval elapse between your departure and his arrival, you will instruct Mr. C. S. Smith to represent the Agency.

"I am, etc.,

(*Signed*) " ROSEBERY."

APPENDIX B

LETTER OF THE LATE SIR GERALD PORTAL ON MISSION EXTENSION

The following is the letter referred to on p. 399 :—

SIR G. PORTAL TO THE EARL OF ROSEBERY.

(*Received June 27th.*)

"KAMPALA, *April 8th*, 1893.

"MY LORD,

"In continuation of my immediately preceding despatch, I have the honour to report that, on the conclusion of the agreement respecting the territorial and political divisions between Catholics and Protestants in Uganda itself, I submitted to the two Bishops the expediency of arriving at some understanding as to mission extension in the future, which should be a safeguard against the recurrence, in the neighbouring countries within the British sphere, of the lamentable events which have cost so many lives and been such a reproach to Christianity in Uganda itself. Both the Bishops at once admitted that some such mutual arrangement was greatly to be desired, but each added that he was not at liberty to bind himself to restrict in any way his sphere of religious work without the consent of the Vatican on the one side and of the committee of the Church Missionary Society on the other.

"I then suggested that the object might be attained if they could now agree upon a purely temporary arrangement, and that there would be every reason to hope that, if such a · *modus vivendi* were recommended by them to their respective authorities, it might be allowed to remain in force for a limited time, or until the dangerous excitability and fanaticism of the natives had been to some extent calmed by Christian teaching and by the absence of rivalry in the immediate neighbourhood. I was careful to explain that I wished to take no official part in the discussion, and that, if any agreement could be come to, it must be simply in the nature of an understanding between the heads of the mission themselves. Monseigneur Hirth then suggested that the Church Missionary Society should, for the present at all events, undertake to work only eastward of the Nile, and towards the Indian Ocean, leaving all the north and west to the Catholics. Bishop Tucker demurred to this, and it soon appeared that each mission was desirous of establishing a station near Mount Ruwenzori, in the district of Toro. As the people of this region are in constant communication with Uganda, and are reported to be of a similarly excitable nature, it appeared more than probable that the simultaneous establishment of rival missions there would be the precursor of fresh troubles. I therefore explained that should these plans be carried into execution, and should I be responsible for the maintenance of peace in Uganda, I should not feel bound to intervene in any way in the event of riots taking place in Toro, but should simply take precautions against the infection spreading into Uganda, and against any of the Waganda going to aid their co-religionists, so that the people of Toro could fight the matter out among themselves.

"Eventually Bishop Tucker undertook not to send any missionaries into Toro 'for some months to come,' or until he could receive the decision of the committee of the Church Missionary Society on the subject, and added that he would devote his attention and his energies to mission extension in Usoga and towards the east.

"Similarly Monseigneur Hirth gave us to understand that his mission would work either westwards or northwards into Unyoro, and that he would abstain from sending any one into Usoga or any country to the east of the Nile or of the Lake.

"No record was kept of this arrangement, which is to be looked upon as being only a private and verbal understanding between the two heads of the missions, with Captain Macdonald and myself as passive witnesses to the transaction. It is, moreover, clearly understood that this allotment of spheres is subject to the approval of the Vatican and of the committee of the Church Missionary Society. I would, however, submit to your lordship that it is greatly to be desired, in the interests of peace, that these authorities should, if possible, be induced to acquiesce in the conclusion of this or of a similar arrangement for a definite period of five or ten years.

"I have, etc.,

"G. H. PORTAL.'

APPENDIX C

THE WAR AGAINST UNYORO

I append an account of what I said at the annual meeting of the Aborigines Protection Society, on Wednesday evening, May 23rd, 1894 :—

" Rev. R. P. Ashe, who was for some time acting-secretary of the Church Mission in Uganda, after expressing his satisfaction at the establishment of a British protectorate over Uganda, and his gratification at the steady advance of the English flag, the symbol at once of political and religious liberty, advocated, as far as possible, the substitution of peaceable and friendly overtures to native chiefs for more forcible measures, which might involve injustice to those against whom they were put in operation. He then made an important statement regarding the war in Unyoro, against King Kabarega, lately undertaken by the officers sent out by the Government. Without impugning their action, or charging them with making an unjust war, he felt that the information already made public failed in some important particulars to put the question from Kabarega's point of view. The cause of the war, so far as it had been made public, appears to be : (1) That Kabarega attacked and drove out of Toro the chief Kasagama, friendly to the English ; (2) that he sent two thousand guns in pursuit to the frontier of Uganda (whether he actually entered Uganda territory we are not informed) ; (3) that Major Owen marched out and attacked the Unyoro fighting men, and defeated them, inflicting upon them a loss of sixty killed, and losing two of his own soldiers ; (4) that the English Resident then collected an armed force and invaded Unyoro, and deposed the king, Kabarega. What Kabarega would probably say is as follows :—

" '(1) In 1891 an European (Captain Lugard), in company with the people of Uganda, brought an Unyoro prince, Kasagama, a member of my family, and, without reference to me, placed him on the throne of Toro. (2) The Europeans built forts in Toro, and left a large number of Nubian soldiers, who made this the point from which to raid and ravage my country, stating that they were acting under the orders of Kasagama and the Europeans (3) These Nubians eventually retired to Uganda (they were really withdrawn by the humane orders of the English Government). (4) I seized the opportunity of attacking Kasagama, who had harboured my enemies. (5) I pursued him to Uganda, where my troops were attacked by the Europeans and defeated. (6) Mwanga, King of Uganda, is my overlord and suzerain. I had no quarrel with him ; I sent him messengers with tribute—ivory, spades, and salt; I asked him to send envoys to tell me what the Europeans wanted in his country. (7) Why, then, did the people of Uganda invade my territory ? (8) Why am I to be deposed from my kingdom ?' "

It is a significant fact that, though there were a large number of the representatives of the press present, not one newspaper ventured to quote my remarks about the Unyoro war, which had found a prominent place in all the newspapers. In referring to my remarks, they dished up something I had said or written about something else the previous year.

APPENDIX D

CORRESPONDENCE RELATING TO TORO AND UVUMA

The following correspondence relating to Uvuma and the atrocities in Toro took place in 1893 :—

" BROADWAY CHAMBERS, S.W., *September 26th*, 1893.

" MY LORD,

" I have the honour, by direction of the committee of the Aborigines Protection Society, to address your lordship with reference to affairs in Uganda, and especially to the matters dealt with in a letter from the Rev. Robert P. Ashe, dated 13th inst., of which a copy is enclosed.

" Our committee is aware that Her Majesty's Government is not responsible for any measures taken under the direction of the Imperial British East Africa Company, and that your lordship has stated that no decision will be arrived at as regards future arrangements until the results of Sir Gerald Portal's mission to the country have been reported and duly considered. Our committee ventures, however, to hope that your lordship will cause such inquiries to be made concerning the offences alleged by Mr. Ashe as may lead to the prevention of similar abuses.

"It appears that a large number of the Nubian or Soudanese troops who were taken into the service of the Imperial British East Africa Company are now in the employment of the Administration temporarily established by Sir Gerald Portal, and there is ground for fearing that, although some order and discipline may have been introduced among them, they are still a most undesirable element in the government of Uganda and its relations with neighbouring countries.

"It appears, also, that in the recent attack on the people of Uvuma, in Victoria Nyanza, the assistance of undisciplined native auxiliaries was accepted, and that these native auxiliaries were allowed to capture and carry away into slavery many of the islanders.

"Without offering an opinion on the question now being considered by Her Majesty's Government as to the retention or abandonment of Uganda, our committee ventures very earnestly to appeal to your lordship against the employment, under any conditions, of undisciplined natives and mercenary hordes from other parts of Africa in warlike operations against the inhabitants of districts within the sphere of British influence. It is respectfully submitted that such action cannot fail to be attended by much cruelty and grave dangers.

"I have the honour to be, my Lord,
"Your lordship's obedient servant,
"H. R. FOX BOURNE.

"THE RIGHT HON. THE EARL OF ROSEBERY, K.G., ETC.,
FOREIGN OFFICE."

(*Enclosure.*)

Here is a copy of my letter to the secretary of the Aborigines Protection Society :—

"WAREHAM, DORSET, *September 13th*, 1893.
"SIR,
"There are two matters of great importance to the welfare of the natives of the countries in the neighbourhood of Uganda, and of Uganda itself, which I feel ought to be brought before the notice of Her Majesty's Government, and I feel that the Aborigines

Protection Society may be able powerfully to espouse the cause of those for whom I would plead.

"I. The first matter, then, which I would state has reference to (1) the erection in the year 1891 in Toro, and on the borders of Unyoro of a number of forts by the officer representing the Imperial British East Africa Company; (2) the establishment there of a large number of licentious Nubian soldiers and others, the off-scourings of Emin Pasha's rebellious troops. Certain allegations have been made to me by persons on whose words I place the strongest reliance with reference to these Nubians: (i) that these men give out, as a reason for their acts, that they have received *carte blanche* from the British to raid and ravage in Unyoro, with whose king, Kabarega, the British are said to have a quarrel; (ii) that these Nubians are guilty of the most horrible outrages, not only on the people of Unyoro, but on those in the immediate neighbourhood of the British forts in Toro. These outrages include: (*a*) violation of women; (*b*) the subjection of women to the most frightful, horrible, and indecent treatment, in many cases resulting in death; (*c*) the seizure of slaves; (*d*) the forcible circumcision of boys; (*e*) religious persecution.

"These matters were brought by me and my missionary colleagues in Uganda before the notice of the Imperial British East Africa Company's 'Resident,' and a most searching inquiry was promised. Whether this inquiry has ever been made, or if it has been made, how it was conducted, and with what result, I have not yet heard. This matter was laid before the Imperial British East Africa Company's representative in December last.

"II. The second matter is the attack, which I consider quite unjustifiable, made early this year by the Imperial British East Africa Company upon the people of the islands of Uvuma in the Victoria Nyanza. The attack was made in conjunction with undisciplined native auxiliaries (and this is a point which I wish particularly to emphasise, as it is a common practice in these days). The result was the shooting down of numbers of brave and, as I maintain, unoffending people, at a long range with Maxim guns, and subsequently the seizure by the native auxiliaries of a large number of slaves—not the sixty or hundred distributed by the leader of the expedition (at their own request?) among his followers, but those who were carried off by the native auxiliaries on their own private account. As far as I understand, the alleged grounds for the attack were as follows:—

"(1) To gain a safe passage for the Company's boat or boats to

Kavirondo *viâ* Uvuma waters. (2) It was alleged that the people of Uvuma had collected, early in 1892, a large force of canoes to make a hostile demonstration against Uganda, and that the expedition was to punish them for this. (3) It was alleged that certain outrages had been committed by the people of Uvuma on some Uganda gardens or ' shambas,' one or two people having been killed.

"In answer to these: (1) There was no contention on the part of the Company that any boat or boats carrying the Company's flag have ever been stopped ; Uganda boats constantly made the journey to the Nile without any hindrance. (2) The warlike demonstration alluded to had been ordered by the King of Uganda, the ally of the Company, since the Bavuma were his warm allies, having helped him against the Muhammedans.' On the king's flight the canoes quietly dispersed. (3) The shamba or garden outrages, serious as they seem to us, were nevertheless trifling every-day matters, comparatively speaking, and considering the normal state of 'native' countries. Far more serious outrages, and outrages on a much larger scale, were being daily perpetrated by the Muhammedans in Uganda itself, and yet the Company never attempted any warlike measure against them. Moreover, at the very time that the expedition was decided upon, the people of Uvuma were living on friendly terms with the people of Uganda, and coming to buy and sell at the weekly or bi-weekly markets. Hence, unless the Company can show much stronger reason for their hostile attack than the reasons alleged above, in my opinion it has been guilty of a very grave and serious wrong towards a brave and independent people, and has been, although unintentionally, the means of many of them being dragged into miserable slavery. So important and so momentous do I consider these matters, that I earnestly ask for your help and support in procuring that the natives be protected against the repetition of such suffering inflicted upon them in the name of civilisation under the ægis of England.

"I need not say that when in Uganda I protested against this expedition above referred to, as did also Bishop Tucker (who, having only just arrived, was unable to controvert the reasons given above), but with no success.

" Believe me, yours faithfully,

"ROBERT P. ASHE,

" *For some time Acting-Secretary of the Church Missionary* " *Society in Uganda.*"

"FOREIGN OFFICE, *October 4th,* 1893.

"SIR,

"I am directed by the Earl of Rosebery to acknowledge the receipt of your letter of the 26th ult., in regard to the employment of undisciplined native troops against the inhabitants of districts under British influence in East Africa.

"In reply I am to state that measures have already been taken to avert danger from this source. Four carefully selected English officers, speaking Arabic, have been sent out for the purpose of taking command of the Soudanese troops in Uganda, and Lord Rosebery has no doubt that their presence will secure the requisite discipline and control.

"I am, sir, your most obedient, humble servant,

"P. W. CURRIE.

"THE SECRETARY, ABORIGINES' PROTECTION SOCIETY."

INDEX

Alberto, an Uganda chief, journeys with Ashe to Zanzibar, 420; has interview with and receives a present from the Sultan of Zanzibar, 451; his portrait, 447.
Apolo Kagwa, the Katikiro, attacked with a spear by Mwanga, 81; denounces the abominations practised by Mwanga, 94; opposes a proposal to murder Mwanga, 102; on Kiwewa's accession he is appointed to be the Mukwenda, 112; his portrait, 137; attacks the Muhammedans twice with success, 137, 138; is defeated once and wounded by the Muhammedans, 139; his victory over the Muhammedans at Bulwanyi, 143; with Lugard he defeats the Muhammedans at the battle of Kanagala, 177, 178; is appointed leader of the English forces against the Muhammedans, 174; defers judgment about a stolen gun, 215; welcomes Mwanga on his return, 312; listens to Ashe's reasoning on behalf of Sekkibobo, 348, 351.
Arabs, 317-319; hostile to the missionaries, they set Mwanga against them, 68-70.
Arthur, Captain, recalled from Busoga by Macdonald, 403; left in charge at Kampala, 406.
Ashe, Rev. R. P., starts for Uganda, 4; meets Captain Stairs on the Madura, 6; is annoyed by flies, 28-31; visits Mackay's grave, 34; is received by Captain Langheld at Bukoba, 49; proposal of the native chiefs to murder him 78; unwilling to "chat over' political matters at Kampala, 267, 278; received by Walker at Masaka, 261, 262; disturbed by a leopard and the goats, 272, 273; unsatisfactory interview with Lugard, 277, 278; pleads with Apolo Kagwa for Nikodemo, 347, 348, 351; receives Mr. Smith's letter about the incident at Wakoli, 358; accompanies Dr. Macpherson to Kavirondo, 361, 362; reaches Mengo, 368; interprets Captain Macdonald to Mwanga, 374-376; sends in his resignation, 377; reads the Burial Service over Bishop Hannington's bones, 379; tries to prevent the attack on the people of Uvuma, 389; leaves Mengo with Nickisson for Zanzibar, 415, 416; crosses a river on a raft, 423; crosses a swift stream by a rope, 425-428; nursed by Timoteo Kaima, 431; meets Stokes and Muxworthy at Usongo, 432; relieves two natives, 440, 441; entertained at Mpwapwa by Rev. J. C. Price, 442, 443; portrait of Ashe and his party, 451; is entertained at Zanzibar by Sir Lloyd Mathews, 449, 450; interview with the Sultan of Zanzibar, 451; speech at the annual meeting of the Aborigines' Protection Society ignored, 459, 460; writes to the

Aborigines' Protection Society about the unjustifiable attack on the people of Uvuma, 461-463; bicycle, 13, 14, 25, 31, 34, 43-47, 254, 267.

Bagge, an officer of the Imperial British East Africa Company, 205; reaches Uganda, 166; advised by Kühne to return for safety to Bukoba, 284, 286; with Captain Williams, 361.
Baskerville, Mr., 198; missionary of the Church Missionary Society, 206.
Beelzebub, 30.
Bikweamba, Yafeti, Katikiro of Kasagama, of Toro, 182.
Bukoba, Ashe reaches, 49; leaves, 50, 416; boxes left at Bukoba looted by the French faction, 255; Bagge reaches Bukoba, and finds Kühne there, 285; compensation demanded for caravan looted at Bukoba, 387-390; Captain Williams sent to Bukoba to secure Mwanga's nephews, 292, 293.
Budo, a demi-god, 96, 97.
Budu, 97, 136, 162, 188, 303.
Bulamezi, 113, 154.
Bulinguge attacked by Captain Williams, 248; Captain Lugard justified in the attack on, 240; Bishop Hirth's account of the affair, 252-254; Bulinguge Island described, 139.
Buxton, Sir Fowell, a director of the Imperial British East Africa Company, 7.
Bwana Heri, affords a safe passage to Muxworthy's friends, 433; how Muxworthy saved his slave dhow, 434.

Chagwe, 90, 246, 347.
Church Missionary Society, accept Ashe's offer to return as their agent to Uganda, 4; station at Mamboya, 21; abandoned station at Usambiro, 39; in consequence of Stanley's letter they undertake the mission to Uganda, 56; action with regard to compensation from the Imperial British East Africa Company, 277.
Church Missionary Society's Committee failed to appreciate Mackay and his labours, 35; answered the *Times* Correspondent, 376 (footnote); approve of the conduct of Lugard and the Imperial British East Africa Company, 377; letter forces Ashe to resign, 378.
Collins, Mr. Walter, 206; formerly a Wesleyan preacher, starts with Ashe for Uganda, 4.

Deekes, D., nurses Mackay at Usambiro, 32, 143; welcomes Ashe at Mamboya, 444.
De Winton, is placed over the troops enlisted with Selim Bey, 187; invited by the Muhammedans to their camp, 324; dies on the way, 324; is buried on Namirembe Hill, 379.
Dualla, Lugard's Somali interpreter, 218; remonstrates with Mwanga's decisions, 219; his interview with Mwanga, 220, 221.

Edgar, a Freretown mission boy, returns to the coast with Ashe, 420, 426, 430, 431, 438; his portrait, 333, 425.
Elephants, 273.
Embogo, uncle of Kalema and Mwanga, a Muhammedan reader, 171; Muhammedans requested by Lugard to give him up, 175; their refusal, 177; Muhammedan hopes of his becoming king, 320, 321; Lugard's threat to enthrone him, 309, 320, 322; Lugard's interview with him, 322; Muhammedan plot to make him king, 401; Embogo sent to the coast as a prisoner, 407.
Emin Pasha, his opinion of Mukasa, 134; and of Kabarega, 383.
Endumi, the first stage of the journey to Uganda, 10, 13.
English Missionaries, names of, 114, 206; send a protest to Captain Williams, 196; influence with the Protestants, 302.

Enkore, 122, 183.
Entare, the king, 122, 183.
Entebe, or Fort Alice, 103; Selim Bey's letter from Entebe, 402; Captain Macdonald goes there to deal with Selim Bey, 407; Ashe leaves it, 416.

Fadl Maula Bey, an opponent of Selim Bey, 186.
Forster, Mr., had seen military service in Africa, 403.
French Government, the, interest in the Roman Catholic missions in Uganda, 150; they hold the English Government responsible for the actions of the Imperial British East Africa Company, 241, 242.
French Party, Mwanga's sudden hostility to, 200, 201, 305; hopes, to acquire Uganda, 203; build a fort, 205; their desires and hopes, 209, 210; give notice of an attack on Kampala, 224.
French priests, their names, 114; they considered Bishop Hannington's arrival in Uganda unadvisable, 73; attitude, 156; policy, 158; desire of "a fair Catholic kingdom by the Nyanza," 158; are opposed to English political influence in Uganda, 193; proposal about the chieftains who change sides, 195, 198; their preponderance due to their possession of Mwanga, 199; cleverly ask Lugard for a guard, 226.
Freretown, native converts forbidden to wear trowsers, 8; residence of Bishop Hannington, 71.

Gaudibert, Père, a French missionary, 251; Ashe's farewell to, 415.
Gedge, Mr., an officer of the Imperial British East Africa Company, hurries back to Uganda with Mr. Jackson, after Peters' visit, 145; left in Uganda by Jackson, 146.
Gordon, General, never in Uganda. His opinion on the Uganda mission, 159.
Gordon, Rev. E. Cyril, Church Missionary Society missionary, 114; on his way home meets Ashe at Mamboya, 21; starts for Uganda as Mackay's substitute, 86; Mwanga thinks of killing him, 87; his interview with Mwanga, 87–89, 153; his letters in the *Intelligencer*, 94; welcomed by Mackay at Usambiro, 118; advises the Protestants to have nothing to do with Mwanga, 124, 131; leaves Usambiro, 136; had gone with Smith to open a mission at Usoga, 165.
Grant, Mr., an officer of the Imperial British East Africa Company, 206; at Wakoli's, 362; in charge at Kampala, 391.
Greaves, Rev. G., leaves a Birmingham curacy for Uganda with Ashe, 4; has dysentery, 11; is taken back to Zanzibar and dies, 12; news of his death, 21.
Guillermain, Père, a French missionary, 255, 288.

Hannington, Bishop, understands in Africa the meaning of "Beelzebub," 30; visited Nyanza in 1882, and returned as Bishop, 71; tries Thompson's route to Uganda instead of the Unyamwezi route, 71; letters warning him against entering Uganda arrive too late, 72; is seized and imprisoned by Luba, 73; and on Mwanga's advice is murdered, 73; extracts from diary, 74–76; is murdered, 77; his murder counselled by Mujasi, 120; Mwanga fears the consequences of his murder, 85, 311–374; his bones buried at Mumias, exhumed and buried on Namirembe Hill, 378.
Hippopotamus, danger to Walker's boat, 118; shot by Nickisson, 419.
Hirth, Monseigneur, French bishop, a German by nationality, 206; in opposition to Lugard, 164; declares the deprivation of a chief because of a change of creed or politics to be persecution, 196; Lugard's letter to him, 221; his description of the situa-

tion at Rubaga during the battle of Mengo, 223, 224; his view of the negotiations held with Mwanga, 239, 240; advises Mwanga not to return, 241; his views of the Imperial British East Africa Company, 241; his description of the attack on Bulinguge in the *Tablet*, 249, 250; with Mwanga on Lake Nyanza, 252; his flight with Mwanga, 252-254; at Sesse with Kühne, 284, 293; his letter in the *Tablet*, 284; slanders the Protestants, 302, does not attempt to prevent the attack on Uvuma, 371; induced by Sir Gerald Portal to adopt territorial divisions for his missionary operations. 397, 457.

Hubbard, E. H., a student of the Church Missionary Society College at Islington, starts with Ashe for Uganda, 4; his portrait, 42; accompanies Greaves to Zanzibar, 12; stationed at Nassa, 40, 416.

Hutchinson, Rev. E., one of the directors of the Church Missionary Society to Uganda, 56.

Ikungu, 439, 440.

Imperial British East Africa Company, or the I. B. E. A. Company, headquarters at Mombasa, 7; Sirs W. Mackinnon and Fowell Buxton, directors, 7; formed in 1888, 90; Mr. Jackson sends a flag as a guarantee of their assistance, 141; Captain Lugard sent by them to occupy Uganda, 149; their instructions to him, 149-151; the French priests decline to recognise their flag as that of the English nation, 156; the Protestants carry the Company's flag which the Roman Catholics reject, 176; Selim Bey joins them, 186; intention to fine Luba for the murder of Hannington, 165; opposition of the French priests, 194; Sir Gerald Portal's estimate of their influence, 193, 241; a breach between the English missionaries and the representatives as to dealing with the chiefs who change their creed, 196; names of the officers, 206; the directors order Lugard to withdraw from Uganda. 206; missionaries on both sides ignored by their representatives, 207; their fate depends on the battle of Mengo against the French faction, 224; fort at Kampala, 228; the Company's flag floats over Mengo, 232; humiliating treatment by the English Government, 242; hostile and prejudiced witnesses against, 257, 258; receive £16,000 from the friends of missions, 277 (footnote); stockade at Wakoli's, 357; Mwanga's awkward questions about their status, 375; insolent behaviour of the Company's soldiers and servants, 379, 380; demand of ivory from Kabarega, 385; determined to smash Uvuma, 388; the last act in Uganda, 390; employment by them of Sudanese and undisciplined soldiers in Uganda, 461-463; attack the island of Uvuma, 462.

Jackson, Mr., sends messages to Bulinguge Island, has orders not to enter Uganda, belongs to the Imperial British East Africa Company, invited to assist Mwanga, 140; sends to Mwanga a flag of the Imperial British East Africa Company's, 141; hurries back to Uganda with Gedge after Peters' visit, 145; leaves with two chiefs for the coast to find out the intentions of the European powers with regard to the protectorate of Uganda, 146.

Juma, the principal man of the Muhammedans, tries to win over the Sudanese troops, 399; seized as a hostage by Captain Macdonald, 404; sent as a prisoner to the coast, but effects his escape, 407.

Kabarega, King of Unyoro, assists Kalema, 144; Lugard threatens to make an alliance with him, 154; his character and policy, 174; allies himself with the Muhammedans, 174; receives a defeat from the Sudanese troops, 323, 324; relations between Kabarega and Uganda, 383, 384; his fine, 382; Emin Pasha's favourable account of him, 383; his view of the events, and war in Unyoro, 459, 460; his country the scene of cruelties caused by Sudanese and undisciplined troops, 461, 462.

Kagera River, the boundary between the English and the German spheres, 50, 107, 262, 301; Bishop Hirth's flight to the Kagera, 261.

Kaidzi, Jonathan, false alarms about his brother's death, 333, 334.

Kaima, Timoteo, accompanies Walker, 261; left with Ashe, 340, 368, 420; stung by a scorpion, 421, 422; nurses Ashe, 431; discovers two unfortunate persons who have lagged behind a caravan, 439, 441; his portrait, 447.

Kakonge, Ashe's cowman, shot in the arm, 365; attacked with dysentery, 366; his farewell of Ashe, 420.

Kalema, Mwanga's brother, brought to the throne by the Muhammedans on Kiwewa's deposition, 121; puts his brother Kiwewa to death, 126; attacks Mwanga, 132; assisted against the Christians by Kabarega, 144.

Kampala, the Imperial British East Africa Company's fort, its situation, 228; an anxious night, 154; intended attack by the French faction, 224; an offer of a shelter for missionaries, 226; reception of Muhammedan messengers by Lugard, 321, 322; fever in the fort, 352; rude conduct of the Sudanese guards stationed at Kampala, 380.

Kamswaga, King of Koki, 136, 202, 209, 286.

Kanagala, the battle of, between the Christians and the Muhammedans, 177, 178.

Kangao, Chief of Bulemezi, 112, 117, 154, 262, 308.

Kangiri, Jimmy, accompanies Walker, 261; and Ashe, 420–431; his portrait, 448.

Kasagama, King of Toro, 182, 183, 184, 326.

Katonga river, 276, 305.

Kidza, a martyr, 81.

Kilimo, little boy at Mazengo's, 14, 15, 444.

Kituka demised, 96.

Kitakule, Rev. Henry, Hannington's favourite boy, preaches at the opening of the Protestant Church 344; author of an unfortunate letter to Captain Lugard, 344; his portrait, 137.

Kiwewa, the, Mwanga's eldest brother, in spite of precedent, succeeds as king, 104; official appointment by eating Buganda, 111, 112; liberal promises, 114; is alarmed by the Arabs, 116; refuses to be circumcised, 119; afterwards consents, 120; kills Mujasi with his own hand, 121; is made a prisoner, 121; put to death by Kalema, 126.

Kiziba, other side of Kagera river, 51.

Koki, 136, 202, 247, 286, 306.

Kühne, Sergeant-Major, second in command to Captain Langheld at Bukoba, 48; sent by him with Mr. Bagge to see the representative of the Imperial British East Africa Company, 281; effects the rescue of Mwanga and Monseigneur Hirth, advises Bagge to return for safety to Bukoba, 284, 285; at Bukoba, 286; receiving a forged letter hands over to the French faction the Church Missionary Society caravan, left at Bukoba by Ashe, 289–291; thwarts the removal of the Uganda princes, 295.

Kyambalango, Pokino, 97.

Langheld, Captain, the German officer at Bukoba, 48, 49; accompanies Ashe from Bukoba, 50; sends Sergeant-Major Kühne with Mr. Bagge to see the representative of the Imperial British East Africa Company, 281; away from Bukoba, 291.

Leakey, an English Missionary, 403.

Leopards, 272, 331, 334, 444.

Lions, 441, 445, 446.

Livinhac, Monseigneur, a French missionary, 114; letter to Mackay about Mwanga's return, 124, 125; his account of the arms imported into Uganda, 203–205.

Lourdel, Père, a French missionary, 114, 396 (footnote); writes to Jackson in Mwanga's name, 140; his over zeal, 208.

Luba, at Mwanga's instance, imprisons and murders Hannington, 73; Imperial British East Africa Company determine to fine him for Hannington's murder, 165.

Lubareism, the heathen religion of Uganda, 95-7.

Lugard, Captain, sent out by the Imperial British East Africa Company to occupy Uganda for them, 149; instructions, 149-151; enters Uganda, 152; first interview with Mwanga, 152, 153; attitude to all parties, 153; threatens to make an alliance with Kabarega, 154; anxious Christmas, 154, 155; attitude of the French priests towards, 156; assisted by Captain Williams, 156; ignorance of the real feeling of the English and Protestant party, 157; attitude, policy, and expediency, 160; decree as to the turn-coat chiefs, 162, 163; view of the claims of missionaries to interfere in politics, 164, 165, 167, 181, 277, 457; proposals to the Muhammedans, 175; proposals to the two factions about the Imperial British East Africa Company's flag, 176; marches from Uganda to Selim Bey, 182; proposes that Selim Bey should enlist in the Imperial British East Africa Company's service, 186; re-enters Uganda, 188; ordered to withdraw from Uganda by the Imperial British East Africa Company, 206; is unable to establish a *modus vivendi* for the missionaries, 207; his assurances of neutrality, 212; his letter to Bishop Hirth, 221; secretly arms the Protestant party, 223; receives notice of a French attack on Kampala, 224; the French priests cleverly ask him for a guard, 226; attempts no pursuit after the battle of Mengo, 232; Bishop Hirth promises him to influence Mwanga to return, 238, 241; fails to warn or help Walker during the war, 267, 268, 274; unsatisfactory interview and relations with Ashe, 277; indifference to the Protestant chiefs, 301; welcomes Mwanga on his return to Mengo, 312; proposes to accept Embogo as king, 309, 320; he accepts Mwanga as king, 321; receives the Muhammedan envoys, 322; interview with Embogo, 325; introduces the Muhammedans into Uganda, 326; departs for England, 340.

Macdonald, Captain, of the Railway Survey, reaches Mengo, 336; re-enters Uganda to inquire about the cause of the outbreak of fighting, 373; interview with Mwanga, 375; Mwanga's awkward question about the status of the Imperial British East Africa Company, 375, 376; helps Captain Williams against the people of Uvuma, not as a Government Commissioner but as a friend, 391; is left by Sir G. Portal as representative of the administration in Uganda, 397; has to settle who are the governors of Uganda, 403; tests the loyalty of the Sudanese troops to the Government, and disarms them, 404, 405; secures hostages from Embogo, 404; arms the Protestants, 406; goes to Entebe to deal with Selim Bey, 416.

Mackay, news of his death in 1890, 3; his grave at the abandoned Church Missionary Society station at Usambiro, 34; estimate of his work and character, 34; appreciated by Mr. Eugene Stock and not by the Church Missionary Society Committee, 35; attended by Deekes in his last illness, 32; one of the first missionaries sent out to Uganda, 56; carried back to the coast from Ugogo, 56; visits Lukonge, crosses the Nyanza and thus reaches Uganda 60; is heard gladly by Mutesa, 63; personal outrage on him by the Arabs, 69; informs Mwanga of Hannington's visit, 72; retires from Uganda, 86; welcomes Gordon and Walker at Usambiro, 118; advises Mwanga to stay where he is, and writes to Monseigneur Livinhac that he will have nothing to do with Mwanga, 124; his fears about the restoration of Mwanga, 131 (footnote); Mwanga's letter, 135; his death, 143; Mutesa's opinion of him, 143.

Mackay, the Christian name of an African surnamed Sembera, 225, 230.

Mackinnon, Sir William, a director of Imperial British East Africa Company, 7; considers Uganda the key of the Nile valley, 149.

Macpherson, Dr., officer of the Imperial British East Africa Company, 206; reaches Uganda, 166; marches with Lugard from Uganda, 182; ill with fever, 360; he leaves for the coast, 361; his record, 366.

Madura, The, steamship in which Ashe sailed from Naples to Zanzibar, 5, 6; discomforts of the voyage, 10.

Maloney, Dr., a Roman Catholic prejudiced witness against the Imperial British East Africa Company, never in Uganda, 258.

Mamboya, Ashe stays at the Church Missionary Society station at, 21; is welcomed on his way home by Deekes, 444.

Martin arrives with a caravan, 166; brings letters from the Imperial British East Africa Company ordering Lugard to withdraw, 206, 209; reaches Mumias, 365, 379.

Masaka, the capital of Budu, 262; Walker stationed here, 48; description of Walker's house, 262; Ashe leaves, 269, 270.

Mathews, Sir Lloyd, chief European adviser of the sultan of Zanzibar, 9; entertains Ashe and party at Zanzibar, 450.

Mazengo, 14, 15, 444, 449.

Mengo, Lugard arrives at, 152; Bishop Tucker, 155; Walker and Ashe, 277, 368; situation, 228; the battle of Mengo, 229-231; the Imperial British East Africa Company's flag set up, 232; Mwanga's return to Mengo, 312, 313; arrival of Captains Macdonald and Pringle of the Railway Survey, 336; departure of Sir Gerald Portal, 396; departure of Ashe and Nickisson, 415; Letter of the *Times* correspondent, 400, 401.

Millar, Mr., an English missionary, 403.

Missionaries pleased at Mwanga's succession to the throne, 67; Mwanga's deputations to them, 135; agreement between the English and French missionaries, Lugard's view of their proper claim to interfere in politics, 164, 165, 181, 277; Captain Williams secures their good offices to restrain their converts, 197; are ignored by Lugard, 207; a shelter offered to them at Kampala, 266; unjust sneers, 369; Sir Gerald Portal proposes to confine their operations to particular spheres, 395, 396, 457, 458.

Mombasa, headquarters of the Imperial British East Africa Company, 7.

Mpwapwa, a station of the German Government and meeting place for caravans, 22; Ashe encamps at, 442; Rev. J. C. Price baptises at, 442.

Muhammedans, in opposition to Mwanga, 95; Mwanga's plot to kill all their readers, 97; alarm Kiwewa against the Christians, 116; wish to force Kiwewa to be circumcised, 119; defeats, 138, 143; become troublesome under Embogo, 171; Lugard's proposals, 174, 175, 177; introduction into Uganda, 180, 326; envoys received by Lugard at Kampala, 320, 321; understanding with the Sudanese troops, 323, 324; burglaries, 381, 382; do not welcome Sir Gerald Portal, 393; are bent on fighting, 398; refuse to work for Mwanga, 398; plot, 400, 401; mutiny ended, 408, 411.

Muhuma, cattle-keeping tribe, 419.

Mujasi, urges Mwanga to persecute the Christians, 80, 81; warns Kidza to fly, 71; excuse for not obeying Mwanga, 99; his record, 120; is killed by Kiwewa, 121.

Mukajangwa, Mutesa's executioner, kills the Muhammedan pages, 65.

Mukasa, declines to join Mwanga's plot to kill the Muhammedan and Christian readers, 97; appointed Katikiro, 98; his death and character, 134, 135.

Mukwenda, Chief of Singo, 102, 117, 126, 139, 162, 272.

Mumias, 365, 378.

Munyaga, a martyr, 81.

Mutatembwa visited by Captain Langheld, 50; is interested in Ashe's bicycle, 51; receives Mwanga, 301, 305.

Mutesa, like Herod, hears Mackay gladly, 63; welcomes the Arabs and begins persecutions, 63; dies in 1884, and is succeeded by his son Mwanga, 65, 66; attempts to become lord of Uvuma, 386; failure of his expedition against Uvuma. 387 murders the guests from Uvuma; 387, 388.

Muxworthy, a partner with Stokes, and a prejudiced witness against the Imperial British East Africa Company, 258; Ashe meets him at Usongo, 432; his version of the rescue of Bwana Heri's slave dhow and its consequences, 433, 434.

Mwanga succeeds his father as king, 66; is under the influence of the Arabs, 68; attacks Apolo Kagwa, 81; starts a persecution at the suggestion of Mujasi on the Christians, 80; record, 82; interview with Gordon and Walker, 87-89; Walker's description of him, 89, 90; portrait, 91; royal progress through his kingdom, 90; tyrannies, 93; fears and enemies, 94; Christian and Muhammedan opposition, 95; plots with the heathen party to murder all the Christian and Muhammedan readers, 97; disobedience to his orders leads to his expulsion, 99-102; proposal to kill him, 102; the question of his successor, 104; Mwanga is betrayed by Mukasa's contingent, who join Kiwewa, 106; proposal by the Christians to restore him opposed by Gordon and Mackay, 123, 124; Mackay fears his return, 131; received by the Sesse islanders, 132; he sends deputations to the missionaries, 135; translation of his letter to Mackay, 136; Lugard's instructions in dealing with him, 150; Lugard's first visit to him, 152, 153; is desirous of joining the Protestant party, 199; the offer refused by Williams, 200; the French party suggest Mwanga's deposition, 201; Lugard's unhappy interview with him, 218; the value of his person, 238, 244; wishes to return, 238, 239; with

Index

Bishop Hirth, 283; the bishop advises him not to return, 241; retires to Mutatembwa, 301; desires a change of masters, 305; Stefano arranges and carries out his escape from the French party, 310-312; returns, 312, 313; is replaced as lawful heir to the throne, instead of Embogo the Muhammedan, 321; attends in state the Protestant church, 343, 344; proposes to send an envoy to England, but is dissuaded by the Resident, 373, 374; is frightened at Captain Williams allusion to Hannington's murder, but is comforted by Roscoe's assurances that it is condoned, 374; Captain Macdonald's interview with him, 375; awkward question about the status of the Imperial British East Africa Company, 375, 376; friendship with the people of Uvuma, 388; the Muhammedans refuse to work as his subjects, 398, 399; Government instructions to Sir Gerald Portal as to his attitude, 455, 456.

Namasole, the King's mother, 63, 82.

Namirembe Hill, its situation, 228; the site of the new Protestant Church on it, 228; opening of, and portrait of the Protestant Church, 343-345, 355; funeral service over Bishop Hannington's bones, 378, 379.

Naples, visited by Ashe *en route* for Uganda, 5;

Nassa, Hubbard is stationed at the Church Missionary Society's mission here, 40, 416; illustration of mission boys, 417; the return journey, 416, 419.

Nickisson, comes to Uganda with Bishop Tucker, 378; leaves Mengo with Ashe, 415; his farewell to Ashe at Nassa, 420.

Nyanza, Lake, Ashe desires to return there, 4; Bishop Hirth with Mwanga on the Lake, 252; a fair Catholic kingdom, 158;

Mwanga escapes in a canoe, 311, 312; how supplied by water (*see* " Perils of Water ").

Nzitiza, the King's messenger, 304, 307.

O'Flaherty, Rev. P., a Church Missionary Society missionary, 70, 78; leaves Uganda, 79.

O'Neill, Mr., one of the first missionaries to reach Uganda, 56; is massacred by Lukonge, 60.

Owen, Major, leads an expedition into Unyoro, 386, 439; he fights the Muhammedans by the banks of the Mpanga, 409.

Peters, Dr. Carl, leading a German Emin relief expedition, goes to Uganda, 141; he concocts a treaty with the French priests for Mwanga, independently of the Protestants who refuse it, 144, 145, 158.

Pilkington, G. L., an English missionary, 206; arrives in Uganda with Bishop Tucker, 155; letter in the *Church Missionary Society's Intelligencer*, 198, 199.

Pokino, Chief of Budu, 97, 114, 162, 188, 262, 266, 275.

Pompeii, visited *en route* to Uganda, 5.

Portal, Captain Raymond, brother of Sir Gerald Portal, died in Uganda, 397.

Port Said, passed *en route* to Zanzibar, 6.

Portal, Sir Gerald, his opinion of Zakaria, 180; he considers the political position of the missionaries, 181; enters Uganda as the Government Commissioner, 393; his awards, 394; recommends that the operations of missionaries should be confined to particular spheres of influence, and induces Bishop Hirth to agree, 395, 396, 457, 458; leaves Mengo for England to report upon Uganda, 396; leaves Captain Macdonald as representative of the administration, 397; Muhammedans aggrieved at his

awards, 397; is recalled by Captain Macdonald, 403; he notices the small influence of the Imperial British East Africa Company, 193, 241; instructions on his appointment as Government Commissioner to Uganda, his attitude towards Mwanga and Uganda, 455, 456; letter to Lord Rosebery on mission extension, 457, 458.
Price, Rev. J. C., a Church Missionary Society missionary at Mpwapwa, 442, 443.
Pringle, Captain, of the Railway Survey, reaches Mengo, 336.
Protestants, Lugard's ignorance of the real feeling and position of the Protestants, 157; carry the flag of the Imperial British East Africa Company, 176; the party for English interests, 194, 195; relations to the turncoat chiefs, 198; Mwanga's offers to join them, 199; support the Imperial British East Africa Company, 211; their courage, 250, 251; Bishop Hirth's estimate of their character, 254; prejudiced witnesses against them, 257, 258; Lugard's indifference to them, 301; are armed by Captain Macdonald, 406.

Railway Survey, 336, 338.
Reddie, Mr., a Government officer, sent for by Captain Macdonald, 403; is taken to Entebe, 407.
Ripon Falls, 367.
Robinson, Sergeant, attendant of Captain Stairs, and a hostile critic of the Imperial British East Africa Company, 258.
Roga, a little chief interested in Ashe's bicycle, furnishes porters, 47.
Roman Catholics, as patriotic upholders of Uganda, desire war, 209, 211, 221, 222; farther concessions for them, 402.
Rome, visited by Ashe *en route* to Uganda, 5.
Roscoe, J., a Church Mission Society missionary, 206, 254; reasons for his early arrival at Luba, 165, 361; sees Lugard at Kampala, 288; assures Mwanga that Hannington's murder has been condoned, 374.
Rubaga, the mission station of the French priests, 104, 156; their church in flames, 230; its situation 228; incidents during the battle of Mengo, 223, 224; intended attack by the Muhammedans, 400.

Sadaani, opposite to Zanzibar, 10, 11; Ashe receives hospitality from the German officers, 449.
Samwili, translated copy of his letter to Bishop Tucker, 335.
Sayyid Hamid bin Thwain, Sultan of Zanzibar, 451.
Schintz, Père, military officer and French missionary, died in 1891, 206.
Sebwato Nikodemo, afterwards Sekibobo, 238, 350, 411.
Selim Bey, in charge of Emin Pasha's Sudanese soldiers, 179, 184; description, 185; enlists in the service of the Imperial British East Africa Company, 187; influence over the Sudanese soldiers, 400; position and character, 400, 401; his impossible position, 402; in opposition to the Government, 404; Captain Macdonald goes to deal with him at Entebe, 406; he is arrested, and dies on his way to the coast, 407, 408.
Sematimba, Mika, a Protestant, 270; is disturbed by a leopard, 272; leaves Uganda with Walker, 340.
Sembera, a Protestant convert with the Christian name of Mackay, 225; he is shot, 230.
Semliki River, crossed by Lugard, 183, 187.
Sesse Islands declare for Mwanga, 132; Mwanga flees thither, 132; the question of dividing them between the French and English, 161; Messrs. Bagge and Kühne, and Bishop Hirth here, 284, 285;

Index

occupied by Captain Williams, 306.
Shergold Smith, R.N., one of the first Church Missionary Society missionaries to Uganda, 56; is massacred by Lukonge, 60.
Siegel, Mr., the German Governor, his conversation upon the Wanyamwezi, and the Africans 32.
Singo, a province, 117, 162, 303.
Smith, Dr., one of the first Church Missionary Society missionaries to Uganda, 56; dies from dysentery, 60.
Smith, F. C., a Church Missionary Society Missionary, 267; opens a mission in Usoga, 165; is disturbed by leopards and goats, 272, 273; reaches Mengo, 277; adventurous interview with Wakoli, his danger with the natives, 353-368; letter to Ashe, 362; his portrait, 359.
Smith, Major Eric, reaches Mumias, 365; brings notice of the Government's intention to subsidise the Imperial British East Africa Company, 366; goes to Uganda with a Maxim gun, 366.
Smithies, Bishop, 450.
Songoro, a runaway slave, afterwards captain of the mission ship, *James Hannington*, 416; his death, 417.
Stairs, Captain, Ashe's acquaintance with him on the Madura, a conversation about Africa, 4; Ashe falls in with his caravan, 16.
Stanley, H. M., his letter induces the Church Missionary Society to undertake the Uganda mission, 56; has no great faith in Mwanga, and refuses to help the exiled Christians, 136; assists Mutesa in his war against the people of Uvuma, 386, 387.
Stefano, meets Mwanga, 310; arranges and carries out his escape, 310-312.
Stock, Eugene, a director of the Church Missionary Society mission in Uganda, 56; supported

Mackay on the Church Missionary Society Committee, 35.
Stokes, formerly a missionary, now an ivory trader, helps the restoration of Mwanga, 124; welcomes Ashe, 432.
Stuhlmann, Herr, 166; a witness hostile to the Imperial British East Africa Company, 258.
Sudanese, 323, 399, 401.
Sultan of Zanzibar, a description of him, 9; allows Ashe and Alberto an interview, 451.

Taborah, Unyanyembe, 32.
Tetze Fly, 29, 30, 31.
Times correspondent, 397; formerly an agent of the Imperial British East Africa Company, reaches Uganda, 376; his criticism answered, 376, 377; his version of the intended Muhammedan attack on Kampala, 400, 401; sent for by Captain Macdonald, 403; takes charge of Selim Bey, Juma, and Embogo as far as Kavirondo, 407.
Toro, 385, 395, 458, 459, 462.
Tucker, Bishop, arrives with Pilkington at Mengo, 155; fails to grasp the situation 193, 194; copy of Samwili's letter to him, 335; his arrival with missionaries, 377; Ashe sends him his resignation, 377; his funeral address at the interment of Bishop Hannington's bones, 379; tries to prevent the attack on the people of Uvuma, 389; engages not to send for some time missionaries into Toro, 458.

Uganda, discovered and described by Speke, and visited by Stanley, 55, 56; the Uganda mission taken up by the Church Missionary Society in consequence of Stanley's letters, 56; weapons, instruments, and utensils illustrated, 58; described 59, 264-266; Arab traders welcomed by Mutesa, 63, 65; rumours of European aggression, 68, 94; martyrdom of three young converts, 69; Bishop Hannington warned of the dangers of entering, 71; chiefs order his murder, 73; Mackay withdraws and Gordon arrives, 86; the formation of the Imperial British East Africa Company destined to influence Uganda, 90; Kiwewa king, 104; representatives of the English and French Missions, 114; the Arab plot to seize Uganda, 116, 117; Mr. Jackson has orders not to enter, 149; Dr. Peters makes a treaty with Mwanga, 141; commencement of the building of the first Christian church, 146; Captain Lugard, of the Imperial British East Africa Company, sent to occupy Uganda, 149; his instructions with regard to it, 149; the interests of the French Government in the Roman Catholic Missions here, 150; Lugard enters, 152; the policy of the French priests to gain possession, 158; General Gordon's opinion on the Uganda mission, 162; Lugard's awards of the chieftainships, 162; politics and religion inextricably entangled there, 164, 303; the Muhammedans raid into Uganda, 171; method of fighting, 178; danger of fanatical Muhammedans, 180; an order from the Imperial British East Africa Company to withdraw Lugard, 206; English influence established, 313; entrance of the Muhammedans, 326; the practicability of a railway and the cost of carriage, 336, 337; Lugard, Walker, the staff of the Railway Commission, and Dr. Wright leave Uganda, 340, 352, 359; Captain Macdonald ordered to re-enter, 373; treated as a conquered country, 380; Kabarega's relations with it, 383; he sends messengers, 385; his whole fighting force gathered against the people of Uvuma, 389; Sir G. Portal, as Government Commissioner, enters, 393; instructions to Sir G. Portal as Commissioner, 467, 468; the proposed territorial divisions between the Catholics and Protestants, 469, 470; the use of undisciplined and Sudanese troops there, 474-476.

Ugogo, description of, 24; description of the people, 25.

Unyoro, 144.

Usambira, Mackay dies of fever at, 3; Deekes ill with fever, 32, 143; the now abandoned Church Missionary Society station, and the scene of Mackay's labours, 34; Walker and Gordon welcomed by Mackay, 118; arrival of Stanley with Emin Pasha, 136.

Usoga, the tragedy on Smith's visit to Wakali, 351, 352, 354, 356.

Usongo, Stokes' village, passed by Ashe, 33, 432, 437.

Uvuma, Mutesa attempts to conquer it, 385, 387; Mwanga's friendship towards the people of Uvuma, 388; hostility of the Imperial British East Africa Company, 388, 389; attack on its people, 389, 390.

Wakirenzi Mulondo, 408.

Wakoli, the chief of Usogo, Smith's tragic interview with, 353-358, 362; is shot by a porter, 354; his death, 358.

Walker, R. H., Archdeacon, at Masaka, 48, 261; joins Gordon in Uganda, 86; plot to kill him, 87; interview with Mwanga, 87-89, 153; his description of Mwanga, 89; welcomed at Usambiro by Mackay, 118; leaves Usambiro, 136; describes the commencement of the building of the first Christian church in Uganda, 146; letter in the *Church Missionary Society's Intelligencer*, 197, 198; meets Ashe, 261; description of his house at Masaka, 262; receives news of the war at Mengo, 267; no communication or assistance sent to him by Lugard, 267, 268, 274;

leopard and goats at night, 272, 273; Lugard complains of his message to Ferag Effendi, 275; leaves Uganda with Sematimba to visit England, 340.

Walukaga, a martyr, 81.

Williams, Captain, is sent to assist Lugard, 156; left in charge at Kampala during Lugard's absence, 194; receives a protest from the English missionaries, 196; the difficulties of his position, 197, 382; the Roman Catholics demand religious liberty from him, 198, 199; Bulinguge, 248, 249; is sent by Lugard to Bukoba to secure Mwanga's nephews, 292, 293, 306; is sent by Lugard to occupy the Sesse Islands, 306; has an attack of fever, 352; attacks Uvuma, 390.

Wilson, Rev. C. T., one of the first Church Missionary Society missionaries to reach Uganda, 56.

Wilson, an officer of the Imperial British East Africa Company, 206; is in charge of their boat, 360, 361; his portrait, 359.

Wolf, Herr, a witness hostile to the Imperial British East Africa Company, 258; a German newspaper correspondent, 366; with Captain Macdonald at Kampala, 374.

Wright, Dr. Gaskoin, leaves a lucrative practice, and starts for Uganda as a medical missionary, 4, 206; has dysentery, 11; he extracts from the throat of a native a huge piece of meat, 347; suffers from fever, 352; leaves Uganda, 359.

Wright, Rev. Henry, a director of the Church Missionary Society mission to Uganda, 56.

Yafeti, Bikweamba, the Katikiro, 182, 395.

Zakaria, belongs to the English party, 180; Sir Gerald Portal's opinion of him, 180; marches with Lugard from Uganda, 373; is selected as an envoy by Mwanga, 373.

Zanzibar, or Unguja, a description, 8; is a free port, 9; status of British Indian residents, 10; Mr. Greaves is brought back, 12; the Universities' Mission, 12, 449; the Custom Houses, 203 (footnote); Ashe arrives on his way home, 449; entertained by Sir Lloyd Mathews, 450; Ashe interviews the Sultan, 451.

BOOKS, MAGAZINES, ETC., QUOTED IN THIS VOLUME

Blackwood's Magazine.
June 1894 (*re* Zanzibar), 9.
Two Kings of Uganda, by Rev. R. P. Ashe (Sampson Low & Co.).
Page 145 (with reference to the murder of three converts in Uganda), 69.
(for Ashe's view of the claim of missionaries to interfere in politics), 165.
Notes on Uganda (Waterlow & Sons).
Page 130 (about the arms imported into Uganda), 203-205.
Page 59 (to show, in Bishop Hirth's opinion, the value of Mwanga's person as regards the propaganda), 244.
Page 102 (to show how Kühne thwarted the removal of Mwanga's nephews), 293.
Page 27 (to show the attitude of the missionaries), 278.
The British Mission to Uganda.
Pages 144, 145, quoted (for Sir G. Portal's opinion of Zakaria), 180.
The Church Missionary Society's Intelligencer.
January 1888 (contains Mackay's account of a trying period in the Uganda Mission), 86.
November 1888 (contains an account of Walker's interview with Mwanga), 87-89.
September 1888 (contains Gordon's letters and accounts of a troublous period in Uganda), 93, 94.
February 1862 (contains Walker's and Pilkington's letters about the turncoat chiefs), 197-199.
July 1892 (contains Bishop Hirth's account of the affair at Bulinguge), 249-253, 284.
Lugard's Rise of our East African Empire.
Lugard's crossing the Nile, 152.
The word "Protestant," 153.
Lugard's partial justice, 161.
Lugard's complaint of the want of assistance from the missionaries, 166.
Lugard's explanation for not sending assistance to Walker, 267, 268.
Lugard's statement about the Imperial British East Africa Company's compensation to the Church Missionary Society, 277.
The priests bearing messages to Mwanga, 304.
How Lugard had lost confidence in the English party, 307.
Lugard's reception of the Muhammedan envoys, 322.

How the Muhammedans had tempted the Sudanese troops to join with them, 323.
Lugard's Rise of our East African Empire—*continued*.
Lugard's assertion that the Church Missionary Society's Committee approved of his conduct in Uganda, 377.
The Tablet.
June 1892 (Bishop Hirth's account of the affair at Bulingugc), 249-253, 284.
The Times.
(*Re* Fadl Maula Bey), 400, 401.
Sir G. Portal's Journal.
About the proposal to confine missionary operations to particular spheres, 396.

INDEX OF NATIVE WORDS AND PHRASES.

Abaprotestanti (*Protestants*), 153.
"Asinze" ("*He is great*"), 96.

Bafransa (*French*), 153.
Bamboa (*executioner*), 100.
Bambeja (*princesses*), 105.
Bafulasa (*French*), 153, 319.
Bangereza (*English*), 153, 317.
Bakabaka (*kings*), 373.
Bazungu (*English*), 153.
Baloza (*British agent*), 433.
Boma (*enclosure*), 445.
Bwerende (*the monthly Sabbath*), 99.
Butaka (*possession*), 66.

Dawa (*medicine*), 16.
Dini (*religion*), 104.

"Emboozi" ("*It is the goats*"), 273.

Gabunga (*chief of Sesse*), 94.
"Gwangamuje ju Junju!" ("*Nation! come for Junju!*"), 224.

Jahazi (*dhow*), 433.

Katikiro (*prime minister*), 66.

Kauta (*chief cook*), 67.
Kigya (*sacred temple*), 67.
Kasanga (*tusk of ivory*), 88.
Kikase (*drums*), 96.
Kulagula (*to foretell*), 98.
Kimbugwe (*keeper of the royal enclosure*), 113.
Kibare (*regent in king's absence*), 225.

"La Illāha ill' Allah Muhammedu rasul Allah ("*God is God, and Muhammed is His prophet*"), 318.
Lwanga (*the jaw*), 67.
Lyato (*canoe*), 262.

Mulamba (*king's doormaker*), 67.
Manoga (*king's tailor*), 67.
Musalosalo (*the engineer*), 94.
Mayembe (*sacred horns*), 99, 153.
Mujaguzu (*the royal drum*), 104, 113.
Mumbeja (*princess*), 105.
Mapera (*French missionaries*, corrupted from *mes pères*), 105.
"Mutuse bananga" ("*You have come, my friends*"), 120.

Index of Native Words and Phrases

Mulangira (*prince*), 126.
Magezi (*cleverness*), 267.
Muli (*reed-like grass*), 343, 380.
Masala (*cleverness*), 425.
Muzungu (*Englishman*), 425.

"O sinze" ("*You are great*"), 96.
Omwanika (*storekeeper*), 94.
"Oli musaja dala" ("*You are a man*"), 143.

Pokino (*ruler of Budu*), 97.

Senkole (*the man who lighted the fire at the accession of the king*), 66.

Scruti (*chief butler*), 67.
Sebalija (*chief herdsman*), 67.
Sensalira (*second in command to Sebalija*), 67.

"Tujage Kaya" ("*Let us go home*"), 433.
"Tweanze" ("*We thank you*"), 352.

Ugali (*porridge*), 445.

Wankakı (*gateway*), 88.
Woza musango (*to plead a case*), 374.

www.ingramcontent.com/pod-product-compliance
Lightning Source LLC
Chambersburg PA
CBHW020833020526
44114CB00040B/604